E THIRD WORLD

ichard Harris

h Dependency

Joel C. Edelstein

Africa
rris

nd Southeast Asia
arney

evelopment

au

LENCZOWSKI, George, ed. Political elites in the Middle East. American Enterprise Institute for Public Policy Research, 1975. 227p il tab (United States interests in the Middle East) 75-10898. 9.50, ISBN 0-8447-3164-1; 3.50 pa. ISBN 0-8447-3163-3

Seven carefully researched and interestingly written essays are contained in this volume on political elites in the Middle East. Each of the contributors to studies of the politically ascendent in Iran, Turkey, Egypt, Iraq, Syria, Israel, and Lebanon is a recognized scholar on his respective country. In a useful introductory essay, editor Lenczowski describes the origins of elite theory and argues convincingly for the place of elite analysis in studies of the region's domestic and foreign politics. Despite the contributors' varying approaches in identifying and describing national decision-makers, the largely common reference in the essays to social backgrounds, informal groupings, and elite cultures suggests the special validity and productiveness of these analytic dimensions. The volume in part overlaps geographically the thematic *Political elites and political development in the Middle East,* ed. by Frank Tachau (CHOICE, Oct. 1975); however, neither book is a substitute for the other. Together, the two volumes help replace many less comprehensive and often more impressionistic descriptions of political leadership in the Middle East. A general and name index is included. Recommended for university libraries.

STATES AND SOCIETIES OF T

A Schenkman Series Edited by

Latin America: The Struggle
and Beyond
Edited by Ronald H. Chilcote a

The Political Economy
Edited by Richard

Politics and Modernization in Sout
Edited by Robert N.

Political Elites and Politica
in the Middle E
Edited by Frank T

Political Elites and Political Development in the Middle East

Edited by Frank Tachau

Schenkman Publishing Company Inc.

HALSTED PRESS DIVISION
JOHN WILEY AND SONS
New York — London — Sydney — Toronto

Copyright © 1975
Schenkman Publishing Company, Inc.
Cambridge, Mass. 02138

Distributed solely by Halsted Press, a Division
   of John Wiley & Sons, Inc., New York

Library of Congress Cataloging in Publication Data
Main entry under title:

Political elites and political development in the Middle East.

   (States and societies of the Third World)
   1. Near East—Politics—Addresses, essays, lectures.
2. Elite (Social sciences)—Near East—Addresses,
essays, lectures.   I. Tachau, Frank, 1919-   ed.
JQ1758.A31974P64   320.9'56'04   74-20507
ISBN 0-470-84314-4
ISBN 0-470-84315-2 pbk.

Contents

Contributors   vi

Preface   ix

Introduction: Political Elites and Political
Development in the Middle East   1
FRANK TACHAU

1   Elites and Modernization in Turkey   23
JOSEPH S. SZYLIOWICZ

2   Egypt: Neo-Patrimonial Elite   69
SHAHROUGH AKHAVI

3   Syria: Downfall of a Traditional Elite   115
MICHAEL H. VAN DUSEN

4   Saudi Arabia: Survival of Traditional Elites   157
MANFRED W. WENNER

5   The Political Elite of Iran: A Second Stratum?   193
MARVIN ZONIS

6   Israel: The Persistent Elite   219
EFRAIM TORGOVNIK

7   Algeria: A Post-Revolutionary Elite   255
I. WILLIAM ZARTMAN

8   Conclusion   293
FRANK TACHAU

Editor

FRANK TACHAU (Ph.D., University of Chicago) is Associate Professor of Political Science at the University of Illinois at Chicago Circle. He is also Treasurer of the American Research Institute in Turkey. He is the author of *The Middle East*, editor of *The Developing Nations: What Path to Modernization?*, co-editor and co-author of *Electoral Politics in the Middle East* (forthcoming), and has written numerous articles and essays on Turkish politics.

Contributors

JOSEPH S. SZYLIOWICZ (Ph.D., Columbia University) is Professor of Middle East Studies at the Graduate School of International Studies, University of Denver. He has published numerous books and articles on various aspects of political change in the region including: *Political Change in Rural Turkey, Education and Modernization in the Middle East, A Political Analysis of Student Activism: The Turkish Case,* and has co-authored and co-edited *The Contemporary Middle East,* and the forthcoming *The Energy Crisis and U.S. Foreign Policy.*

SHAHROUGH AKHAVI (Ph.D., Columbia University) is Assistant Professor of International Studies, Department of Government and International Studies, University of South Carolina. His publications include: "Egypt's Socialism and Marxist Thought: Some Preliminary Observations on Epistemological Theory," a monograph titled, *The Theory and Practice of Egypt's Socialism,* to be published under the auspices of the Research Institute on Communist Affairs, Columbia University, and the forthcoming *Comparative Studies in Society and History*

XVII. Dr. Akhavi has delivered papers to the Middle East Studies Association annual conferences in 1971, 1972, and 1974.

MICHAEL H. VAN DUSEN (Ph.D., Johns Hopkins University) has worked as editorial assistant for the *Middle East Journal* and has traveled extensively throughout the Middle East. His publications include several articles and book reviews. Dr. Van Dusen is currently Staff Consultant to the Subcommittee on the Near East and South Asia of the Committee on Foreign Affairs of the United States House of Representatives.

MANFRED W. WENNER (Ph.D., Johns Hopkins University) is currently Associate Professor of Political Science at Northern Illinois University. He is the author of *Modern Yemen 1918-1966*, and a contributor to a number of textbooks, encyclopedias, and journals on Arabian peninsula subjects and affairs. His current research is on comparative ethnic and minority politics, using materials from the Middle East and Western Europe.

MARVIN ZONIS (Ph.D., MIT) is currently Associate Professor of Social and Behavioral Sciences, University of Chicago. He was Director of the Middle East Studies Center, University of Chicago and President of the American Institute of Iranian Studies. He is currently chairman of the American Council of Learned Societies-Social Science Research Council, Joint Committee on the Near and Middle East. He is the author of *The Political Elite of Iran.*

EFRAIM TORGOVNIK (Ph.D., New York University) is presently chairman of the Department of Political Science, Tel Aviv University. He is author of the book' *Determinants of Managerial Selections*, and of numerous articles, including: "Non-Party Political Organizations in Israel," *Western Political Quarterly*, "Election Issues and Interfactional Conflict Resolution," *Political Studies*, and "A Perspective on Central Metropolitan Relations," *The Journal of Comparative Administration.*

I. WILLIAM ZARTMAN (Ph.D., Yale University) is Professor of Politics and Director of the Center for Research in International Studies (CRIS) at New York University, and Executive Secretary of the Middle East Studies Association (MESA). His most recent work includes three books he has edited and co-authored: *Man, State and Society in the Contemporary Maghreb, The Analysis of Negotiations*, and, with Marvin Zonis, the forthcoming *The Study of Elites in the Middle East*. He has alwo written two books on Morocco, two works on African international relations, and a textbook on North Africa.

Preface

The essays which follow are original contributions prepared specifically for this volume. Preliminary versions of most of these chapters were presented as papers at the annual meeting of the Middle East Studies Association at Binghamton, N.Y. in November 1972. They represent some variation reflecting both different interactions of elite processes with the process of modernization and some differences in approach and perspective among individual authors. Hopefully, the nature of the subject matter and the attempts to emphasize common themes in the Introduction and Conclusion will help clarify the common basis underlying this effort and enable the reader to draw meaningful comparisons.

Individual authors have recorded their own acknowledgments. It remains to note here that a joint effort of this type involves a number of handicaps or obstacles. Among these are the peripatetic nature of the academic profession, particularly of those concerned with foreign cultures such as the Middle East, and the sheer problem of communication over long distances. The cooperativeness of the contributors helped immensely in overcoming these obstacles. Special thanks are also due to I. William Zartman, whose helpful comments on individual chapters as well as general editorial matters were well beyond the call of duty. Manfred Wenner and Marvin Zonis similarly gave freely of their time and energy.

FRANK TACHAU
CHICAGO, ILLINOIS
NOVEMBER 1974

Introduction: Political Elites and Political Development in the Middle East

Frank Tachau

The authors of this group of essays seek to analyze the inter-action of political elites with forces of social, economic, political, and cultural change. The societies which form our context are located in the Middle East. We define the Middle East to include the countries lying generally to the east and south of the Mediterranean Sea. This area is characterized by a predominantly Muslim culture, a common history molded by its physical position at the juncture of major lands and seas (Eurasia to the north and east, Africa to the south; the Mediter-ranean and Atlantic to the north and west, the Indian Ocean and its elongated arms—the Persian Gulf and Red Sea—to the south), and certain major features of climate and topography (the juxtaposition of mountains, coastal plains, inland deserts, and two major river systems, the Nile and the Tigris-Euphrates). Border areas shade off into adjoining regions. There are, for example, close affinities between the Middle East and the Muslim areas of Soviet Central Asia, Afghanistan, and Pakistan on the one hand, and of east, central, and west Africa on the other.

We have chosen not to deal with each of the countries of this area, nor with the region as a whole. Instead, we limit ourselves to seven countries: the Arab states of Algeria, Egypt, Saudi Arabia, and Syria, and the non-Arab states of Iran, Israel, and Turkey. These cases enable us to examine a variety of patterns of elite structure and interaction. They run the gamut from

1

relatively traditional social and political systems (Saudi Arabia) to highly modern ones .(Israel). They include relatively stable systems (Israel, Saudi Arabia) as well as highly unstable ones (Syria). There are among them systems which have remained quite authoritarian or closed (Iran) and some which are relatively open and competitive (Turkey, Israel). Some have undergone political revolutions (Algeria, Egypt) while others have experienced more gradual institutional change or evolution (Turkey). While all of them have experienced at least a minimum degree of social and economic change they show a wide variety of types of elites and interactions among elites as well as between elites and masses. Some of these elites are rather narrowly defined and persistent over long periods of time (Israel, Saudi Arabia); others are more volatile (Syria, Turkey). Our purpose is to examine the interaction of political elites in these seven states in the context of rapid socio-economic and political change. Our analysis will hopefully enable us to draw some inferences and raise critical questions about the political future not only of these seven societies, but of other societies confronting similar problems elsewhere in the Middle East and beyond.

SOCIETAL CHANGE:

Each of the societies analyzed here has its own unique set of traditions. Each of them has also experienced to some degree a series of rapid and fundamental changes in its cultural, social, economic, and political systems. These changes have certain general features which are manifested in some form not only in these societies, but in other societies around the world. Culturally, these changes have tended to replace a system heavily permeated by religious or sacral values with one of a more secular nature. Socially, systems dominated by primary groups of relatively local scope and largely parochial in nature have tended to be overshadowed by secondary associations of broader scope, more specific functions, and at least in theory permitting of a relatively higher degree of social mobility. Economically, systems based on barter exchange and subsistence production are being replaced by systems based on monetary exchange, a complex division of labor, and commercial institutions. Politically, systems characterized by government for the rulers and with a minimal amount of political involvement of the ruled, have tended to be replaced with systems with greater, if sporadic, involvement of the masses in politics and a proclaimed concern of the rulers for the general welfare.

These changes appear to be related to one another, although the precise nature of the relationships among them remains a matter of dispute. The term *modernization* has been widely adopted to describe this process of large scale change. We may summarize the process of modernization or modernizing change as involving increasing control over man's physical and social environments through reliance on inanimate sources of energy and the application of complex tools and scientific methods. The results appear to be social, economic, and political institutions of vastly enlarged scope and capacity, more highly differentiated societies with great potential for the mobilization and integration of larger numbers of people than ever before, and finally, the opportunity for amassing economic, social, and political power of virtually unprecedented proportions.

It should be emphasized that, although modernization involves certain inherent general features regardless of social context, the manner in which these changes manifest themselves in particular societies is subject to almost infinite variety. In effect, the specific pattern of modernization in a given society is the result of interaction between elements of tradition and pressures for change. Since each society has its own unique tradition, and receives pressure differently, the product of this interaction is bound to be unique at least in certain respects, while at the same time reflecting the general features of modernization.

POLITICAL ELITES:

Elites are discrete elements which, in D. A. Rustow's words, offer "a concrete island of refuge" in a bewildering sea in which "old abstractions" have foundered and a new "more seaworthy set" remains to be constructed. This is so for several reasons. First, emphasis on legal institutions has not only been abandoned by political scientists, or at least de-emphasized, but is particularly unsuitable for the high degree of flux characteristic of the contemporary Middle East. Second, the reality of most of these countries indubitably includes rule by oligarchies. Third, even in highly revolutionary situations, elites provide a realistic and coherent analytical thread on which to base an analysis of the ongoing process of change. Thus, to borrow Rustow's phrasing once more, "while constitutions and other formal arrangements would project a false image of stability, individuals and groups can be seen as a 'binding link' from regime to regime."[1]

The interaction between elites and the process of modernization varies. Some elites may be threatened or undermined. Some may attempt to adapt to the changes wrought by modernization with varying degree of success. Some may seek to initiate and/or gain control over the process of modernizing change as a means of improving their society, or their power within the society. Others are themselves the product of modernization. Moreover, no matter how particular elites relate to modernization, they interact with other elites who are also caught up in the processes of change. Thus, one may find a variety of elites in societies undergoing modernization: non-adaptive traditional elites, adaptive traditional elites, transitory (catalytic), or more permanent modern elites. Finally, elites may emerge from various groupings or strata, such as ethnic groups, social classes, or functional or skill groups. Analysis of changing social backgrounds, education, occupational distribution, political commitments and values, political behavior, etc., can thus provide meaningful insights into the relation between the socio-economic changes characteristic of modernization on the one hand and political change on the other.

We cannot proceed without a definition of the phenomenon we propose to analyze. We might begin with Lasswell's terse statement: "The study of politics is the study of influence and the influential. . . . The influential are those who get the most of what there is to get. . . . Those who get the most are *elite*; the rest are *mass*."[2] Put more succinctly, "the elite are the influential."[3] These statements imply several assumptions. Two in particular are worth mentioning explicitly: first, the assumption that influence and power are unequally distributed in a group or society; and second, that elite status is basically defined in political terms by possession of influence or power, or participation "in the formation and execution of policy."[4]

Lasswell's definition requires some further elaboration for our purposes. It should be noted, first, that the influential elite is not necessarily a homogeneous or well integrated group. Rather, highly complex societies and societies in a state of flux are characterized by competition and conflict over influence and power among a variety of groups. While it may be possible to identify which specific group is dominant at any given moment, there is less certainty about how long that group is likely to retain predominant influence or power. Second, we must be careful to avoid mistaken inferences concerning the scope of influence of dominant groups. If we assume that a single group dominates politics, it might be inferred that this group determines policy on all issues which enter the political arena. In fact, however, there are many societies and many situations in which particular groups exercise dominant influence only on certain issues while they lack such power on other issues.

We stress competition for power and influence among elites. Power is a complex phenomenon. To attempt a rigorous definition which would take account of all its ramifications is beyond the scope of this work. Suffice it to say that power is a relationship between or among individuals or groups "such that the behavior of one actor(s) alters the behavior of another actor(s)," in an intended direction. This relationship involves a number of elements and dimensions, among them the following:

The Influencer:	the actor who alters the behavior of another actor.
The Influencee:	the actor whose behavior is altered by another actor.
Influential Behavior:	the set of behaviors of the influencer which alters the behavior of the influencee, e.g., bribery, speechmaking, voting, violence, paying wages, etc.
Scope:	the number or variety of issues or affairs (sets of behavior) over which the exercise of power by the influencer is effective.
Domain:	the number of people, space (territory) and/or resources over which the exercise of power by the influencer is effective.[5]

It may be noted that the power of ruling elites in modern political systems is generally greater than that of pre-modern or non-modern (traditional) governments.[6] It is also clear that groups in a given society will vary in terms of the power at their disposal. Moreover, there are likely to be variations in any or all of the dimensions of power for specific groups over varying periods of time. These variations are most noticeable during times of great flux, such as is represented by the process of modernization.

If the elite consists of the influential—that is, those who share or participate most in the exercise of power—then we are confronted with a complex analytical problem. The problem is best perceived when we consider two aspects of modernization mentioned above: increasing differentiation, and increased political power. In essence, the process of modernization tends to make greater power available, but a greater variety of groups demand participation in the exercise of that power. Moreover, these demands are heightened because, as Clifford Geertz has pointed out,[7] the stakes are greater; i.e., the availability of greater power offers the possibility of heightened effectiveness and rewards to power seekers. And, in a situation of rapid change, acquiring power may be easier than in a more stable social environment. Conversely, the costs of political defeat in a situation of flux are likely to be significantly greater than in conditions of stability.

Political analysis of societies dominated by a small, homogeneous and externally differentiated elite is a comparatively simple matter. Such societies are likely to be relatively non-modernized or traditional. More complex, relatively modernized societies are likely to include a greater variety of groups, and these groups are likely to engage in activities of varying scope. These activities may be primarily economic, social, scientific, moral, or cultural in character. Nevertheless, such groups become involved in the struggle for power to varying degrees and in different respects at various points in time. Determining the political impact of discrete groups at particular points in time, or over periods of time, is a formidable task.[8] In particular, unlike more simple, traditional societies, complex social contexts are less likely to embody homogeneous or stable political elites. In short, *politically significant elites* may emerge from social classes, ethnic groups, kinship groups or tribes, occupational or skill groups, or some other social segment or stratum. Nor is it certain that a particular class or social stratum always and invariably dominates the political system. Thus, we cannot speak of a ruling *class* unless we can show that the political system is, in fact, dominated or controlled by a particular social class.

What we have said about the process of modernization does suggest certain gross tendencies, however. It leads us to expect, for example, that traditional societies are more likely to be dominated by kinship groups and that such domination is likely to be undermined by the process of modernization. That is, kinship groups are likely to be replaced in positions of political prominence or dominance by certain types of occupational or skill groupings (e.g., lawyers, soldiers, businessmen, technocrats). At the very least, we would expect politically prominent elites to partly reflect the changes of modernization. And, in fact, the societies analyzed in this volume graphically illustrate this point. The case of Algeria, for example, manifests the replacement of a colonial elite (which itself had displaced a traditional indigenous elite) by a wholly new indigenous elite. In Syria and Turkey, groups from relatively low rungs on the ladder of social prestige and power have begun to challenge and penetrate older political elites at the apex of the national system. On the other hand, in Egypt, new elements have seized the top positions in the political hierarchy, reflecting basic changes in the social system, but the operation of the political system has not been greatly modified from traditional patterns. Finally, Saudi Arabia and Iran are examples of traditional elites which have attempted to maintain their dominance by incorporating modern occupational and skill groups, and/or by attempting to master such newly important skills themselves.

As a matter of fact, it is possible to derive insights into the modernization process in a given society by analyzing the politically salient elites in that society. If membership in these elites is based largely on such ascriptive criteria as kinship or heredity, if the membership is relatively small and socially and culturally homogeneous, if its educational background and value commitments do not include modern elements or skills, it is a reasonable assumption that the societies dominated by such elites remain traditional. On the other hand, if modern skills and values appear among elite members, this may be taken as an indication that modernization has at least begun. In other words, changes in elite structure, composition, value commitments, skills, and behavior reflect changes in the society.

While we may be able to specify the kinds of changes which

modernization induces among elites and in societies at large, it is difficult if not impossible to predict precisely how such changes will manifest themselves. In other words, while we may recognize the process of modernization, we cannot predict in other than very general terms how specific elite groups or societies will initiate or respond to its manifestations, nor whether they will survive.

The manner in which these changes and challenges manifest themselves is of utmost importance. They may come about gradually and almost imperceptibly, hardly appearing to affect the system for a considerable length of time. Conversely, there may be spasms of rapid and radical change, transforming basic institutions in a relatively short span of time, sometimes accompanied by outbreaks of violence, as in revolutions and coups d'état. The relationship between the political system and its environment is of critical importance in this regard. Frederick Frey has suggested the term "capillary action" to describe the slower, more gradual process. In his analysis of the membership of the Turkish Parliament between 1920 and 1957, he found such capillary action to be characteristic of the institution. He elaborates the process in these terms: "the lowest levels of leadership are affected first. If the pressure continues, the middle leaders are then altered, and only after a noticeable time lag is there a seepage into the highest levels of leadership and the cabinet." This type of gradual change works well "when the demands of the environment are not severe." "In purely political terms, the gradual infusion of new personnel from lower levels of power to higher levels probably promotes maximum continuity in policy and reduces the strains resulting from change." On the other hand, "if an alteration in the environment, or in other parts of the system itself, demands rapid change in recruitment, the type of process that we have broadly christened 'capillary action' is unlikely to be adequate. Phased gradual absorption may simply be too slow a process under certain conditions, and the pressures demanding more rapid change may burst out elsewhere in the body politic, not infrequently rupturing vital organs at the same time."[9]

These considerations suggest that we must study the interaction between political elites and the process of modernization in an empirical context. That is to say, we must examine individual cases to determine how politically salient elites attempt to initiate or manipulate modernizing change, or how they respond to such change as it impinges on their status or position in the social and political systems. This is what we attempt in the present volume.

ELITE ANALYSIS:

What do we need to know about politically salient elites for purposes of our analysis? Basically, we must know their identity; i.e., *who* they are, what *positions* they occupy, what they *do* or can do, how they achieved both the skills and the position they now hold, what *values* they harbor and what *behavior* patterns they adhere to.[10] Moreover, we must examine the interaction of various elites, whether they be conflictual or cooperative. Finally, we must incorporate a longitudinal perspective by noting changes over time. Let us elaborate on these points.

First, how are we to recognize politically salient elites? The political scientist's traditional answer to this question was unequivocal: occupants of high official posts such as Cabinet ministers, members of Parliament, the judiciary, etc., constituted the political elite. This answer assumed that power came with position. We cannot rest on such an assumption. There is no doubt that such positions are important—important enough to provide a starting point in our attempt to identify elites. But we must also ascertain the dimensions of power exercised by incumbents in these positions in the societies in question, rather than assuming it. We must further relate the characteristics of those who exercise power with the outcomes of that exercise.[11] It is significant, for example, that the Iranian *Majlis* which failed to enact land reform legislation at the behest of the Shah was dominated by wealthy landowners. Their stubborn resistance, however, ultimately resulted in the disbandment of the *Majlis* and enactment of the reform through royal decree. Similarly, it is significant that the advent of multi-party competition in Turkey coincided with a fundamental change in the composition of Parliament, with a decline of civil and military officials and a rise in the proportion of businessmen, free professionals, and members of local or regional elites. Concurrently, the relative positions of President, Prime Minister and Parliament shifted substantially, as did the relations between previously dominant bureaucratic and military elites and those with political and social bases in the small towns and cities of the hinterland.

In answering the question of identity, elite studies often emphasize the social background of elite members. This is perhaps partly explained by the relative availability of such data as family background, date and place of birth, education, marital status, and occupation or profession. The weakness of analysis based solely on such data is that it cannot in and of itself explain value commitments or policy outcomes to which the elite members in question may contribute, nor the behavior patterns to which they adhere. Therefore, social background data must be linked with available evidence concerning the value commitments of elite members. Where direct evidence is not available, patterns of socialization and recruitment, particularly through formal educational institutions, may provide indirect indications which are more readily available, particularly in societies where such institutions possess fairly well defined cultural and behavioral norms of their own, and where they provide clear channels of access to elite status.[12]

Middle Eastern educational institutions have played a crucial role in the process of elite formation and identification. More than perhaps any other single set of institutions, they have provided skills, forged social links, and inculcated values and behavioral norms to and among elite aspirants. Changes in the educational system have often presaged or heralded changes in elite structure and function. Thus, before the advent of modernization, the traditional mosque schools and seminaries (madrassahs) constituted one of the principal channels of access to elite status. This reflected the dominance of the Muslim religion in culture and society, and was reinforced by the prominence of the religious elite (ulema). With the advent of modernization, however, new educational institutions of an increasingly secular and specialized character were established. In time, they came to overshadow the religious institutions, and in some cases entirely replaced them. The skills and values inculcated in these schools were, of course, at sharp variance with those favored by the traditional institutions. The character of the elites which emerged from them was correspondingly very different from that of the traditional elite. Not only were they different in terms of skills and value commitments, but often their social origins were also distinct.

The development of new educational institutions often led to unintended results. Thus, for example, the Ottoman Military Medical Faculty of the late nineteenth century produced a disproportionate number of political activists. Yet the purpose of the institution clearly was not to train a new *political* elite. What seems to have occurred is that ambitious young men of humble social origins gravitated toward the Faculty because it offered a new channel for upward mobility. Having achieved higher status upon graduation, they found themselves in a position to turn their energies to politics.[13] Similarly, the expansion of the system of secondary education in Syria had the perhaps unintended effect of creating new political elites—significantly with different value commitments, policy preferences, and political bases of support from those of the older elite.

Educational training and experience provide one means by which aspirants may achieve elite status. As educational facilities expand and proliferate, however, their effect on student aspirants to elite status is also likely to shift. The Istanbul Military Medical Faculty may have produced an outstanding crop of elite aspirants with modern value commitments because it was one of a relatively few such institutions at the time, and a relatively small one at that. With the proliferation of medical training facilities in contemporary Turkey, the proportion of graduate MD's who move from the practice of medicine into the practice of politics is much reduced, although the absolute number of such doctors may have remained the same, or even increased somewhat. The law of supply and demand operates in this situation: as the demand for elite members with modern skills and values expands, the educational access channel will initially act as a narrow funnel. Those who come through the funnel will find opportunities and attractions in seeking a place within the political elite. As the funnel widens, however, with the extension of the educational system, the supply of elite aspirants with the requisite skills and value commitments also expands, and individual opportunities to attain elite status are proportionately reduced.

The expansion of the educational system may have one other consequence. As long as those undergoing training constitute a relatively small group for whom the very opportunity of acquiring training in modern skills represents a significant advantage in terms of upward mobility, the effect is likely to be the creation of a rather cohesive peer group. Individual members of such a restricted peer group are likely to experience great personal pressure to develop value commitments in conformity with those of the group and the institution. As the institution is enlarged, however, or as the system expands and new institutions of similar character are established, the peer group similarly grows. With expansion, peer group pressure is likely to be diluted. Indeed, one may expect to find smaller more discrete peer groups forming within the enlarged institutions. These smaller groups may represent the products of particular towns or regions, or particular secondary schools, each with its own identity and tradition. These more parochial and particularized groups are likely to prove more resistant to the pressure for more modern value commitments emanating from the faculty or university in question. The result may well be elite groups or aspirants with training in modern skills, but harboring parochial and generally traditional values.[14]

Obviously, the educational system does not operate in a vacuum. The analyst must therefore take into account the general nature of the social and political system within which the educational institutions are initially established for purposes of defensive modernization. The intention in such cases is typically to provide a cadre of professionally trained functionaries, or technocrats, who can bolster the society's ability to resist further encroachment from more modern alien sources (that is, Europe). Insofar as these cadres become imbued with modern values, however, they find themselves at odds with the more traditional political elite. If these conflicting values cannot be adequately reconciled, a confrontation or clash will ensue. This most often takes the form of a struggle for national independence or liberation from colonial rule, or a coup which overthrows the traditional elite and places some faction or representative group of the new elite in power. Among the countries analyzed in this volume, such clashes have occurred in Algeria in the form of an anti-colonial nationalist upheaval, in Egypt in the form of the Free Officers' revolt of 1952, in Syria in the form of revolt against the French mandate in the 1940s and in elite changes in the late 1950s, in Israel in the form of the achievement of independence in 1948, and in Turkey in the form of an extended nationalist revolt against the Ottoman dynasty culminating in a war against foreign occupation armies in 1919-1923. In Iran and Saudi Arabia, no such clash has yet taken place.

The new elite, characterized by modern education and value commitments, unlike its more traditional counterpart, is frequently committed to bringing about far-reaching social and political change. Part of its effort is usually devoted to extending and enlarging the educational system. But, as we have noted, the law of supply and demand prevails. The number of elite positions cannot be expanded indefinitely. Indeed, in many cases the number of such positions does not expand sufficiently quickly to accommodate all the products of the newly established educational institutions. The result, as I. W. Zartman has noted in this volume and elsewhere, is likely to be impeded access to elite status, or more simply put, unemployment or underemployment of trained personnel. This has been notably characteristic of Egypt, and explains that country's role as a supplier of school teachers to other Arab countries in the region. Obviously, one likely result of such a situation of blockage is heightened social and political tension and instability.

These considerations bring us to the question of elite changes over time. Analysis of a political elite at a given point in time is analogous to a snapshot: it freezes the action at the instant the shutter clicks. If no allowance is made for change over time, not only do we impose a static image on a dynamic process, but we run the risk of misjudging the present on the basis of the patterns of the past, and/or misapprehending the future on the basis of the patterns of the present.

Elite analysts beginning with Mosca have been conscious of this danger. Indeed, Mosca himself coined the phrase "elite circulation" to describe changes in elite composition over time. For our purposes, the concept of elite circulation may be understood in two senses. First, it may refer to the socialization and recruitment of *individuals* to elite positions. This type of circulation implies relative stability. Changes may occur in both the socialization (educational) process and in patterns of recruitment of individual aspirants to elite membership. The elite as a whole will change only gradually as new members displace outgoing or old members individually. Dominant value commitments and behavior patterns among the elite are not likely to change very much, for the process of socialization continues even after the individual achieves elite status, and the pressure to conform to existing norms is likely to be overwhelming, especially if the supply of aspirants exceeds the number of available positions. We have already noted that Frey refers to this type of change as "capillary action." A second type of elite circulation is more abrupt and probably more fundamental. This is the displacement of an established elite by a challenging group, or counter-elite. This displacement may, though it need not, involve violence or revolution. It does, however, embody change which is at least more compressed in time than the changes inherent in the more gradual infiltration of established elites by new individuals.

It is misleading to suggest that the two types of elite circulation are diametrically opposed to one another. Both may produce entirely new elites with new value commitments, policy preferences, constituencies, and behavior norms, but the one produces these changes rapidly, while the other takes more time and works more subtly. The two types are, indeed, related to each other in that the more rapid type of elite displacement is most likely to occur—and most likely to assume violent or revolutionary forms—precisely in cases where existing elites fail to respond to demands for access from non-elites. In other words, if the reigning elite fails to respond to pressures for social change from below, it runs the increasing risk over time of forceful displacement. If it does respond, it may lose its dominant position as the number of new recruits from humble origins increases to the point of overwhelming the old guard. On the other hand, even the relatively abrupt replacement of one elite by another does not necessarily mean wholesale social revolution or transformation. The new elite may, in spite of overt commitments to change or reform, fail to follow through successfully on such commitments and, in fact, may well perpetuate the institutional, behavioral, and value patterns established by its predecessors. It may also dig in and monopolize the seats of power, producing no change except its own advent to power.

The variety of possible combinations of factors is amply illustrated in the chapters that follow. For example, in Egypt, the displacement of the political elite occurred abruptly in 1952. The new elite was distinguished from the old by its social background, its socialization patterns and experiences, its value commitments and behavioral norms—indeed, by virtually every indicator one might imagine. And yet, as Akhavi argues, the political patterns which have prevailed since 1952 are not substantially different from those that prevailed earlier. Algeria, by contrast, is the only case of truly revolutionary transformation in the entire Middle East in this regard as in so many others. Zartman suggests a generalized pattern common to colonial societies which relates various changes in elite strategies to differing forms of political organization. Saudi Arabia and Iran constitute cases in which reigning elites have attempted to stay ahead of pressures for change by attempts to accommodate potential challengers, while discouraging overt opposition. Syria and Turkey represent cases in which gradual infiltration of the national elite by local or regional elites with somewhat different institutional and experiential backgrounds produced instability and confrontations from time to time. Israel, finally, suggests a pattern in which a cohesive elite group remains entrenched in power after more than two decades, and in which a potential counter-elite has not yet formed, although pressures from below have been manifested in recent years.

The lack of a viable counter-elite in Israel suggests a further question. A ruling elite cannot simply be removed as if by fiat. Something or someone must replace it. Several observations are in order. First, there is no guarantee that because a dominant elite has lost popularity or support it can easily be replaced. The outcome of such a situation depends on such factors as the availability of a counter-elite, the character, composition, and abilities of that counter-elite, and its social and political position relative to other potentially aspiring groups. A counter-elite may be willing and able to step in to replace a discredited ruling group, but may lack support from other groups in the society. This may prevent its bid for power from succeeding. Alternatively, it may trigger a struggle for power among contending groups. Obviously, in such a situation, the incumbent ruling group has opportunities to strive to hold on to power.

Another of the tasks of the elite analyst is to identify actual or potential counter-elites, estimate the probability of a challenge being mounted against the ruling elite, and calculate the possibilities of success should such a challenge materialize. Retroactively, he may gain extremely useful insights into the character and position of the currently dominant elite by examining its rise to power.

Zartman has elsewhere[15] suggested that elites and counter-elites may be characterized or distinguished along four dimensions: ideological (i.e., in terms of ideas chosen or rejected), generational (age), socio-economic (by profession or occupation), and geographical or spatial (in terms of place of origin or present location). Classification on the basis of these attributes or characteristics depends on the way that elite members "define themselves as bearers of demands." More importantly, Zartman hypothesizes that "the greater the coincidence among dimensional cleavages, the more intense the challenge to the incumbent coalition" (assuming equal weight among the various dimensions); and further that "the greater the concentration of incumbent elites into a particular category of any one dimension (and the narrower the category), the more intense the reaction to them." This restatement of the notion of cumulative cleavages may be linked to our discussion of elite circulation. It leads us to expect once again that the gradual type of circulation would have the effect of preventing the accumulation of cleavages along these dimensions, and thus averting a build-up of tension culminating in a revolutionary overthrow.

MIDDLE EASTERN ELITES:

What are the bases of Middle Eastern elites? In the most general sense, they are the same as those that prevail in other societies, for example, force, descent, wealth, and/or skill. In the traditional Middle East, a combination of force and descent (kinship or lineage) formed the basis of elite status among nomads, while a combination of descent, wealth, and religious knowledge or function formed its basis in village and urban sectors. Possession of relevant modern skills may be added as a further basis for contemporary societies in the Middle East. A perusal of the chapters that follow suggests that varying combinations of these factors form the basis of elite status in each of the seven societies in question. The more traditional the society, the more prominent is descent likely to be in the identification of the elite; the more modern the society, the more prominent are skills likely to be in its identification. The power factor will be found to have shifted in large part from small, localized communities to the larger community, more or less corresponding to the state. Similarly, to the extent that wealth is a factor, its source is shifting from landowning to commercial property and investments in several of these countries.

We do not maintain that skills have *replaced* descent as a basis for elite status. On the contrary, in most of the societies in question, descent remains an important identifying feature of elites. The point, rather, is that elites defined by such traditional ascriptive criteria increasingly find it necessary to acquire objectively defined skills to maintain their status. In some cases they face challenges from aspiring non-elite groups. A common response is to attempt to monopolize the new bases of access to elite status (e.g., commerce, acquisition of technical skills through formal training) or at least to compete with challenging groups. In western Turkey, for example, in the 1960s, members of a traditional landowning elite found that landownership was no longer a reliable basis for the maintenance of their economic, social, and political status. They shifted rather energetically into other forms of investment, among them touristic facilities. Moreover, they discovered that domination of their local district or region was also no longer sufficient to maintain status; it was now necessary to seek a power base in the national economic, social, and political system as well. In both instances, they faced competition from those who were formerly social inferiors.

The military is a good example of the intermixture of traditional and modern bases of Middle Eastern elites. They have traditionally played a prominent role in the Middle East. This is undoubtedly due at least in part to the physical location of the area, which has attracted the attention of alien forces and has frequently produced military threats from outside the region. The important role of the military is attested to by the frequency with which military power has been transformed into political power, and by the explicit recognition of war as an acceptable instrument of the Muslim community. In recent times, it was by military means that Europe first impinged upon the Middle East in the form of the Napoleonic expedition in Egypt and Palestine, and continuing encroachment of Russian power on Ottoman territories throughout the eighteenth and nineteenth centuries. Modern arms continued to pose one of the most obvious and basic threats to the survival of Middle East societies well into the twentieth century; indeed, perhaps the most traumatic shocks suffered by these societies have been the series of military defeats inflicted by Israel on its Arab neighbors after 1948.

It is thus no accident that modernization in the Middle East has often begun with the military. They are the last defense of the physical integrity of the society; there is no appeal from force of arms. Moreover, more than any other social institution, the military is necessarily judged not by the standards of the domestic society but by the yardstick of other, potentially hostile armies. Thus, a relatively traditional society seeking to defend its independence must be prepared to field an army as modern and as capable in terms of technology and efficiency as those that potentially threaten from abroad. Finally, because of its heavy reliance on hierarchy, discipline, and rationality, the army is capable of adjusting to the demands of modernization more easily than many other social institutions. On the other hand, although the military have formally adopted such modern principles of organization as universalistic and achievement criteria (e.g., promotion based on merit), several of the countries under review in this volume reveal a variety of vestiges of more traditional elements as well. Examples are the recurrence of traditional types of factionalism in Syria and Turkey, evidence of ethnic and kinship ties in Syria, and kinship as a basis of high rank in Saudi Arabia. Finally, it should be noted that in a relatively stable traditional political system, modernization of the army may have the apparently paradoxical effect of neutralizing the military as a political force. This appears to be the case in Saudi Arabia, as Wenner argues below.

Evidence of the amalgamation of modern and traditional values appears in other contexts as well. As Zartman points out, when the logic of a colonial or quasi-colonial relationship gives rise to a Great Coalition dedicated to the achievement of national independence or liberation, the commitment to modernity of some elements of such a coalition is necessarily diluted by the generally opposed commitment of other elements to traditional values. Among the cases examined below, this point is illustrated not only in Algeria, but also in Egypt from 1922 to 1952, Turkey from 1918 to 1923, and even, in a sense, in Israel to the present day in the form of the politics of coalition building at the Cabinet level. Among the specific groups which may produce aspirant elite cadres we may list civil servants or bureaucrats, technocrats (such as engineers, econo-mists, management experts), free professionals (primarily doctors and lawyers), businessmen and merchants; labor union leaders;

ethnic groups; landowners; and traditional religious functionaries. Examples may be found in the chapters which follow.

Finally, we must say a word about elite-mass relations. It has been argued that elite analysis ignores pressures for change from below and thus is inappropriate for an explanation of the process of modernization.[16] But this argument could just as easily be turned around to say that it is difficult if not impossible to understand mass behavior without taking into account the role of leading elements both of discrete groups and of whole societies. While it is indubitably true that challenges and pressures for change often originate among the masses, it is also true that the outcome of such challenges depends heavily on the response from the elite. It is also indisputably true that elites exist; in fact, they are by definition the most influential individuals and groups. Consequently, analysis of their composition, background, value commitments, and behavioral patterns as well as channels of access and recruitment to elite status, and changes in all of these factors over time, offer useful explanatory insights into the societies that are the subjects of our interest. The following chapters constitute our attempt to provide such insights.

NOTES

1. D. A. Rustow, "The Study of Elites: Who's Who, When, and How," *World Politics* 18, 4 (July 1966): 692, 695.

2. Harold D. Lasswell, *Politics: Who Gets What, When, How* (New York, 1936), p. 13, as quoted in D. A. Rustow, "The Study of Elites," p. 690.

3. H. D. Lasswell, Introduction to H. D. Lasswell and D. Lerner, eds., *World Revolutionary Elites* (Cambridge, Mass.: MIT Press, 1965), p. 4.

4. Ibid., p. 5. Theoretically, Lasswell suggests, "if influence is equally shared, every participant in the situation belongs to the elite," which is to say there is no elite.

5. This paradigm is based on unpublished notes of F. W. Frey, and on Karl W. Deutsch, *The Analysis of International Relations* (Englewood Cliffs, N. J.: Prentice-Hall, 1968), pp. 22ff.

6. Although this is generally true, some qualifications may be introduced. Thus, Deutsch notes, the power of modern governments in international affairs has declined. Similarly, the range of influential behavior may also decrease under certain conditions in domestic affairs, as, for example, in the tendency to restrict capital punishment in many contemporary societies and the elaborate procedural rules applied particularly in criminal cases.

7. Clifford Geertz, *Old Societies and New States* (New York: The Free Press, 1963), p. 120.

8. Suzanne Keller, *Beyond the Ruling Class: Strategic Elites in Modern Society* (New York: Random House, 1963), p. 4, uses the term "strategic elites" in arguing this point.

9. F. W. Frey, *The Turkish Political Elite* (Cambridge, Mass.: The MIT Press, 1965), pp. 282-284.

10. Compare this list of elite attributes with that of Lasswell: "social origins, special skills, personal traits, subjective attitudes, and sustaining assets such as symbols, goods and violence," *World Politics and Personal Insecurity* (Glencoe, Ill.: The Free Press, 1950), p. 3.

11. On the problem of identifying political elites, especially in "societies whose political processes are less institutionalized within the formal structures of government," see Marvin Zonis, *The Political Elite of Iran* (Princeton, N.J.: Princeton University Press, 1971), pp. 5-9 and Appendix I. Zonis hypothesizes that "the less representative (accountable, democratic) a political system is estimated to be, the less the correlation between formal position and actual power is likely to be." P. 5. Although the chapters that follow do not focus specifically on this problem, they do provide a number of illustrations or manifestations of it.

12. A striking example of this type of analysis is given by Michael Brecher in *The Foreign Policy System of Israel* (New Haven: Yale University Press, 1972) in his comparison of the Foreign Service Technical Elite (i.e., the professional staff of the Foreign Ministry) with the Parallel Technical Elite (i.e., officials concerned with foreign policy matters in other ministries). The former tend to be predominantly of central European (i.e., German) or Anglo-Saxon background, and to have migrated to Israel no earlier than adolescence (thus to have received all or most of their formal education outside of Israel); by contrast, the latter are predominantly of Eastern European extraction, and migrated to Israel at earlier ages, receiving most or all of their education at Israeli institutions. Moreover, the Parallel Technical Elite tends to be more heavily infiltrated by former military officers, and a larger number of its members tend to go into partisan politics upon leaving the bureaucracy. These contrasting profiles may reasonably be associated with the apparent policy preferences of the two groups: the Foreign Ministry staff tends to stress diplomacy and conciliation, while the parallel group tends to favor military capacity and self-reliance as primary foreign policy instruments. On the other hand, these general profiles obviously do not apply to all individuals in the system. Thus, the contrasting approaches to foreign policy are personified by the country's first two prime ministers, David Ben Gurion and Moshe Sharett, whose backgrounds are quite similar.

13. Doctors have been politically prominent in a number of societies at various times, e.g., the eighteenth century U.S., and more recently in Iran and Syria. The point may apply to other professions as well. It has been suggested that with greater professionalization, such individuals gravitate towards politics less frequently. See William A. Glasser, "Doctors and Politics," *American Journal of Sociology* 66 (Nov., 1960): 230-245, cited in Zonis, *Political Elite of Iran*, p. 194n.

14. The effects of the expansion of the educational system in culturally heterogeneous societies have been noted by James S. Coleman, who suggests that one result is likely to be intensification and exacerbation of local parochialism. See *Education and Political Development* (Princeton, N. J.: Princeton University Press, 1965), pp. 39-40. The analysis of Syrian political elites by Michael Van Dusen in this volume makes the same point by implication. So also, the new, more parochial political elite of Turkey, particularly since 1960, represents a combination of modern technical skills and traditional values.

15. See Zartman and Zonis, eds., *The Study of Elites in the Middle East* (Princeton, N. J.: Princeton University Press, forthcoming).

16. See, for example, James A. Bill and Robert L. Hardgrave, Jr., *Comparative Politics: The Quest for Theory*, (Columbus, Ohio: Charles E. Merrill, 1973), p. 173.

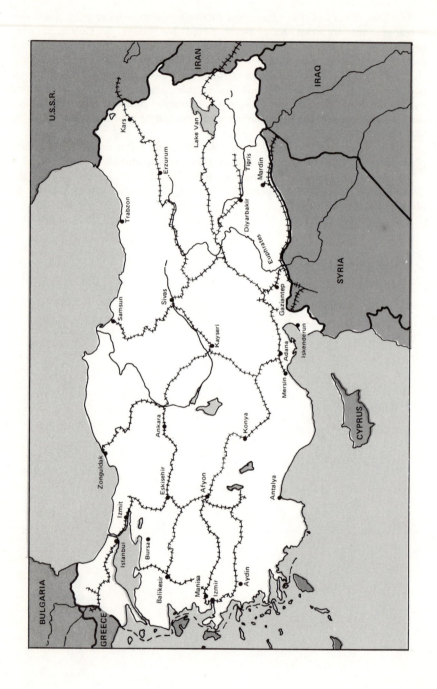

1

Elites and Modernization in Turkey

Joseph S. Szyliowicz*

INTRODUCTION

Although Istanbul has been a Turkish city for over 500 years the history of the modern Turkish Republic extends back only to 1923. Until that year Istanbul was the capital of the Ottoman Empire, a major factor in the European state system, whose boundaries at its zenith included all of the Middle East and North Africa (except Iran) and much of Europe. The shift of the capital from Istanbul to Ankara and the transformation of the latter is symbolic of the changes that have taken place in the past half-century. The creation of the Turkish Republic from the wreckage of the Ottoman Empire after its destruction in World War I, the implementation by Mustafa Kemal Atatürk, the founder of the Republic and the creator of modern Turkey, of a program of political, social, and economic transformation designed to create a strong new nation, and the shift from a one party to a multi-party system after World War II, combine to make the Turkish case of particular interest to all persons concerned with problems of modernization in the Middle East and elsewhere.

Although one might expect such changes to produce a marked degree of discontinuity in elite patterns and processes, one knowledgeable analyst has insightfully pointed out that:

*I am grateful to Dr. George Harris who took time from a busy schedule to read and comment extensively and insightfully upon an earlier draft of this paper and to the editor who also contributed many valuable suggestions.

23

A transformation in cultural content of such scope and speed was made possible through a remarkable degree of continuity in political leadership and political method. It has been characteristic of Turkey's gradualist pattern of political development that its political elite changed most drastically at times when political institutions underwent little change (e.g., 1908-18 and since 1950), and that its political institutions were extensively recast (in 1919-1925) when the composition of the elite remained essentially unchanged.[1]

The degree to which continuity has in fact characterized elite and leadership patterns in the Ottoman Empire and Turkey since the onset of modernization, represents the basic question to be explored in this chapter. We shall examine the available data pertaining to specific elites, though as will become evident, only fragmentary information is available on many important aspects of this topic while others have not yet received any systematic treatment at all. We shall approach the subject from two separate though interrelated perspectives. First, we shall trace the changes that occurred in the structure and composition of the societal center or social core over time.[2] Second, we shall examine changes in the composition, characteristics, and attributes of particular elites, specifically those that have been politically salient in various epochs. Throughout we shall regard elites and social core groups as both dependent and independent variables; that is, we shall examine the consequences for their structures, processes, and dynamics that flowed from political, social, economic, and cultural developments as well as the relationship between changes in social core group patterns and elite patterns and processes. We shall place our analysis within a historical framework beginning with a discussion of the Young Turk era, for many of the subsequent developments had their beginnings in this period.

THE YOUNG TURKS

As the name given to this period suggests, the 1908 revolution represents a watershed with the past. Former patterns and processes were disrupted in numerous ways and important changes inaugurated in many aspects of social and political life. Among the most significant was the transformation of the social core group for though weak sultans had been commonplace in

Ottoman history, never before had power resided with a political elite whose legitimacy was based upon control of the military and administrative institutions. Moreover, the composition of this political elite was very different from that of any other social core group in Ottoman history. The Young Turks were not of upper-class backgrounds but were recruited essentially from junior officials and officers, professionals, and intellectuals.

How radical a departure from previous patterns this represented can readily be seen if we consider the character of the traditional Ottoman system and the changes that it had undergone during the nineteenth century. In its classical period the Ottoman Empire was a patrimonial system par excellence. The most powerful administrative and military posts were filled largely by non-Muslim youths who had been recruited through periodic levies (*devşirme*). After conversion to Islam they underwent a rigorous process of academic and practical training and, depending solely upon ability and merit, could become the most influential officials within the state. At all times, however, they remained dependent upon the ruler; their lives and fortunes could both be forfeited at his command. Religious affairs (including law and education), however, were not controlled by the Sultan's "slaves." The religious hierarchy represented an autonomous career staffed overwhelmingly by persons of free Muslim-Turkish backgrounds. Recruitment into this elite was also determined on the basis of achievement criteria following long and rigorous training in a complex of religious schools (*medreses*)*. The holders of the highest religious posts were men of great influence and power within the Empire and should also be considered as members of the social core group.[3]

There was also a bureaucratic elite but its members, who were mainly freeborn Muslim Turks, could not aspire to fill the highest and most powerful official positions within the state since these were reserved largely for the "slaves" of the Sultan. Hence, the bureaucratic elite ranked below the palace-military and religious elites in terms of status, wealth, and power.

In the course of centuries, however, this pattern underwent considerable change and a ruling class emerged as processes of aristocratization and hereditarization became the norm. Increasingly members of specific elites successfully established

*Also known as madrassahs.

themselves and their families and by the end of the eighteenth century, channels of mobility within particular careers became largely restricted to members of families who were powerful and influential.[4] New criteria of blood, kinship, and connections were of prime importance in achieving membership in the religious, military, and administrative elites.[5]

At the same time that a ruling class was emerging at the center, change was also taking place on the periphery. There, a rural elite emerged with its own power base and interests as the changes at the center and the decay of the Empire permitted a marked shift away from the patrimonial system and towards a feudal one.

Developments during the nineteenth century, when policies of modernization were initiated, affected but did not destroy these patterns. Though many persons of non-ruling class background were able to achieve rapid career mobility by engaging in such innovative and un-Ottoman behavior as acquiring a modern education and learning foreign languages, the upper class proved flexible enough, after a short time lag, to engage in such activities themselves. Thus, essentially the impact of "westernization," in terms of stratification and elite processes, was limited to a broadening of the ruling class.

As we have emphasized, the 1908 revolution represented a benchmark in Ottoman social history, for now power was vested in a political elite, and with this change in the structure and composition of the social core group came important changes in policy. Although the Young Turks had sought power merely to restore the constitutional government that had existed in 1876, they increasingly adopted policies with radical consequences in order to maintain their own position and to save the Empire. Within a few years, parliamentary government was replaced by one-party rule and the triumvirate of Talat, Cemal and Enver swept the Empire into World War I. The new circumstances led to the adoption of major reforms in such areas as women's rights, legal reform, municipal and provincial administration, and the rapid expansion of educational opportunities, particularly for girls.[6]

Concomitantly, important changes took place in the political system. The political party emerged as a major institutional factor, branches were opened throughout the Empire, and as a result of its activities, political processes were transformed.

Political rallies and demonstrations became commonplace, meetings at local and national levels were also regular events, and a significantly larger number of persons came to participate in the Empire's political life. Politicization was enhanced by growing tensions among different groupings, by their efforts to mobilize popular support, and by the continuing expansion of literary and journalistic activities which often focused on political issues. In this manner, the circle of politicized elements grew ever larger. Concomitantly, the character of the political game became more ruthless, the penalties associated with defeat escalating from exile to execution.

To what extent and in what manner these developments affected elite patterns and processes, however, is not clear for little detailed information is available. One would expect that patterns of recruitment into various elites would become more diversified than heretofore and there is some evidence to suggest that the pool of recruitment did expand. The representation of non-Istanbul students at the Mülkiye (the training school for the civil bureaucracy) increased from 42 percent to 53 percent in this period and though many of these students were the sons of military and administrative personnel, the percentage of students whose fathers were members of these elites apparently declined.[7] On the other hand, it is also known that in the Foreign Ministry, no attempt was made to promote the rise of new elements or to change existing patterns. Thus, persons of upper-class backgrounds continued to be heavily represented in this particular elite. Moreover, all foreign ministers but one came from families with a legacy of government service.[8]

To what extent such continuity characterized the rest of the bureaucracy as well as the military and the religious elites awaits further study, but given the orientation of the Young Turk leadership, it is quite possible that little change in composition occurred, apart from the removal of some persons who had been closely associated with the former sultan and his policies. The Young Turks were, after all, driven to assume power to restore the status quo ante and their radical innovations and reforms were essentially the result of pragmatic responses to particular needs.

Of all the changes that did occur in this period, perhaps the most radical in terms of discontinuity with past patterns was the emergence of ideology as a major political factor. All aspects of social, cultural, religious, economic, and political affairs were debated, the fundamental issue being that of political identity. This question had been forcibly brought to the attention of all politically conscious elements during the preceding century, as nationalism had entered the Empire and quickly and deeply affected the non-Muslim inhabitants, leading to the transformation of one province after another into a new independent state. Essentially, three ideological currents vied for supremacy: a vigorous debate ranged among those who felt that the empire should remain a multi-racial, multi-national state (Ottomanism), those who believed that Islam represented the foundation of the state and that it should include only Muslims (Islamism), and those who argued for a Turkish state encompassing Turks everywhere (Pan-Turkism).

The loss of the Christian provinces culminating in the disaster of the Balkan wars, which virtually stripped the Empire of all its lands in Europe, eliminated Ottomanism from practical consideration. Now, the struggle was between those who advocated Islamism and the Turkish nationalists. The latter were deeply influenced by the West; indeed, not only was nationalism itself a western concept but it was the growth of European studies in Turcology which had fueled the new sense of pride in Turkish culture and Turkish history. This cultural revival, which quickly assumed political overtones, represented a radical innovation for the word "Turk" had heretofore been used with contempt. By the beginning of the twentieth century, however, Pan-Turkism had become a powerful ideological factor, strengthened by the large influx of exiles from Russia as that state extended its control over formerly Turkish areas. After 1908, nationalist sentiment spread rapidly. The *Türk Derneği* (Turkish Society) was organized soon after the revolution, followed by the *Türk Ocağı* (Turkish Hearths) in 1912. Their activities and publications, particularly the journal *Türk Yurdu*, were extremely influential in disseminating the nationalist ideology and in winning adherents to the nationalist cause. Pan-Islamic feelings also retained considerable strength. In 1912, however, the Albanian Muslims, for centuries one of the most loyal and significant groups in the Empire, rebelled. This uprising greatly weakened those who believed in Islam as a unifying force and spurred the further development of Turkish national feelings. Hence, the Young Turks increasingly came to adopt policies of Turkification, policies that created resentment in the Arab provinces and thus, in turn, promoted the growth of Arab nationalism and ultimately ensured the destruction of the Empire and molded the shape of the modern Middle East.

THE ATATÜRK REVOLUTION

The victory of the Allies in World War I struck the final blow against the Ottoman Empire. The events of 1919–1920 demonstrated the strength that Turkish nationalist feelings had acquired in Anatolia (Asia Minor), the sole remnant of a once great empire. The Sultan's government, even though supported by the victors, proved unable to withstand the nationalists who rallied to the banner of Mustafa Kemal. By 1922 Atatürk had defeated the Greek invaders and expelled the Allies who had planned to enjoy the fruits of victory in a very practical manner by dividing up Anatolia.

All of these events were important socializing experiences for the relatively homogeneous new state that emerged out of the wreckage of the Ottoman Empire: a deep sense of national identity was forged by the hardships and common experiences of leaders and followers in their harsh struggle for independence and survival. Moreover, as a result of his inspired leadership, Mustafa Kemal acquired a powerful charisma which legitimized the new regime and permitted him to implement his vision of a modern nation.

To accomplish such a goal was an immense task. To begin with the country was underdeveloped, its people exhausted by years of fighting, most of its meager resources destroyed. Only the largest towns had been affected by western values and technology and many townpeople still clung to traditionalism. Most importantly, no consensus existed among the nationalists who included persons of all ideological persuasions in their ranks. Indeed, only a minority of those who had fought with Atatürk to achieve independence were committed to the radical changes that he envisaged. In the first Assembly (Parliament, 1920–1923), for example, the Kemalists, who were by no means united, numbered 197 deputies; 118 deputies were organized in opposition as the "second group"; and 122 deputies were unaffiliated.[9]

Fortunately for the future of his country, Mustafa Kemal

was a master strategist. He moved with consummate skill to consolidate his power and to deal with advocates of different policies. Above all a non-ideological pragmatist, Atatürk adopted an incremental policy that permitted him to present an image of moderation while ably employing such techniques as conciliation, negotiation, discussion and co-optation to disarm and neutralize his opposition. His first priority was to establish control over major institutions of power. He did this by destroying the basis of the religious hierarchy, separating the military from politics, and vesting power in the top leadership of a new institution, the Republican People's Party (RPP). He then embarked upon a program of transformation that was designed to change not only the structure and functioning of institutions but the very way of life and mentality of the people as well.

In some ways the Atatürk era can be regarded as the culmination of developments that took place in the Young Turk era. Many of the programs that he adopted had their roots in the earlier period and Atatürk himself had been deeply influenced by those turbulent years. Moreover, there appears to have been a remarkable degree of continuity in both the social core group and in the composition of particular elites. The social core group remained a political elite and though the leaders of the former regime were discredited, many members of the political elite were of upper-class background. As Dankwart Rustow has pointed out:

> The political associates whom Kemal ralled around him in Anatolia in 1919 ... mostly came from good families: Ali Fuat Cebesoy was the son and grandson of a Pasha; Rauf Orbay's father had been an admiral and a senator; and Kazim Karabekir's a gendarmerie officer.[10]

Moreover, Atatürk inherited military and bureaucratic institutions that had developed during the nineteenth century, institutions which represented the pillar of his rule and from which were recruited most members of the political elite. Most administrators had continued to serve the Istanbul government while the Turkish Republic was being born but they changed loyalty easily and many important posts were filled by them. Unfortunately it is difficult to assess the degree of continuity that occurred, for little detailed information is available apart from the Foreign Ministry. Traditional considerations of family background remained important in the Foreign Ministry. Problems of missing data somewhat obscure this vital point but a recent study concludes: ". . . the Kemalist regime preserved a striking amount of continuity with the past. What transformation there was was evolutionary and gradual, with a minimum disruption of the old . . . The foreign service remained through Atatürk's lifetime a closely knit elite corps . . ."[11]

Such findings corroborate what little is known about Atatürk's personnel policies. He did purge some former high level administrators who had been closely identified with the previous regime and brought in newcomers, often at a very young age; one person, for example, became head of the Agricultural Bank at 22 and Minister of Education at 29. Most high officials, however, were products of the Ottoman bureaucracy and of upper-class backgrounds. Even in those cases where Ottoman administrators did not find favor with the new regime, many were able to maintain their positions through marriage and wealth; illustrations abound of young officials of non-elite backgrounds who married the daughters of their Ottoman predecessors.[12]

In view of such data one may hypothesize that Atatürk relied primarily upon established elements within the society to implement his policies—indeed what other groups possessed required skills—but that he also moved to broaden the pool of recruitment and increasingly to bring in younger men who had been socialized and educated during the Republican era. Such a hypothesis is buttressed by the shape of enrollments at the Mülkiye. The importance of this school is evidenced by the fact that about 70 percent of all civil servants who served in Parliament in this period were graduates of this institution. From the available data it appears that there was a marked increase in the number of students of non-elite and non-official backgrounds attending the school during the Atatürk era and that these students came from towns in Anatolia. The shift in fathers' occupations is particularly striking—the percentage of students with military fathers almost doubled in this period while the percentage whose fathers were bureaucrats dropped from 66 percent in the Young Turk era to 26 percent. This shift and the growth in the number of students with non-official backgrounds may perhaps be due partly to changing patterns of occupational prestige and opportunities which may have encouraged persons of upper-class background to seek non-official posts and partly to Atatürk's desire to recruit new men into the bureaucracy. Moreover, almost half of these students who graduated between 1920 and 1931 subsequently came to occupy high administrative posts, thus suggesting that a marked change in the composition of the bureaucratic elite occurred in later years.[13]

Continuity can also be discerned in the military, which provided the backbone of the nationalist struggle. Only a small minority of senior officers had remained loyal to the Sultan. The great majority, particularly the young military commanders who were veterans of World War I, were nationalists. Atatürk did, however, usher in one major change for the military elite— he isolated it from politics. He did so partly in order to eliminate threats to his own position, for not all high ranking officers shared his orientation, and partly because of his experience during the Young Turk period when military influence had so frequently made itself felt in policy making, usually with unfortunate results in Atatürk's eyes. Thus, when he faced growing opposition to his personalist consolidation of power by many of his military colleagues, who were active in the Progressive Republican Party, he moved step by step to bring the military under his control and to eliminate his opponents' ties to it. Essentially, Atatürk divided his military opponents, separated those who chose politics from the military and then neutralized them completely.[14]

Though a new tradition of civilian supremacy and military separation from political affairs was thus established, Atatürk continued to use former army officers in important administrative and economic posts. They were heavily represented in Parliament, serving both as deputies and in leadership roles. The military group accounted for about 20 percent of all deputies but held 30 percent of the important posts. Many also held important Cabinet offices for long periods.[15]

Their importance declined steadily, however, as the country underwent a profound social and economic transformation that brought other social groups to prominence. This change is evident in the available data concerning the composition of the officers corps, for Atatürk's emphasis upon creating a dynamic civilian sector deeply affected the occupational and prestige structure of the society. During the twenties and thirties, despite the importance accorded to national defense, the status of the military profession was not high and the career became to some degree hereditary; it also appealed mainly to persons of middle- or lower-class backgrounds. Most youths preferred a career in the professions or in the administration but not all—particularly persons of non-elite backgrounds—possessed the necessary perquisites to obtain appropriate training. As one scholar has remarked: ". . . only the fortunate could choose. Hence a poor boy, or a middle-class son from a more remote part of Anatolia might be able to obtain an education only in a professional military school."[16] That the officer corps was in fact composed of such persons is suggested by the background of those deputies who were formerly officers. Almost half of them had fathers who had themselves been military men; another 28 percent came from families in agriculture or trade.[17]

Atatürk dealt with the religious elite by isolating it from politics altogether. He moved resolutely to secularize the state and thus destroy what he and his associates considered a major obstacle to modernization. Despite its decline in the nineteenth century the religious institution still possessed formidable political resources based on the considerable prestige and support that it continued to enjoy throughout the country. Ataturk's political ability and resoluteness were clearly demonstrated by the manner in which he implemented his policy. He was most careful to avoid a break with the religious elite until he had fully consolidated his position. He deliberately gave the nationalist movement, during the days of the War of Independence, a religious flavor to counteract the support accorded to the Sultan's government by many religious leaders. Not only were about 20 percent of the deputies of the first Grand National Assembly members of the *ulema* but they were as well represented in the Kemalist faction as in the opposition.[18] Once the secular republic was established, however, this situation changed dramatically. Atatürk moved step by step. First, he abolished the Sultanate and created a "spiritual Caliphate," an institution unknown to the Islamic world. Then, the following year, confident of his position, he pressured the Grand National Assembly to abolish the Caliphate. Simultaneously, a new executive department to regulate religious affairs was created and within a short time religious schools, courts, and dervish orders were closed, the Ottoman script was replaced by the Latin alphabet, the visual distinction between Muslim and non-Muslim eliminated by the passage of the hat law, and European law codes displaced Islamic law. As a result of these reforms, religious affairs were brought directly and completely under the government's control, and the power base of the religious elite eliminated. Yet, although the political saliency of the religious elite at the center was destroyed, many religious personages remained influential in rural areas where stratification patterns remained essentially unchanged.

This lack of change has been attributed by some scholars to the distribution of power within the state and particularly to the strength of the rural elite, which was well represented within the Republican People's Party (RPP). This was the institution through which Atatürk exercised power. Its highest positions at the center were essentially filled by officers and bureaucrats. At the local level, on the other hand, all the important positions were controlled by the rural elite whose power had not been adversely affected by developments at the center. In fact, the rural elite benefitted from the establishment of the Turkish Republic for those important local personages had been among the most active and effective supporters of Mustafa Kemal during the War of Independence. Their affiliation with the RPP when it was organized was thus quite natural. Such cooperation between nationalist leaders and rural elite grew out of a shared concern—to preserve the independence of the Turkish heartland against the threat of division and colonization posed by the Allies and the Greek invaders after World War I. The alliance was cemented by the benefits that accrued to both sides: Atatürk gained a vital base of support, first against the invaders, later against his opponents, while the social and economic position of the rural elite was legitimized and strengthened as it now possessed the opportunity to achieve material benefits from the country's development.[19]

Thus, the new Republic was characterized by two separate and in many ways conflicting cultures, one at the center increasingly oriented towards modernization in all its aspects; another, with far more traditional values and orientations, in the rural areas. This cleavage between center and periphery did not receive detailed attention from the political elite until the 1930s. Many scholars have sought explanations as to why rural development in general and land reform in particular were so neglected during these years. Some scholars have suggested that the reason lies in what has been termed the "implicit tradeoff" that materialized between the political elite and the rural elite.[20] Such an analysis, however, probably represents an oversimplification, particularly since it is widely accepted that land reform was not a major issue in these years and that the rural elite did not possess much power or influence at the center.[21] Thus, although various economic and social concessions may have been made to maintain the loyalty and support of the rural elite, it is not likely that such a major policy decision was ultimately determined by their role in the party and the state. A somewhat different, though related, analysis suggests that Atatürk deliberately adopted a strategy of neglecting the peasant mass and concentrated his efforts on building a strong elite committed to his vision of modernity. This implies that he was aware of the awesome problems of transforming the country's rural areas and therefore not only perpetuated but deliberately "exploited" the urban-rural gap.[22]

This hypothesis is more plausible for it directs our attention back to Atatürk's political acumen. However, it, too, represents an oversimplification for it is difficult to find the kind of coherent policy outputs that one would expect if Atatürk had, in fact, made such a fundamental decision. It appears, for example, that Ataturk evidenced a continuing concern with rural affairs though he lacked real knowledge and understanding of peasant realities, and believed that land reform was not necessary since ample land was available within Turkey.[23] His naivete is also demonstrated in the Village Law of 1924 which was to promote rural development through self-help by the peasantry. Thus, further evidence is required to substantiate the thesis that the "benign neglect" of the peasantry which characterized this period actually stemmed from specific political calculations by Ataturk.

There is also little evidence to suggest that a policy of building loyal and dedicated elites was in fact pursued. If one looks at educational policy, it is difficult to understand why higher education expanded so slightly during the twenties or, more importantly, why the *Darulfünun* was ignored for so many years. It was an important elite training institution which was noted for its intellectual weaknesses and for its lack of sympathy with many aspects of modernity—in fact the faculty did not cooperate with Atatürk in any way and actually opposed many of his reforms covertly or overtly.[24]

Any attempt to understand this period must begin with an examination of Atatürk's perceptions, knowledge, and experiences. He was a pragmatist with a vision who always considered political realities, particularly the actual and potential power configurations affecting and affected by any policy. In this sense, the power of the rural elite may have been a consideration. But it should also be noted that Atatürk did not hesitate to sponsor policies opposed by powerful groups. Thus, in the first decade of his rule he sought above all to establish the basis of a strong and independent state, a state that possessed Western institutions and Western culture. He paid little attention to economic or social transformation at any level, and though his sweeping and far-reaching wave of reforms—the hat law, the adoption of the Western alphabet and calendar, the enactment of new law codes on European models—had the most immediate and penetrating effect upon urban dwellers, they do not reflect a coherent strategy designed to build a modern, unified elite. Rather, they involved primarily structural transformation and cultural secularization and were aimed at building the institutional and cultural base of a modern Turkey bereft of all vestiges of Ottoman traditionalism.

One should neither neglect the context of the times nor forget that the kinds of sophisticated and integrated approaches to economic and social development that are now current were developed after, and to some extent because of, Atatürk's achievements. Most of his reforms essentially implemented ideas that had been discussed for many years. Although Atatürk possessed a clear view of the kind of state that Turkey should become, he was not always certain as to what the particular conditions in various fields were or the kinds of policies that should be adopted, a fact which, as we have already noted, may well explain his policy in the field of rural development.

Moreover, if one looks at the whole period of Atatürk's rule, one is struck by the differences between the twenties and thirties. In the first decade he created a new state structure, a new culture, and a new ideology; in the second decade he changed his priorities and found the resources that were necessary to embark upon a bold and innovative program of economic and social change. New institutions such as the Village

Institutes and the People's Houses (which we will discuss below) were established, designed to build a new elite, transform the society, including the rural mass, and bridge the elite-mass gap.

For such a fundamental change in policy to occur Atatürk had to be flexible and pragmatic enough to adopt new emphases, new priorities, and new policies to achieve his goals. This reassessment may well have been spurred by two significant events, one that began in 1929 and lasted for several years, the other that began in 1930 and lasted only a few short months. The first of these was the world depression which had a significant impact upon the Turkish economy and forced the government to reappraise its basic economic policy. The result was the adoption of the principle of *étatism* and a new role by the state in sponsoring economic development.[25]

The second event which deeply influenced Atatürk and led to the adoption of policies of social transformation was the decision to experiment once again with the democratization of the polity. At the end of the twenties Turkey seemed to have lost its earlier momentum and dynamism. There was widespread disaffection with the intensity and content of the revolutionary changes that had been implemented in a few short years. These feelings, which were more or less shared by elites and masses alike, were aggravated by deteriorating economic conditions. The onset of the world depression also led to shortages and high prices which further spurred dissatisfaction. In this environment Atatürk decided to establish a "loyal opposition" which could serve as a safety valve for discontent, provide him with more adequate insights into the state of public feelings, and enable him to move towards his goal of genuine democracy.

The experiment lasted only three months. The new party, the Liberal Republican Party, though run by Atatürk's close associates, quickly attracted widespread and often fanatical support. It soon became apparent that a significant threat to Atatürk's objectives could emerge and the experiment was ended. The significance of this event, however, should not be underestimated for the demonstrations and other incidents that occurred revealed vividly to Atatürk the limited degree to which his reforms had penetrated the country and the need for additional change if a modern society was to be created.[26]

Accordingly, after an intensive period of reflection and a personal inspection of conditions throughout the country,

Atatürk moved to deal with the major problem areas that he had defined. The first of these was the weakness of the RPP which had become rigid, inflexible, and an ineffectual channel for upward communication. Now a degree of decentralization was initiated and greater freedom of discussion and choice permitted at lower levels. The composition of the Assembly reflects this change as the percentage of "official" deputies declined markedly (from 57 percent in 1927 to 23 percent in 1931) and the percentage of those with professional, trade, and other economic backgrounds increased correspondingly—from 17 percent to 41 percent. The younger intellectual elements within the party were also given more voice. They dominated the "Independent Group," a highly artificial opposition that was organized within the RPP. Although this group was not itself a genuine opposition it may have been established in order to prepare the country for the ultimate democratization of the polity.[27]

The second important change occurred in the area of elite training and socialization. Long a stronghold of conservatism, factionalism, and low academic standards, the *Darulfünun* was closed in 1933 and the completely new Istanbul University opened a short time later. The change was more than one of mere nomenclature. The new institution was staffed largely by professors from Germany; only a minority of the faculty from the former university was rehired. Research and modern values were emphasized and students overtly indoctrinated with Kemalist ideology.

Another significant reform in this area was the closing of the Turkish Hearths and the establishment of the People's Houses. Originally founded in 1912 the Turkish Hearths had played an important role in the development of Turkish nationalism. Their philosophy, however, accepted the role of Islam in the national culture. This diverged from Atatürk's views. Accordingly, they were replaced by new institutions, the People's Houses, which were officially opened in 14 provinces in 1932. The People's Houses were explicitly designed to serve as agencies for political communication and socialization: their constant emphasis was upon the Kemalist ideology—nationalism, secularism, development. They were also intended to help bridge the elite-mass gap and engaged in activities that brought townsmen into contact with villagers. Though the impact of such programs was minimal, the concern with this problem led to the extension of the People's Houses into rural areas in 1940 with the establishment of People's Rooms. By 1945 over 400 People's Houses and 2,338 People's Rooms had been established.[28]

The third significant change reflected a new awareness of the need to raise the educational level of the masses so as to facilitate the inculcation of Atatürk's ideology and the achievement of his reform program. Accordingly, educational opportunities were greatly expanded and this decade witnessed a marked increase in the number of students enrolled at all levels. The number of students attending primary schools, which had risen from 332,000 in 1923 to only 500,000 in 1930, reached almost a million ten years later; the number of students in the middle and secondary schools, which had climbed from 6,000 to 27,000 and from 1,200 to 5,700 in this period, now reached 95,000 and 25,000 respectively. Even more striking was the increase in the number of students receiving higher education: 2,300 in 1923, 2,900 in 1930 and 12,850 by 1940.[29]

The problem of rural education was also tackled in a decisive and innovative manner. The Village Institute movement proved to be a landmark in the country's developmental efforts. Opened in the late thirties, the Institutes represented a bold attempt to transform rural life through education. Village youths were trained as teachers and change agents and sent to serve in rural communities. Altogether about 25,000 graduates were produced. The importance of this program cannot be underestimated. One expert has pointed out that as a result of this program "there were approximately *three times* as many rural children for secondary education as there had been urban *primary* school graduates in 1935."[30] Moreover, the movement served to arouse a traditional peasantry and laid the foundation for its effective participation within the polity for:

> Not only were the Village Institute students and their graduates in a position to tell their co-villagers of their constitutional rights, but also the spotlight cast upon rural Turkey by the Movement endowed the majority electorate with a sense of its power.[31]

Such an assessment, however, is probably somewhat exaggerated. Unfortunately, this project was never reinforced by other programs, although Atatürk shortly before his death urged the passage of land reform legislation. The eruption of World War II, however, brought other priorities to the fore and questions such as this were temporarily ignored. Thus, many parts of rural Turkey remained untouched by any vestige of modernity and isolated from national developments except for occasional visits from the gendarmerie and the tax collectors, both of whom were feared and hated. Economically, the consequences of such a situation were of course profound; as one scholar has pointed out: "the neglect of agricultural development might be deemed the original sin of the whole system of planning. . . . Agricultural production did not increase, and only a limited labor force was released for urban industries."[32] The political consequences were to prove even more significant for the gap between town and country which had, as we have emphasized, always been wide, may well have become wider in view of the changes that had taken place in town and city. The size of the cleavage and the attitudes of intellectuals towards the peasantry can be highlighted by the comments of a student from Istanbul who visited a village school teacher several years after the death of Mustafa Kemal.[33] "Mahmut—my dear fellow," he said, "the squalor, the primitive conditions in this village—they're indescribable: What do people mean by having houses and stables in these conditions? It might be the Stone Age, which one only reads about in history books!"

The elite-mass gap was not the only problem area. In fact, the very character of the political system itself was to be brought into question as a result of the very success of the Atatürk reforms in the urban areas. Changes in social stratification patterns accelerated greatly. Developments in industry, communications, and culture led to the proliferation of new roles and to an increase in the number of persons in these roles. Now, numerous businessmen and entrepreneurs, artists and writers, journalists and teachers, managers and workers, ballet dancers and opera singers were active in Turkey. In the course of these decades the structure of occupational opportunities and prestige changed markedly. We have already noted how the composition of the military elite and of the Parliament reflected this trend.

From a political viewpoint, however, the most important consequence of these developments was the growth and emergence of the commercial sector. Under the Ottoman Empire the minorities had monopolized trade and commerce. The break-up of the Empire, the transfer of the minorities, and the new concern with national development all led to the emergence of a group of Turkish entrepreneurs and businessmen. Although new in Turkish society, this group soon proved to be "self-confident, self-reliant and ambitious." Its members included many persons who were solidly established within the state and who possessed considerable political power. Many owed their new success to the important administrative and military offices they had previously occupied, or the close ties they enjoyed with persons in such offices. Another important segment of this new elite was already prominent in political affairs, having entered politics after achieving economic success. As a result the new group, whose emergence "was radically changing the political balance of forces in the country and affecting even the traditional social ethos," became a major political actor.[34]

Thus, by the time of his death Atatürk had resolved two of the major crises that have been defined as critical by students of political development. He had created a new nation whose identity was clearly defined and its authority firmly established. What remained to be resolved was the question of participation. The business community would inevitably demand a greater voice in policy making. The response of the political elite to this de-mand would shape the polity for many years. Similarly, despite developments in the thirties, only a limited degree of penetration had occurred. Much of the rural populace as we have seen, re-mained largely isolated from national trends. Thus Atatürk's suc-cessor and close associate, İsmet İnönü inherited a situation in which serious problems, especially possible inter- and intra-elite conflict, could be expected.

THE MULTIPARTY ERA

With the end of World War II such conflicts erupted into the open. Divisions within the country and within the party over the shape of the future were soon evident. For various reasons, including the desirability of gaining Western support, the expectation that the RPP with its strong institutional base and proud heritage would remain the dominant party, and the genuine acceptance of Atatürk's ideal of democracy, President

İnönü made a momentous decision. Rather than suppress the dissidents or attempt to co-opt them, he declared on November 1, 1945, that the country had achieved political maturity and expressed the hope that an opposition party would be founded.

Shortly thereafter the Democrat Party (DP) was formally established by four leading members of the RPP. It contested the elections held in July 1946, electing 61 deputies. It promptly raised charges of fraud and called for reforms to ensure a fair and honest election. Though some irregularities did occur, notably in Istanbul, these were not sufficient to change the overall results. The next election, held in 1950, was without precedent and marked a turning point in Turkish political development. Eighty-nine percent of the eligible voters went to the polls and the DP, which had established a powerful and effective organization throughout the country, won 54 percent of the vote, electing 416 deputies out of a total of 487. The RPP won 40 percent of the vote and 76 seats. It was turned out of office after 27 years.[35]

Many groups united under the banner of the DP to voice their discontent with the RPP and its policies. Joining the business community, who demanded a move away from etatism towards private enterprise, were intellectuals who wanted democracy, religious conservatives who hoped for a return to Islamic principles, elements of the rural elite who were dissatisfied with the distribution of power within the RPP and the state, and the peasantry which felt neglected and abused by a tyrannical administration—in short all those persons (and after twenty-seven years there were many) who harbored resentments against or who had suffered from or disapproved of the policies of the RPP. The DP leaders displayed a remarkable organizational ability and quickly created a political organization with strong roots throughout the country that successfully mobilized rural support and inducted the still largely traditional peasantry into politics.

Once in power the DP moved to carry out its campaign promises. It embarked upon an ambitious program of economic development, financed to a large degree by US aid, and the country prospered. Private investment expanded greatly. Agricultural production boomed as a result of price supports, the mechanization of farming, and very favorable weather. The highway building program and the concomitant availability of transportation gave the country a new unity; large numbers of villagers began to visit market towns where they were exposed to new ideas, attitudes, and values and many persons migrated permanently to urban centers. The overall result was that the peasantry became increasingly market-oriented and integrated into the national economy.

Equally rapid advances were made in communications, and radios were soon to be found in every coffee house or party local. The army, reorganized and modernized with American support, proved to be an important means of reinforcing the changes taking place in rural areas for the peasant draftees became part of a new environment in which they were exposed to modernism.

All these factors led to rapid change in rural life and to the emergence of the peasant as an important actor in the political arena. Long isolated from national life, the rural masses now began to develop a political awareness and, as a result of the DP's organizing efforts, gained a channel through which to articulate demands. Before long villagers were demanding schools, roads, and drinking water and the relationship between the central bureaucracy and the peasants, traditionally one of domination and subservience, began to change in the direction of a service orientation. This process was in many ways a painful one for the administrators who were now subject to political pressures of all sorts. The DP, for its part, reacted quickly and flexibly to this new situation and moved in various ways to meet rural demands. Quite naturally the DP won an even larger victory in the 1954 election than four years earlier. It emerged with almost 57 percent of the vote and 503 seats as compared with the RPP which won only 35 percent of the vote and 31 seats in Parliament.

These developments had profound consequences for patterns of elite composition and for inter-elite relationships. Most importantly the composition of the political elite had changed drastically as a new group swept to power in the "ruralizing election" of 1950 and strengthened its position in 1954. An indication of the change is given by the transformation of the membership of Parliament, a critical and central institution of the political system. Heretofore, the Assembly had been dominated, as we have noted, by persons of military and bureaucratic background; now representatives of such occupational categories as "trade," "agriculture," and the "free professions" became dominant. This change has been summarized as follows: "Along with the provincial lawyer, the small-town merchant or tradesman seems to typify the changed Assemblies of the Democrat Party's decade of control, just as the official and the officer typified the Kemalist epoch."[36] A second change was in the increased localism of the new assemblies; more than ever before in Ottoman-Turkish history rural interests were influential in national policy making; local and provincial elites had in effect emerged as major political actors at the center.[37]

That such a transition could be achieved so easily and smoothly was truly remarkable. Unfortunately, the new political elite proved quite insensitive to the concerns and aspirations of its predecessors. It adopted policies that adversely affected the position of the military, the bureaucracy and the intellectuals. Moreover the new government, headed by Prime Minister Menderes, was unable to sustain its ambitious program of economic development because of inadequate and haphazard planning, a shortage of capital, the allocation of substantial resources to the armed forces, adverse terms of trade, and inclement weather. Thus, within a few years the economy was characterized not by growth but by a drastic inflation and a scarcity of consumer items. The urban elements were particularly affected; in addition, the government's fiscal policies directly favored the peasantry by exempting it from taxation so that the salaried groups bore a still heavier burden.

Moreover, throughout this period developments that had already become obvious during the Atatürk era, such as the increasing correlation of status with economic power, continued and expanded so that the relative prestige of bureaucrats, intellectuals, and military officers dropped markedly (despite the policy of material rejuvenation of the armed forces). Thus groups which had enjoyed high social status and, at least until 1950, a preponderant role in decision-making now not only lost their power but saw their social and economic position seriously threatened by the policies implemented by the new political elite.

The military was particularly affected. The new government possessed "a thinly veiled contempt for the officer corps."[38] It accorded the military little voice in decision-making and permitted its prestige and standard of living to deteriorate. How officers felt about this situation is vividly attested to by one scholar who reported: "Many of the officers I interviewed ... complained that in the 1950s some landlords would not even bother to show them houses for rent, for 'they could not afford it'; some store owners looked annoyed at the prospect of showing expensive items to this impoverished group; waiters with an eye on tips preferred to serve richer customers; and even mothers, who had once been highly honored to have officers as sons-in-law, often advised their daughters not to marry men with 'shiny uniforms but empty pockets.' "[39] Even more serious, in the eyes of many officers, was the change in their social status and prestige. One officer emphasized this point in the following words: "The prestige of the army was declining. Money seemed to be everything. An officer no longer had status in society. . . . It was not that we needed money, for officers had always been ill-paid, but we had had honor and respect in the past. Now these are gone."[40]

Bureaucrats too were affected by such considerations. Inflation was no new phenomenon in Turkey; during the war the country had watched prices rise rapidly. In those years, however, bureaucrats—and army officers—were provided with assistance in the form of specific goods to offset the consequences of inflation. Now such supplementary income was no longer forthcoming.[41] Particularly affected was the bureaucratic elite. The DP government sought to reduce the differential between the higher and lower echelons of the administration. Thus it was the purchasing power of the elite which suffered most. Between 1952 and 1957 their purchasing power fell by 69 percent whereas the lowest grades suffered only a 43 percent decline.[42] As was the case with the military, their status also declined markedly. Businessmen, for example, had formerly accorded officials the highest prestige; now they ranked official positions merely above the "worker" category. Nor was administration the preferred career that it had once been: 49 percent of the students surveyed in one study accorded most prestige to the free professions, while only 12 percent felt that way about the combined category of government and politics.[43]

These trends are reflected in the available data concerning the composition of the administrative elite and recruitment patterns into the administration. It appears that the pool of recruitment changed during these years with significant numbers of persons from humble backgrounds entering the administration. One study conducted in the mid-fifties showed that 20 percent of provincial governors (*Vali*) were the sons of farmers, peasants, small traders, artisans and the like as compared to 38 percent of the sub-provincial governors (*kaymakam*). Similarly a later study revealed the 12 percent of officials holding the highest posts at the center came from such backgrounds whereas 30 percent of officials in the middle ranks had fathers in these occupations. If we assume an age differential between persons serving at these two levels it appears that the trend in provincial administration towards increased recruitment from humble backgrounds also holds for the center.[44]

Moreover, a detailed study of career patterns had indicated that as the central ministries lost status a marked exodus of officials from those ministries into new, more economically oriented institutions occurred. Particularly affected was the Ministry of the Interior whose administrators, especially those serving in the provinces, were subject to the greatest strains and pressures as a result of the redefinition of roles that occurred after 1950.[45] As we have seen, a new relationship evolved between bureaucrat and peasant. Similarly bureaucrats had to reorient their views of businessmen whom they had heretofore tended to dismiss as "thieves with a neck-tie."[46]

A third grouping that was affected by developments in this period were the intellectuals, composed primarily of faculty and students but also including journalists and writers. At first they supported the DP. But as economic conditions deteriorated and the new political elite increasingly adopted policies that, though popular in rural areas, were viewed as representing retrogression from Atatürk's principles, the intellectual community moved steadily into opposition. The expectations of the early fifties were rudely dashed and the DP government increasingly came to be viewed as a regime that was concerned only with maintaining itself in power. Its policies, particularly the relaxation of religious control, which was accompanied by a wave of conservative reaction in many places, deeply worried many members of the Atatürk political elite and their supporters, particularly the intellectuals. It seemed as though the fundamental bases of Atatürk's Turkey were being endangered.

In this atmosphere criticism of the government's policies expanded rapidly but the new political elite, led by President

Bayar and Prime Minister Menderes, proved highly insensitive and intolerant. It unwisely moved to extend its control over centers of opposition by limiting the rights of free speech, assembly, campaigning, and the autonomy of the universities; as early as 1954 the DP passed laws that gave it the right to retire and dismiss civil servants, including judges and professors under certain conditions. It also moved to neutralize the student opposition by extending its influence over student organization, a policy that was to have disastrous consequences for the character and development of the Turkish student movement.[47]

Thus between 1954 and 1957 the tone and temper of Turkish politics deteriorated steadily and the stage was set for severe inter-elite conflict. The result was acute polarization. A reaction set in within the DP itself; in 1955 its liberal and intellectual members resigned or were expelled. They formed the short-lived Freedom Party which later merged with the RPP. Hence, those groups which had formerly enjoyed power were now allied together: the bureaucrats, the military, the intellectuals. On the other side was the new political elite consisting of landowning and provincial elites and businessmen who had assumed leadership in the DP. As the economic situation degenerated, however, there were some signs that even the business elite was becoming alienated from the DP. Many businessmen chafed under the government's onerous controls and its ineffective economic measures and apparently no longer supported the DP.[48]

In the 1957 elections, the government, concerned with the continuing erosion of its popularity, amended the electoral law to prevent the opposition from forming a united front. As a result, although the DP won only 48 percent of the vote, it elected 424 deputies out of a total of 610 as compared to 41 percent and 178 seats for the RPP. These results further increased tensions and aggravated inter-elite conflict. The DP reacted vigorously to charges of fraud and electoral manipulation and retaliated with vituperation against the RPP and its leaders. Though the DP's tactics did enable it to get a majority of the seats in Parliament it should be noted that the RPP contributed to its own defeat through its ineffectual and static organization and campaign.[49] In any case, the RPP responded to the DP's attacks in kind, condemning the imposition of ever stricter government controls over the opposition and the press. It strongly attacked Prime Minister Menderes and President Bayar and accused the government of dictatorial intent, warning that its leaders would be held accountable.

Thus, the dangerous cycle accelerated and the delicate fabric of political civility was strained to the breaking point as partisan bitterness and invective became normal means of political discourse. As conditions continued to deteriorate the government attempted to use the army to prevent İsmet İnönü from making a speaking tour and established, in early 1960, a commission with extensive powers. This move was widely regarded as part of a policy to abolish all opposition and institute dictatorial rule. This action proved to be the catalyst that sparked student demonstrations in April which led directly to the military takeover the following month. These developments have been well summarized by one scholar who wrote: "Both Republicans and Democrats alike contributed to the vital process of destroying the credibility of the civilian regime. ... The RPP heightened the Democratic leaders' determination to hang on to power at all costs ... The continued refusal of the DP to risk elections and the immediate threat that the RPP would be closed ... created the specter of civil war."[50]

As early as 1954 some military officers were plotting to overthrow the government. In 1957 one plot was actually uncovered. This may have contributed to the DP's reactions, but these early efforts at conspiracy did not yield appreciable results until the legitimacy of the government had dropped much further and until the government itself forced the military to choose between two painful alternatives by attempting to use the army for its own political ends. Much has been written about the factors responsible for the military's decision to intervene and different scholars have identified different causes. One analysis attributes the military's unrest primarily to the fact that in sharp contrast to the situation under Atatürk, when the military had been static and the civilian sector dynamic, "the army's dynamism was not matched by the civilian sector. This tended to make the army's programs dysfunctional; its satisfactions turned into frustration."[51]

Such a view, however, cannot be supported by the available data concerning either the character of the military institution, particularly its career patterns, or the structure of opportunities within the civilian sector which became more dynamic than ever. Moreover, one cannot underestimate the factors that we have discussed; many officers felt a strong kinship with administrative and intellectual elites, shared their concern with policies that seemed to negate Atatürk's principles, and increasingly lost confidence in the new government over which they had little influence.[52]

Similar problems arise when considering the hypothesis that the "deeper sources of dissatisfaction" of the military lay in their concern with the social injustices of the DP's policies owing particularly to their own socio-economic backgrounds.[53] As we have seen, most officers traditionally came from lower-class families. At least 11 of the 29 officers who comprised the National Unity Committee, the junta which ruled the country after the revolution, came from such backgrounds; none of the others were of elite backgrounds.[54] Nevertheless, as is noted elsewhere in this volume, it is difficult to relate such background data to value orientations or behavior. Subsequent experiences must be taken into account, particularly in cases such as this where officers underwent a thorough socializing experience through military schools and the military career itself and probably acquired new orientations and attitudes. Certainly it is known that the administrative elite, a group that did not include the same high percentage of persons of lower-class origins in its ranks, shared the orientations of the military. Moreover, the revolutionists did not represent a cohesive group but encompassed a wide variety of political orientations running the gamut from left to right. The plotters possessed no clear objectives other than overthrowing the existing government. As we shall see, once that had been accomplished serious dissensions broke out among them concerning the nature and direction of policy.[55]

Thus, the roots of the 1960 revolution are ultimately to be found in the social and political changes that we have described, particularly in the disintegration of the broad elite consensus that had existed under Atatürk's dynamic leadership. The new political elite never understood the importance of this consensus, not did it adopt policies to ameliorate the inevitable strains that accompanied the realignment of political, social, and economic power which followed democratization and the transformation of the peasantry into an active political force. Instead, it proved remarkably insensitive to the frustrations of elite groupings that still retained considerable power and abetted by its opponents, polarized the society and increased tensions to such a degree that civil strife might easily have resulted. The actual military intervention was thus only a matter of timing. It came on May 27, 1960.

FROM REVOLUTION TO INTERVENTION

The aftermath of the coup vividly revealed not only the degree to which the fundamental cleavage between center and periphery remained the dominant feature of the Turkish political system but also the degree to which the military, bureaucratic and intellectual elites were divided among themselves. Once jubilation over the coup had died down the junta found itself confronted with such serious problems as legitimizing the revolution in the rural areas, where it was treated with passivity if not resentment. There was also pressure to resolve the conditions which had sparked the conspiracy. As a result, although the military junta which took the name National Unity Committee (NUC), had naively anticipated that it would be able to restore power to civilian hands within three months, it did not do so for nearly one and a half years.[56]

Greatly complicating the junta's task were divisions within its own ranks and within the military in general, as well as dissension between the junta and non-military elites. Several cliques could be discerned within the NUC. The radicals, led by Colonel Alpaslan Türkeş, were more concerned with implementing fundamental social and economic reforms than with restoring civilian rule. This group consisted of the original conspirators. They were younger and of lower rank than the moderates, led by General Gürsel. In the ensuing power struggle, Türkeş and his followers were defeated. Further adding to dissension among the military was the early decision on the part of the junta to purge about 7,000 officers, including 235 generals, ostensibly to "rejuvenate the army." Unrest remained evident, sometimes dramatically so, as in 1962 and 1963, when attempted coups against the new civilian regime were suppressed.[57]

As for tension between the junta and non-military groups, the case of the intellectuals is instructive. Initially, there was close cooperation between the two groups, especially in the preparation of a number of reform proposals. However, the decision to apply the instrument of the purge to the universities in order to oust unqualified and incompetent professors, backfired badly, destroying the rapport which had existed earlier. Indeed, this clumsy attempt at reform of the institutions of higher learning had the paradoxical effect of ousting many qualified individuals, and served only to heighten existing tensions.

Equally troubled were relations between the junta and the political parties. Various elements within the army held differing views of the RPP and the desirability of permitting it to gain power. And, although the party, confident of its ability to win, desired early elections, it did not wish to be too closely associated with an increasingly unpopular military regime.

The new constitution and electoral law that were drawn up were specifically designed to prevent past abuses and overcome the fundamental cleavages within the country. It soon became evident, however, that consensus could not be achieved through structural and institutional changes. In the referendum on the new constitution, 38 percent of the voters who bothered to cast ballots openly voiced their disapproval with the junta and its policies by rejecting the new arrangements.[58] In the general elections held later that year (1961) the degree to which the country remained polarized was further indicated by the fact that the RPP polled only 37 percent of the vote; two new parties, the Justice Party (JP) and the New Turkey Party (NTP) which focused their appeal on the former DP electorate, received 35 percent and 14 percent respectively.

In their zeal to restrict the power of the government, the authors of the new constitution rendered such institutions as the universities, the judiciary and the broadcasting system virtually immune from outside control and guaranteed extensive personal liberties. They also provided for a system of checks and balances including a bicameral legislature, the upper house of which would include members of the NUC for life. A constitutional court was also provided for. Whether such arrangements prevented the government from implementing its policies effectively and permitted these institutions to display political partisanship as the JP leaders later claimed, particularly after the 1965 election, remained a debatable topic.

Above all, the leaders of the NUC were concerned with legitimizing the revolution and with preventing a resurgence of the factors that had forced them to intervene. Accordingly, the DP was outlawed and its leaders imprisoned and tried; Prime Minister Menderes and two of his associates were executed; thirty-one persons were sentenced to life imprisonment and 402 others to prison terms ranging from two to twenty years. Thus a new issue entered the political arena, the question of amnesty for the imprisoned DP leaders which, for most of the sixties, served to increase political tensions. On this issue, too, a split within the military became evident. While former NUC members were uncompromising, the armed forces in general seem to have supported the moderates in the two major parties, the JP and the RPP, who came close to agreement on this question as early as 1962. The conservatives in the JP and in the minor parties, particularly local organizations, were the strongest supporters of amnesty.[59]

Civilian rule was resumed in the fall of 1961 in the form of a coalition between JP and the RPP, formed after the intervention of General Gürsel, who was elected President. İsmet İnönü became Prime Minister. Disagreements over the question of amnesty and the nature of social and economic policy soon led to the demise of the coalition. Two other coalitions were formed with difficulty by İnönü without the JP. They did not produce stability or the kinds of basic reforms that had been anticipated by the military junta either.

Throughout this period the strength of the JP increased steadily and the fundamental issue was whether the military would permit government by a party that possessed such close ideological and generational ties to the outlawed Democrats.[60] The Chief of Staff, and later President, General Cevdet Sunay, in 1965 issued a well publicized warning against the actions of political parties who were dividing the country and alienating the people from the army. Since this statement came shortly before the JP was to elect a new leader it was obviously directed against that party, particulary its powerful conservative wing headed by Mr. S. Bilgiç. What role this message played is unclear but subsequently Süleyman Demirel, a moderate, was elected head of the JP, and in February of that year he engineered the defeat of İnönü's coalition. In the new coalition, he served as Vice Premier under a political neutral, a move designed to allay popular fears that the military elite would never permit the JP to rule.

Tensions within the country were particularly heightened by the emergence of new ideological issues in this period and with the realignment of parties along a conservative-liberal continuum. Throughout the fifties the primary concern of the military, bureaucratic, and intellectual elites was for the preservation of Atatürk's principles and the prevention of authoritarianism. Now questions of social and economic justice increasingly occupied the attention of various elements of these elites. The saliency of ideological factors is well illustrated in the post-1960 struggle within the RPP to define that party's orientation. As we have seen, the party consisted essentially of a coalition of the bureaucratic and military elites on the one hand and local gentry on the other. But this alliance was being subjected to increasing strains. The party was being prodded by critics, particularly intellectuals, both within and outside its ranks. They claimed that it was betraying the principles of Atatürk and of the 1960 revolution by its willingness to compromise on fundamental social and economic questions. Contributing to this kind of pressure was the increasing realization that the party's chances of electoral success were not bright. Moreover, by the mid-sixties the RPP had lost the support of some of the intellectual elite which favored the Marxist Turkish Labor Party (TIP) which had been newly organized in 1961 and which seemed more dynamic and attuned to contemporary problems. Its proclamations that "socialism" provided the key to rapid development found ready acceptance within the universities and among many journalists and writers, as did its bitter attacks on the United States for alleged imperialism.

These pressures combined to push the RPP slowly but surely to the left. The party's new orientation was officially announced before the 1965 elections when İnönü proclaimed that the RPP was a "left of center" party. This proclamation did not eliminate dissension within the party; on the contrary, it alienated the more conservative elements and several important resignations occurred. One indication of the lack of agreement on fundamental issues that characterized the RPP in this period is provided by the opposition of several deputies to the party leadership's decision in favor of land reform legislation.

While the RPP was evolving its new stance the JP moved to consolidate its position among conservative and centrist elements by further concessions on religious matters and by openly identifying itself with the DP. Thus "communism" and religion became major campaign issues in the 1965 elections; some JP candidates attacked the RPP on the ground that it was pro-communist or at least paving the way for communism and that it was anti-Islamic, a party of infidels. RPP and TIP candidates did not hesitate to respond in kind with charges that the JP was the party of reaction, that it betrayed Atatürk's principles, and that its leaders were puppets of the US. The electoral campaign was thus marked by violent demagogery.

When the ballots were counted the JP emerged with a major victory. It received 53 percent of the vote as opposed to 29 percent for the RPP—by far the smallest percentage that party had ever won. Contributing to the RPP's crushing defeat was the persistence of former political cleavages and the introduction of new ones which further served to draw votes away. Not only was the RPP viewed as responsible for the 1960 revolution, despite its continuous protestations, but it was held culpable for the lack of attention that the coalition governments under its leadership had paid to rural needs. In particular, the attitudes and behavior of gendarmes and bureaucrats apparently regressed towards the pattern that had existed prior to the establishment of the multi-party system, and this aroused deep-seated resentment. Thus the rural masses voted strongly for the JP which they regarded as the true heir of the DP. Nor did the RPP win many new voters elsewhere. It was condemned for the failure to enact concrete reforms after the revolution; its new ideological stance alienated many former supporters but did not enable the party to win back the intellectual elements who leaned toward TIP. That party gained 3 percent of the vote, most of which was centered in urban areas.

Despite these results the RPP remained committed to democratic socialism. In 1966, Bülent Ecevit, the able leader of the "progressive" group was elected General Secretary, despite considerable opposition from the party's conservative elements. The following year 52 senators and deputies, headed by Turhan Feyzioğlu, resigned and formed the new Reliance Party (RP). This exodus weakened the RPP greatly; it was left with only 130 representatives in Parliament. This also marked the end of the traditional alliance between local notables and nationalist elite that had characterized the party since its inception. The new dynamic leadership moved promptly to revitalize the party's moribund and ineffectual organization and to recruit new sources of support. Hitherto the RPP's electoral strength had been derived from the least developed parts of the country where notables continued to exercise considerable influence over voting behavior; now it was clear that the party could no longer count on such support. TIP in the meantime became increasingly ineffective as its leaders divided over questions of ideology and strategy and different personalities sought to gain control of the party. These cleavages were soon reflected among its supporters in the universities and elsewhere, and were particularly evident among the students and their associations.

The JP too was characterized by considerable dissension in these years. Though Prime Minister Demirel managed to avoid an open split he had to maintain unity among a heterogeneous amalgamation of a few intellectuals, the business and landowning elites, peasants and workers. Within the party's ranks were to be found representatives of viewpoints ranging from reactionary to moderate. Demirel often made concessions to the conservatives to maintain his position. Such concessions, particularly those involving religious affairs, further antagonized other elements and served to aggravate tensions. Moreover a rapid inflation was again evident even though the overall rate of economic development was about 6 percent a year.

This situation was highly reminiscent of the late fifties, but significant differences were also evident. The most important of these was the dissolution of the former entente between the intellectual, military, and bureaucratic elites. While many intellectuals proved highly receptive to Marxist ideologies, their receptivity was not matched by most of the military and bureaucratic elites. Also contributing greatly to the military's changed stance was the policy followed by Demirel. Aware of the DP leadership's errors in this regard he always accorded a high priority to maintaining good relations with the military elite. He did not permit the standard of living of the officer corps to be damaged by the inflation; in fact, their economic position improved markedly during these years. He was also careful to maintain the status and prestige of the military and consulted frequently with high ranking officers. Thus the military elite participated actively in decision-making. Their power was further enhanced by the fact that since 1960 the office of President of the Republic was the preserve of senior military officers.[61]

The position of the bureaucratic elite also differed markedly from that of the earlier decade. The performance of the military after the 1960 revolution did not arouse any more enthusiasm among the bureaucrats than elsewhere in the society; indeed, the attitude of the bureaucrats toward the military was quite reserved. In a survey of Political Science Faculty graduates conducted in 1965 only one of the respondents felt that one could benefit his country most by serving in the military. The authors of the study concluded: "Although both the civil servants and the military had been under similar pressures in the late 1950s few enduring psychological ties between these two groups were noted. . . . The ties between administrator and military officer may have been eroded by social change and the experience of military rule."[62]

Equally significant results were evident in the attitude of bureaucrats towards their own profession and towards other groups in society. They evaluated their own roles modestly and evidenced a new appreciation of both businessmen and politicians.[63] This finding requires further examination, however. It is known that a large turnover occurred in the bureaucratic elite in the sixties as the JP government sought to place friendly personnel in important posts. This made for considerable unrest within the bureaucracy. Whether it sufficed to overcome such other factors making for satisfaction as the opportunities for career mobility that were created by the process of economic development must await further study.[64]

While the military and bureaucratic elites were quiescent the intellectual elite remained active in opposition, although its influence was weakened by fragmentation between the RPP and various TIP factions, each with its own ideological variant. Various attempts were made to unify and integrate the "socialists" however, and the fundamental cleavage in this period lay between the left and the right. The latter was usually supported by conservative elements in the JP and the National Action Party (MHP), a strongly nationalist party headed by Colonel Türkeş, the former leader of the radical group in the NUC.

Militancy plus organization soon led to increasing violence, and pitched battles, often involving armed students, became frequent occurrences. One particularly bloody event occurred in February 1969 when a demonstration organized by radical students and trade union members to protest the visit of the US 6th Fleet was attacked by reactionary elements. The toll was several dead and over 200 wounded.

The fact that workers were involved indicates that this group is becoming an important new factor on the Turkish political scene. In 1964 they numbered almost a million, 34 percent of whom were unionized. Although the history of the Turkish labor movement can be traced back to 1871, only after the 1960 revolution, when unions were granted new rights, did the labor movement become a potent economic and political force. The largest confederation, Türk İş, was founded in 1952. By and large it is considered sympathetic to the RPP and hostile to TIP. A rival confederation, DISK was founded in 1967 by 17 unions with 84,000 members who disapproved of Türk İş's political stance. DISK may be considered more leftist than Türk İş; it had close ties to TIP.[65]

Thus the second half of the sixties witnessed the growing politicalization, polarization, and fragmentation of various groups and elites within the society. The 1969 elections did not serve to halt this process but probably accelerated it. Fewer voters turned out than in any other general election (64 percent). Factors such as the plenitude of elections and campaigns since 1960, apathy, resentment, or satisfaction, and inclement weather may also have been responsible. The JP's vote dropped to 47 percent, although it elected 57 percent of the deputies. The RPP received 27 percent of the vote, a slight decline from 1965, but it gained some additional seats, electing 32 percent of the deputies. This result was in fact quite promising for the RPP since it made up the losses that it suffered from defections such as those to the RP (which gained almost 7 percent of the vote). The minor parties each polled between 2 percent and 3 percent of the vote. Surprisingly, in view of the saliency of ideology and the popularity of leftist thought, TIP polled only 2.7 percent of the total. This poor showing can be attributed to its fragmented leadership and its uncompromisingly doctrinaire approach to Turkey's problems. A new party, the Unity Party (UP) which based its campaign on appeals to the Shiite minority received almost 3 percent of the vote.[66]

Despite its victory the JP continued to be wracked by tensions between its two wings. Finally in February 1970, 41 supporters of Mr. Bilgiç joined with other parties to defeat the government's budget. A wave of expulsions and resignations ensued and the conservatives formed a new party, the Democratic Party (DP), a name chosen for obvious reasons. Equally blatant was the new party's policy of recruiting members from the old DP, including former P. M. Menderes' son.[67]

Though Mr. Demirel was able to attract enough deputies from among independents and various minor parties to form a new government, the weakness of his position served as an added incentive to various groups within the country to try to unseat the government. Thus the level of violence continued to increase. Between July 1969 and March 1970 eight youths were killed in struggles between leftists and rightists and the number continued to grow as the legitimacy of the government continued to erode. Mr. İnönü, P.M. Demirel and the National Security Council all denounced the violence but the precarious position of the government spurred the activities of extremists, and another dozen persons or so lost their lives in clashes between ideological extremists.[68] From December 1970 onwards, an organization called the Turkish People's Liberation Army began to engage in bank holdups and kidnappings in order to acquire funds to free the "Turkish People from American Imperialism and its local collaborators."[69] Subsequently, it appeared that the members of this Maoist organization possessed ties with the Palestinian guerrilla movement and that some of its members had received training there. The role of outside forces in inciting students and various youth organizations awaits clarification, but one responsible political leader has charged that: "Professional agents, trained, armed, and directed outside Turkey, were able to transform some leftist student organizations into urban guerrilla units. . . ."[70] It is also probable that the right wing extremists enjoyed external support of various sorts.

In February 1971, Mr. Demirel sponsored harsh new legislation to curb the anarchy but the following month the Chief of Staff and the chiefs of the Turkish armed forces issued an ultimatum demanding that the government resign and that a new non-political cabinet be formed to restore political stability and undertake reforms. Even the military's intervention did not bring an immediate end to violence. But the imposition of martial law and the adoption of repressive measures, including imprisonment of numerous intellectuals accused of leftist proclivities and the capture of most of the guerrilla leaders, led to the restoration of a state of public order.

Thus, 1971 represents another benchmark in Turkey's history. Eleven years after the revolution the military intervened again and ostensibly for the same reasons—to restore political stability and to promote needed reforms. Ironically the intervention came despite Demirel's determined effort to avoid the mistakes of the DP leadership of the fifties. Yet once again the military felt compelled to intervene. Unlike 1960, however, the initiative came not from colonels and majors but from the highest ranking officers within the state who, perhaps partly because of the earlier experience, proclaimed that they did not seek to replace civilian authority with military rule. And, in fact, general elections were held in 1973 which resulted in the defeat of Mr. Demirel and the JP, its vote dropping precipitously to 30 percent of the total. The rejuvenated RPP, on the other hand, increased its total to 34 percent. Each of the other established parties received 5 percent or less of the vote. Two new parties, on the other hand, did very well; the DP received 12 percent, mainly from former supporters of Mr. Demirel, and the National Salvation Party which combined a conservative religious orientation with a forward looking economic program polled the same vote.[71] It subsequently agreed to form a government with the RPP with Mr. Ecevit serving as Prime Minister. These results, together with developments since the mid-sixties reflect the degree of change which has been taking place in Turkish society.

CONCLUSION

The Turkey of the seventies is not the Turkey of former years. At the same time it is clear that important elements of continuity with the past can be discerned in such areas as patterns of elite composition, the potential or actual power of various elites, and the character of center-periphery relations. What is particularly striking is that these aspects of Ottoman society retained their essential characteristics even though the country underwent a marked degree of modernization, experienced a cultural revolution of remarkable scope and intensity, and witnessed the transformation of its political system.

Throughout our discussion, we have made a distinction between social core groups and elites. Change in the former represents systemic transformation. It is at this level that the most radical transformation has occurred since the beginning of modernization. Such a transformation took place in 1908 in the form of the Young Turk Revolution. That upheaval placed power in the hands of a political elite which included bureaucratic, military, and intellectual elements and whose base was control of military and administrative institutions. The transformation of the social core group, however, was not accompanied by radical change in the composition of particular elites or in their power and significance. Many persons of upper-class backgrounds continued to occupy important positions within the state apparatus and former patterns were largely retained. However, the social base of recruitment to particular elites broadened considerably during the Young Turk period as the new political elite adopted policies that further spurred ideological, social, and cultural change. On the other hand, center-periphery relations changed very little. So also, the rural and other elites remained essentially unchanged, apart from the continuing decline of the religious elite.

It was during the years of Atatürk's rule that the power of the religious elite was eliminated at the center. But even during this period of radical social and cultural change a marked degree of continuity can be discerned in the structure and composition of the social core group and particular elites. The society's core remained a political elite, and though the policies followed by Atatürk led to a marked broadening of the pool of recruitment to specific elites, changes in composition appear to have been largely evolutionary: it was a case of what Frey has called "capillary action."[72] The policies followed by Atatürk did, however, markedly accelerate and expand societal differentiation and thus promoted the emergence of new social groups, such as businessmen, professionals, entrepreneurs, and the like. Leading personalities from among these groups came to represent a counter-elite challenging the authority and legitimacy of the existing political elite. When the rules of the political game were altered after World War II to permit open competition, this new elite was able to mobilize the periphery and achieve political power.

Thus, a fundamental shift in the composition of the governing elite and in the core pattern of the society took place in 1950 for Turkey was now characterized by open competition for power between various elites with conflicting interests and values. At first the political system was essentially bi-polar and reflected deep-rooted tension between center and periphery. Now the periphery deeply influenced policy outputs at the center for during this period the peasantry became, for the first time, an important factor in the country's economic and political life and the local gentry and their allies were well represented in the new political elite. Such a fundamental change in the power structure of the society inevitably created tensions, tensions which were aggravated by the insensitivity of the government to the adverse changes in the social and economic position of those groups that had heretofore enjoyed power and influence. Nor did the RPP, the party of the Kemalist elites, hesitate to adopt tactics that contributed to the erosion of civility and consensus.

In 1960 the inevitable occurred and the military overthrew the government. This upheaval, however, did not lead to any fundamental change in either the structure of the center or the periphery. It did create conditions which intensified conflict and led to the emergence of a multi-polar polity. The new atmosphere of freedom facilitated the introduction and dissemination of ideologies that possessed a considerable attraction for those groups in the society concerned with problems of development, equality, and justice. Particularly affected were intellectuals and students but as they became increasingly politicized and sensitive to ideological nuances they not only shifted their allegiances towards the left but fragmented in the process. This development affected the ties that formerly joined them to military and bureaucratic elites, for the latter were not receptive to Marxism.

As new patterns of inter- and intra-elite relationships began to emerge so the political parties were subject to new strains from within and outside their ranks. The RPP found itself increasingly forced to reappraise its position; finally, the traditional alliance between its national and local wings was shattered. Nor did the radical left evidence any unity, for TIP, too, was divided. A similar pattern characterized the JP, whose membership was also fragmented. Ultimately its right wing broke away to form a new party.

In reviewing these developments it is clear that the major impact of modernization appears to have been the emergence of new groupings and concomitant pressures for greater political participation; in terms of individual mobility and changes in the composition of particular elites the pattern seems to be one of a gradually broadening base of recruitment and evolutionary changes over time. In no case has there been a radical transformation as the members of functional elites have proven flexible enough to maintain their position and even to take advantage of new opportunities that were created by the modernization process. The present situation in Turkey is not, however, the inexorable result of an inevitable process of modernization but stems from implicit or explicit political decisions. It is because of these decisions that change and continuity occurred in patterns of elite structure and processes, in the political saliency of particular elites, and in the role that they played in the political process. Thus, since political decisions created conditions of instability, fragmentation and polarization, the successful implementation of other decisions could provide the country with a renewed sense of purpose and national unity. Whether such decisions will actually be forthcoming awaits the verdict of history.

NOTES

1. Dankwart A. Rustow, "Atatürk as Founder of a State." In *Professor Dr. Yavuz Abadan'a Armağan* (Ankara Üniversitesi Siyasal Bilgiler Fakültesi Yayınlarī No. 280, 1969), pp. 567-568.

2. For this and related terms, see S. Keller, *Beyond the Ruling Class* (New York: Random House, 1963).

3. The classical pattern is described in detail in H. A. R. Gibb and Harold Bowen, *Islamic Society and the West* (London: Oxford University Press, 1950, 1957), Volume I, Parts I, II. For an incisive critique see Norman Itzkowitz, "Eighteenth Century Ottoman Realities," *Studia Islamica* 16 (1962): 73-94.

4. Norman Itzkowitz, " 'Kimsiniz Bey Efendi,' or a Look at *Tanzimat* through Namier-Colored Glasses." In *Near Eastern Roundtable*, ed. R. Bayly Winder (New York: Near Eastern Center and Center for International Studies, New York University, 1969), pp. 49-50.

5. Robert Mantran, *Istanbul dans la séconde moitié du XVII siecle* (Paris: Librairie Adrien Maisonneuve, 1962), p. 175.

6. On the accomplishments of the Young Turks in addition to the sources cited see B. Lewis, *Emergence of Modern Turkey* (London: Oxford University Press, 1961), pp. 206 ff.; on political changes see Dankwart A. Rustow, "The Army and the Founding of the Turkish Republic," *World Politics* 11, 4 (July 1959): 541.

7. Joseph S. Szyliowicz, "Elite Recruitment in Turkey: The Role of the Mülkiye," *World Politics* 23, 3 (April 1971).

8. George S. Harris, "The Atatürk Revolution and the Foreign Office, 1919-1931: A Preliminary Study," (paper delivered at the Middle East Studies Association Meeting, Binghamton, New York, November 1972) pp. 9, 12-14.

9. Frederick Frey, *The Turkish Political Elite* (Cambridge, Mass.: M. I. T. Press, 1965), pp. 307-324.

10. Rustow, "Atatürk," p. 352.

11. Harris, "The Atatürk Revolution," pp. 32-33.

12. Doğan Avcioğlu, *Türkiyenin Düzeni* (Ankara: Bilgi Yaymevi, 1968), pp. 155-156.

13. Frey, *The Turkish Political Elite*, p. 115; Szyliowicz, "Elite Recruitment in Turkey," p. 393.

14. Frey, *The Turkish Political Elite*, pp. 334-335. See also his "Arms and the Man in Turkish Politics," *Land Reborn* 11, (August 1960): 5-6; see also George S. Harris, "The Role of the Military in Turkish Politics," Part I, *The Middle East Journal* 19, 1 (Winter 1965): 54 ff.

15. Frey, *The Turkish Political Elite*, pp. 181, 283.

16. *The Military in the Middle East*, ed. S. N. Fisher, (Columbus: Ohio State University Press, 1963), p. 29.

17. Frey, *Turkish Political Elite*, p. 141.

18. Dankwart A. Rustow, "Politics and Islam in Turkey 1920-1955," *Islam and the West*, ed. R. N. Frye, (The Hague: Mouton and Co., 1957), p. 73; Frey, *Turkish Political Elite*, p. 311.

19. Michael P. Hyland, "Doctrinal and Tactical Problems of Turkey's Republican People's Party, (RPP)," (paper delivered at the Middle East Studies Association Meeting, Toronto, Canada, November 14-15, 1969) pp. 14 ff. See also E. Özbudun, "Established Revolution Versus Unfinished Revolution: Contrasting Patterns of Democratization in Mexico and Turkey," *Authoritarian Politics in Modern Society*, eds., S. P. Huntington and C. H. Moore, (New York: Basic Books, 1970), pp. 387 ff.

20. Özbudun, "Established Revolution versus Unfinished Revolution," p. 389.

21. Ibid., p. 388.

22. Frey, *Turkish Political Elite*, p. 41.

23. Özbudun, "Established Revolution versus Unfinished Revolution," p. 388.

24. İlhan Başgöz and H. E. Wilson, *Educational Problems in Turkey 1920-1940* (Indiana University, Uralic and Altaic Series No. 86, 1968), pp. 61, 85.

25. On economic policy see Z. Y. Hershlag, *Turkey: An Economy in Transition* (The Hague: Uitgeverij Van Keulen N. V., 1958) Parts II and III.

26. On the Free Party see Walter Weiker, *Political Tutelage and Democracy in Turkey* (Leiden: E. J. Brill, 1973).

27. Frey, *The Turkish Political Elite*, pp. 210, 343-347, 379-389.

28. On the establishment of Istanbul University see Başgöz and Wilson,

Educational Problems in Turkey, pp. 159 ff; on the People's Houses, Kemal H. Karpat, "The People's Houses in Turkey: Establishment and Growth," *Middle East Journal* 17 (Winter, Spring 1963).

29. These figures are from Başgöz and Wilson, *Educational Problems in Turkey,,* pp. 233 ff.

30. F. K. Berkes, "The Village Institute Movement of Turkey: An Educational Mobilization for Social Change," (Ph.D. Dissertation, Teacher's College, Columbia University, 1960) p. 674.

31. Ibid., p. 671-672.

32. Hershlag, *Turkey: An Economy in Transition,* p. 169.

33. Mahmut Makal, *A Village in Anatolia,* trans. Sir Wyndham Deedes (London: Valentine Mitchell, 1954) p. 162.

34. Lewis, *Emergence of Modern Turkey*, p. 467.

35. On developments in the fifties see Richard Robinson, *The First Turkish Republic* (Cambridge, Mass.: Harvard University Press, 1963) pp. 124 ff, and Kemal Karpat, *Turkey's Politics* (Princeton: Princeton University Press, 1953); see also my "Political Participation and Modernization in Turkey," *The Western Political Quarterly* 19, 2 (June 1966): 275 ff.

36. Frey, *Turkish Political Elite,* p. 183.

37. Frank Tachau, "The Anatomy of Political and Social Change: Turkish Parties, Parliaments and Elections," *Comparative Politics* 5, 4 (July 1973).

38. George Harris, "The Causes of the 1960 Revolution in Turkey," *The Middle East Journal* 24, 4, (Autumn, 1970): 441.

39. Kemal H. Karpat, "The Military and Politics in Turkey, 1960-1964: A Socio-Cultural Analysis of a Revolution," *American Historical Review* 75, 6 (October, 1970): 1663.

40. Ibid., p. 1665.

41. Karpat, *Turkey's Politics,* p. 130.

42. C. H. Dodd, *Politics and Government in Turkey* (Berkeley and Los Angeles: University of California Press, 1969), p. 53.

43. Leslie L. Roos, Jr. and Noralou P. Roos, *Managers of Modernization* (Cambridge, Mass.: Harvard University Press, 1971), pp. 84-85.

44. Dodd, *Politics and Government in Turkey*, pp. 286 ff.; N. P. Roos, and L. L. Roos, "Changing Patterns of Turkish Public Administration," *Middle Eastern Studies* 4, 3 (1968): 262.

45. Roos, Jr. and Roos, *Managers,* pp. 128 ff.

46. Karpat, *Politics,* p. 298.

47. Joseph S. Szyliowicz, "Students and Politics in Turkey," *Middle Eastern Studies* May 1970 and "A Political Analysis of Student Activism: the Turkish Case," (Beverly Hills: Sage Professional Papers in Comparative Politics, 1972).

48. Dankwart A. Rustow, "Turkey's Second Try at Democracy," *Yale Review* (1963): 529-530; Daniel Lerner and Richard Robinson, "Swords and Ploughshares, The Turkish Army as a Modernizing Force," *World Politics* 12, 1 (October 1960): 41.

49. See Joseph S. Szyliowicz, *Political Change in Rural Turkey, Erdemli* (The Hague: Mouton and Co., 1966), pp. 184 ff. for a detailed discussion of electioneering in one province; Karpat, *Politics,* p. 406.

50. George Harris, "The Causes of the 1960 Revolution in Turkey," (paper presented at the Second Annual Meeting of the Middle East Studies Association of North America, November, 1968) pp. 31-32, mimeo.

51. Robinson, *The First Turkish Republic*, pp. 241 ff.; also Lerner and Robinson, "Swords and Ploughshares," passim.

52. Ergun Özbudun, "The Role of the Military in Recent Turkish Politics," (Cambridge, Mass.: Harvard University Center for International Affairs, Occasional Papers in International Affairs No. 14, November, 1966), pp. 11 ff. Dodd, *Politics and Government*, pp. 32 ff.; cf. Tachau & Ülman, "Dilemmas of Turkish Politics," *Turkish Yearbook of International Relations, 1962* (Ankara, 1964).

53. Özbudun, "The Role of the Military," p. 21.

54. Ibid., p. 28.

55. Harris, "The Causes of the 1960 Revolution" p. 442; Dodd, *Politics and Government*, pp. 29 ff. See also Walter Weiker, *The Turkish Revolution, 1960-61* (Washington: Brookings Institution, 1963).

56. Unless otherwise noted I have drawn in this section upon my "The 1965 Turkish Election," *Middle East Journal* 20, 4 (Autumn 1966) for the discussion of events through that election.

57. On these events see Weiker, *The Turkish Revolution*; Özbudun, "The Role of the Military," pp. 30 ff.; according to Dodd, *Politics and Government*, 5,000 were purged.

58. In fact, the votes cast in favor of the new constitution only came to slightly less than 50 percent of the total electorate, though they were a decided majority of the votes cast. For detailed figures, see *Keesing's Contemporary Archives*, March 17, 1962, p. 18649.

59. Dodd, *Politics and Government*, pp. 57-58.

60. Many JP leaders had occupied important positions in the DP's provincial organizations. See Tachau, "Anatomy."

61. Michael P. Hyland, "Crisis at the Polls: Turkey's 1969 Elections," *The Middle East Journal* 24, 1 (Winter, 1970): 4-5; 13-14.

62. Roos, Jr. and Roos, *Managers of Modernization*, p. 161. The quote is from p. 176.

63. Ibid., pp. 132, 161.

64. On Demirel's policies see Dodd, *Politics and Government*, p. 308; on job satisfaction and mobility see Roos, Jr. and Roos, *Managers of Modernization* Chapter 6, 7.

65. Ahmet T. Kışlalı, *Forces Politiques Dans La Turquie Moderne*, (Ankara: Sevinç Matbaası, n.d.), pp. 142 ff.

66. Hyland, "Crisis at the Polls," pp. 9-11.

67. İlter Turan, "Political Perspectives," (Istanbul: Newsletter, Current Turkish Thought, New Series No. 8, June 1971), pp. 4-5.

68. Ibid., p. 2.

69. Ibid.

70. Nihat Erim, "The Turkish Experience in the Light of Recent Developments," *The Middle East Journal* 26, 3 (Summer 1972): 249.

71. Jacob M. Landau, "The 1973 Elections in Turkey and Israel," *The World Today* 30, 4 (April 1974): 170-180.

72. As cited in the Introduction to this volume.

BIBLIOGRAPHY

Cohn, Edwin J. *Turkish Economic, Social, and Political Change*. New York: Frederick A. Praeger, 1970.

Dodd, C. H. *Politics and Government in Turkey*. Berkeley and Los Angeles, Calif.: University of California Press, 1969.

Frey, Frederick W. *The Turkish Political Elite*. Cambridge, Mass.: Massachusetts Institute of Technology Press, 1965.

Heyd, Uriel. *Foundations of Turkish Nationalism: The Life and Teachings of Ziya Gokalp*. London: Luzac, 1950.

Karpat, Kemal H. *Turkey's Politics: The Transition to a Multiparty System*. Princeton, N.J.: Princeton University Press, 1959.

Kinross, Lord Patrick Balfour. *Ataturk: A Biography of Mustafa Kemal, Father of Modern Turkey*. New York: William Morrow and Co., 1965.

Lewis, Bernard. *The Emergence of Modern Turkey*. New York: Oxford University Press, 1961.

Lewis, G. L. *Turkey*. 3rd ed. New York: Frederick A. Praeger, 1965.

Özbudun, Ergun. *The Role of the Military in Recent Turkish Politics*. Harvard University Center for International Affairs, Occasional Paper, no. 14.

Robinson, Richard D. *The First Turkish Republic: A Case Study in National Development*. Cambridge, Mass.: Harvard University Press, 1963.

Roos, L. L., Jr., and N. P. Roos. *Managers of Modernization: Organizations and Elites in Turkey (1950-69)*. Cambridge, Mass.: Harvard University Press, 1971.

Szyliowicz, Joseph S. *Political Change in Rural Turkey: Erdemli*. The Hague: Mouton, 1966.

──────── . *Education and Modernization in the Middle East*. Ithaca, N.Y.: Cornell University Press, 1973.

Weiker, Walter F. *The Turkish Revolution, 1960-61*. Washington, D.C.: Brookings Institution, 1963.

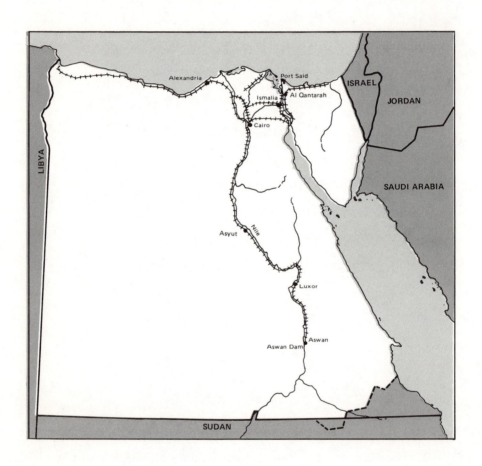

2

Egypt:
Neo-Patrimonial Elite

Shahrough Akhavi*

I. INTRODUCTION

The Egyptian Arab Republic is the successor to one of the world's oldest political systems. An examination of the traditional order, while here limited to developments in the second half of the Ottoman era, should nevertheless look for the roots of contemporary Egyptian politics in the soil of six millenia of history. Actually, the major features of Egypt's politics under what may loosely be called royal rule (1805-1952) have been examined so often that only the barest outline will be sketched in what follows.

"Egypt is the gift of the Nile," said Herodotus. The Nile River Valley and the flat desert vastness of the land are two geographic facts of life that provide the basis for the salient features of Egyptian politics to this day: (1) centralization of authority; (2) ease of political control; (3) political stability; (4) the bureaucratization of power. Egypt is perhaps the most outstanding example of the "hydraulic society."[1] Control of the headwaters of the Nile and of the riverine system (irrigation networks, canals, drainage systems, dikes, barrages and dams) by the authorities easily translated into control over the entire country. The demographic patterns, notably the clustering of the population along the thin ribbon of the Valley and in the Delta region, as well as ethnic,

*I would like to thank Professor S. N. Eisenstadt for calling my attention to the concept of neo-patrimonialism. I am also indebted to Professor Frank Tachau and Professor I. William Zartman for their comments on earlier drafts of this chapter.

cultural, religious and social homogeneity of that population account for relative system stability and facility of political control.

Most observers have indicated that political power in Egypt has been consistently influenced and shaped by the above four features; and that these in turn are related to the water regime. Indeed, it is difficult to analyze power in Egypt by reference to arguments that have no connection to the river's management and control, as, for example, an exclusive stress on Islamic attributes, a class analysis of politics, or the Ottoman system of rule. The argument of the hydraulic society, it is true, has been expounded by a Marxist with a conceptual eye on the notion of the "Asiatic mode of production." It *is* seemingly rooted in class analysis. But the "Asiatic mode of production" is the weakest link in Marx's chain as far as class is concerned. And the Oriental despot apparently governs not so much because the correlation of productive forces and productive relations are in his favor as because of superior administration (a non-class factor).

Apart from the Nile River and the topography, no analysis of the traditional political system will be complete if it ignores the centuries on end of foreign rule over Egypt. The "sons of the land" only came to govern their country after the coup d'etat of 1952. The Military Academy opened its doors to them only in 1936. Issawi's emphasis on foreign domination and occupation merits attention. The list is as impressive as it is startling:[2] (1) the Persians (525 B.C.); (2) the Macedonians (332); (3) the Romans (30 A.D.); (4) the Arabs (642); (5) the Turkic Tulunids (868); (6) the Turkic Ikhshids (935); (7) the Fatimids (969); (8) the Kurds (1163); (9) the Mamluks (1250); (10) the Ottoman Turks (1517); (11) the French (1798); the British (1882).

The fundamental consequence of foreign domination and occupation has been to embed a profound sense of a "we-they" consciousness in the minds of the native Egyptian peasant. In addition, the elite-mass gap under the traditional political system was truly wide and ultimately unbridgeable. The gap persists in the republican era, to be sure, but at least one scholar has indicated that there has been since 1952 a qualitative difference in people's attitude toward it. It has been either ignored as inconsequential or accepted approvingly because of the leadership's autochthonous origins.[3] The we-they mentality, to some extent newly emergent since the June War of 1967, is partly what Lacouture has in mind when he speaks of "une pyramide d'aliénations."

II. THE TRADITIONAL SYSTEM

The Ottoman Empire is a classic example of the patrimonial system of rule.[4] A chief distinguishing trait between patrimonialism and feudalism has to do with the development of corporate jurisdictions and rights on the part of municipalities and other geographical and functional subunits, as well as the growth of the concept of contract. The Ottoman social structure has often been referred to as "feudalism," but it is important to note the absence there of corporate features and time honored rights based on contract. In this way, the ruler's subjects could never reappropriate the rule for themselves, and this is a critical aspect that is particular to patrimonialism. Indeed, Ottoman political culture and ideology enshrined the idea that the Ottoman Sultan owned his realm very much in the fashion of a proprietor who owns his store. According to Shaw,[5] the Ottoman Sultan had the right to consume the resources of the Empire, and he utilized his "staff" (Weber)—the *Osmanlilar* stratum—for the purpose of securing these and exploiting them for the benefit of his Imperial household.

After the conquest of Egypt by Sultan Selim I in 1517 similar attitudes and policies were applied to that territory. In effect, the Ottoman patrimonial system experienced one of those extensions of the household that Weber considered to comprise the growth of such empires. The Sultan appointed as ruler of the new domain a loyal member of his staff. In time, however, emulating the example of military usurpers in classical and medieval Islam, this ruler (Wali, then Pasha, then Khedive, then King, and finally, it will be argued, the President of the Republic) asserted control on behalf of his own patrimony.

During the period when Ottoman rule was undisputed (1517-1819), the Egyptian political elite consisted of the ruler (let us call him Pasha); a number of governors of the various administrative districts of Egypt; the Ottoman officers of the Cairo garrison; salaried notables (sing. *amin*) appointed by the Sultan to oversee the collection of taxes from the land; agents (sing. *'amil*, later to be called *multazim*), actually tax farmers originally serving as subordinates of the salaried notables above-mentioned but quickly securing their own autonomy as the *amins* disappeared from the scene; the religious dignitaries and men of law (plural *'ulama*) whom we may term the intellectuals at that time; urban tradesmen and merchants; the village head-men (sing. *'umdah,* or, in a larger village, *shaykh al-balad*); the village elders (sing. *shaykh*); the artisans, most organized into guilds and sufi orders; the common peasants (idiomatic plural, *fallahin*).[6] One may note that the ascriptive factors of influence, prestige, status, honor, power, wealth and so on served to distinguish these strata from one another.

The classic Ottoman social cleavage, however, separated the Osmanlılar stratum from the non-Osmanlılar groups. The political culture of the Ottoman Imperial Court was a closed culture. Admission into it was also strictly controlled. Therefore, elite movement in this system tended to be a function of whether or not aspirant elites bore the imprimatur of the Ottoman imperial lifestyle, including manners, a knowledge of the idiom of Ottoman Turkish (a thoroughly stylized language), and a number of other ascriptive attributes documented by scholars of Ottoman history.

In Egypt the Pasha, his governors, the military officers of the Cairo garrison, the amins and some of the 'ulama were members of the Ottoman socio-cultural stratum. The 'amils, who were the terror of the Egyptian peasant because of their extortionist taxation policies, were descendants of the slave dynasty (*Mamluks*) that had secured control of Egypt in the thirteenth century. Although they represented a completely illegal develop-ment and hence posed a threat to the Sultan's authority, the *iltizams* (tax farms) did not transform the existing system of rule into a totally new form of socio-economic order. In short, the system, which reached its apogee in the eighteenth century, was a blow to the patrimonial relations and principles by which the Sultan ruled. But patrimonialism itself was sustained.

Needless to say, the *fallahin* actually supported the entire edifice of society through their cultivation. Lewis claims that "in the military empire, at once feudal [sic] and bureaucratic, which they had created, the Muslims knew only four professions—government, war, religion and agriculture."[7] Those professions, trade and industry, which would have stimulated the develop-ment of the market, credit and financial institutions and ultimately classes, were ignored and left to the non-Muslim minorities. Hence, one notes the following twin development: the cultivators supported the government, the military, and the religious institutions by their sheer physical efforts; concepts of private property, contract, corporate autonomy and jurisdictions, credit, and markets played a negligible role in Ottoman and Egyptian social productivity.[8] Egypt was the granary of the Ottoman Empire and played the classically defined role of furnishing the Emperor's staff with food. No more clearcut model of the patrimonial phenomenon could be conceived than the Ottoman Empire and Egypt.

Despite the enormity of the burden with which the peasant masses had to put up, the social system of Egypt was remarkably stable. Even the frequent Mamluk uprisings against the pashas apparently had negligible repercussions in the society as a whole.[9] The peasant masses constituted the broad base of the pyramid in the stratification scheme. The Egyptian fallah enjoyed minimal structural autonomy, a term designating (1) security of tenancy; (2) a high degree of direct relation to the vertical market; (3) a high degree of peasant management over his plot.[10] The literature tends to show that Egyptian fallahin enjoyed no effective property ownership rights over the land they tilled.[11] In other respects, the nature of life in rural Egypt was characterized by communal or primordial relations and exchanges.

In matters of personal status, social relations, and local affairs, government left the peasantry alone according to the Ottoman practice. In this way, villages seemed to be self-contained units with an ecological, social and economic system of their own. The Egyptian peasant's ties to the lands of the village were constructed on the basis of common holding with the other fallahin. One should note, in this connection, that before the mid-nineteenth century village peasants were collectively responsible for rendering tax payments, and public works projects were the collective responsibilities of the peasants in the village.[12]

Change in these patterns from communal to individual ownership and responsibility began around the mid-nineteenth century. Baer cites a number of sources indicating, nevertheless, that even nine or ten decades after that date one could not consider the Egyptian village as a coherent unit characterized by a relatively complex division of labor. A German author writing in 1934 noted the absence of "any organic solidarity on the part of the peasantry, any representational agency of the village community, any community assembly."[13] Jacques Berque was to remark more than twenty years after that: "At no time up to now in our inquiry have we found an organized communal life, not even the municipal fundaments."[14] Father Ayrout underscored the amorphousness of the Egyptian village in the 1940s when he wrote: "The Egyptian village is not a commune in the civic sense of the word, it is not an organism but a mass."[15] Finally, again Ayrout asserted the low level of public cooperation in the Egyptian village: "The ideas of nation, patriotism, are foreign to the fallah, but the idea of cooperation, of public interest and of community life are no less so."[16]

Consequently, even a century after the changes in the patterns of landownership brought about by the successors of Muhammad 'Ali (ruled 1805-1849), the rural social structure failed to evolve toward class stratification. Similarly, in the urban centers of eighteenth and nineteenth century Egypt municipal institutions based on corporate personality and autonomy did not develop. Clot Bey's four "classes" of 'ulama, merchants and proprietors, artisans, and peasants seemed to represent segmented hierarchies based on primordial relations and exchanges. Tomiche quotes one source on the 'ulama that they "in no way gave the idea of being a political body and were hardly a religious one."[17] And while the numerically small merchant group "conserved appreciable vestiges of their former [pre-1805] autonomy,"[18] this autonomy did not refer to quasi-political rights vis-à-vis the royal house of Egypt. Similarly, artisans banded together in handicraft guilds, but once again these communal social and economic solidary groups lacked any true development toward more secular political associations.

III. SOME THEORETICAL CONSIDERATIONS ON SOCIAL STRUCTURE

It seems clear that class analysis is inappropriate for the study of Egyptian social structure. Egypt is an example of what might be called a segmented (composite), not a stratified, society.* As the term implies, such a society is constituted of elements that are not well interlocked, synchronized or integrated with one another in a socio-political sense. Marx put it crudely in the *Eighteenth Brumaire of Napoleon Bonaparte* when he bitingly

*For a further discussion of segmentation and stratification, see Chapter 9.

characterized peasant nations (France) as composed "by the mere addition of homologous magnitudes, much as potatoes in a sack form a sackful of potatoes." Such societies may be termed discontinuous in the sense that an extremely wide elite-mass gap exists.[19]

The vertical segmentation of society exemplified by Egypt over the centuries is, moreover, in accord with the theoretical principles of Islam, which stress the equality of all believers while urging on rulers paternalistic solicitude toward the masses and obedience from these to their overlords. This signifies that the Islamic community, both rural and urban, has traditionally been composed of close-knit, self-contained units (with the clan serving as the nucleus). The relative deprivation in power, prestige, influence and so on on the part of these units *vis-à-vis* the numerically tiny political elite makes for a discontinuous or segmented political system.

Whether one is speaking of village or guild, of urban or of rural groups, in Egypt loyalty and solidarity have traditionally been directed to and within the unit, not across its boundaries, and hence not linking a variety of such units over space. Consequently, the stability of traditional Egyptian society is matched by the lack of "moral familism," as it were; that is, the absence of groups intervening between the family and the state that provide political and economic rights and power to the citizens. In Egypt, we see the lack of corporate jurisdictions and class affiliations, with all the differentiation and articulation that those phenomena involve.

For these reasons when Egyptian Marxists like Ibrahim 'Amir, in his classic work on the peasantry,[20] refer to Egyptian society in terms of the "Asiatic mode of production," they are perhaps unwittingly affirming the existence of a *neo-patrimonial*, non-stratified system. The assertion by Egypt's leading agrarian expert, Sayyid Mar'i, that it was not until 1951 that the peasants made common cause with one another in a country-wide uprising against their masters is crucially important in demonstration of the thesis of patrimonialism.[21] Egypt has known no rural rebellions comparable to the great Taiping Rebellion in China, Pugachov's uprising in Russia or the Jacquerie in France. To be sure, peasant revolts have occurred in Egypt much more frequently than has traditionally been acknowledged by scholars trapped by the myth of the quiescent and passive fallah. These uprisings were aimed against forced conscription for public works projects, high taxes, confiscations of property, increases in rents, and decline in wages.[22] However, the same author who stresses the relative frequency of rural violence in Egyptian history in local milieux cautions elsewhere that "*Fallahs* seldom take organized action for a common cause."[23] In this way one may explain the not infrequent murders and assassinations of unpopular rural notables and officials in such settings. Extensive and deep-seated rebellions against the constituted authority, however, (the closest approximation to which was the 1919 unrest) are another thing entirely.

What of the view of the peasant regarding other social strata? Tomiche stresses their admiration for the 'ulama, who were the only native group that occupied a secure position in society. Sayed and Shayyal assert that these religious leaders were the sole group with which the population could in any sense identify.[24] Moreover, although generalization is risky, the peasantry and urban poor did not seem to bear animus against those forces that neo-Marxists might lump together as the bourgeoisie (the village shaykhs and urban guild leaders and merchants). Strong primordial bonds cut across potential occupational cleavages.

What all this shows is that Egypt has experienced patrimonialism in its social structure and relations. Patrimonialism refers to a type of authority. The notion that the ruler himself cannot hope to govern alone is important. This contrasts with such forms of authority as patriarchalism and gerontocracy, where the need for a staff does not exist. The legitimacy of the ruler's authority rests in the society's ready concession that the prince has the right freely to appropriate the rule over the rest of the community for himself, due to his power, charisma (link with the divinity), and so on. The term "staff" really is symbolic for the larger and more secular concept of "machine". Patrimonialism imposes certain minimal obligations on the ruler. He must meet the minimal demands of equity and right conduct in the eyes of his followers, including the opportunity for them to vent their grievances against local misrule before him. Apart from these considerations, the ruler must fulfill the expectations and requirements of the social myth that has evolved out of earlier patterns of society and politics. There is thus, in patrimonialism, a two-way flow of contact and exchange: from the prince to his subjects, but also from them to him. He is always on notice to discharge his obligations under the terms of the system, so to speak. However, his sway can typically operate far from the daily lives and view of these subjects and ultimately with little direct contact with them. Elsewhere, the persistence of the old into the new era has gone under the rubric, "modernity of tradition" and "post traditional societies."[25] In this case, we wish to talk of the elite since 1952 as a neo-patrimonial elite, thereby emphasizing the fundamental carryover of traditional modes into the political system of republican Egypt.

To recapitulate, Egyptian society has been characterized by vertical segmentation, causing extreme forms of localism and preventing solidarities across the various territories of the domain. The absence of corporate rights and autonomy for what might be termed civic groups and institutions has helped shape Egyptian politics according to the principle of rule by the prince (Pasha, Khedive, King, President), whose ownership of the entire land is rooted in traditional practice. The purpose behind expansion of territory is to enhance the consumption and to aggrandize the pomp of the ruler. It occurs through the administrative staff, or machine, that is beholden to this ruler but which, to be sure, benefits in its own way from the enlargements of the ruler's power and privilege.

Naturally, much has changed in post-1952 Egypt that would make the political system different from the pre-republican era. But the elite today is a neo-patrimonial elite whose military component is so significant as to have led one analyst to coin the phrase "stratiotocracy" (Vatikiotis): that is, rule by the military. The armed forces serve as the leading element of the staff of the President of the Republic. The entry of new forces into the ranks of the elite depend on qualities defined and manipulated by the military in the society.

The ultimate consequence of viewing Egyptian politics according to these concepts is that it helps explain the "ideology-action" of the leadership: an ideology that continues to remain amorphous and unsystematized despite the adoption of the terminology of "scientific socialism" (sic); and action typified by weak, fragile mobilization and integration. In the last analysis, it is felt, the failure of Egypt's socialism to define and articulate itself in relationship to the world rests in the persistence of structural determinants with their bias against class development.

While numerous authorities[26] have been impressed by the "middle-class" or "bourgeois" attributes of the post-1952 military elite, it might be preferable to make the following distinction: Egypt has historically been devoid of an indigenous bourgeoisie, as already noted above. In view of the absence of class stratification in Egyptian society, and given the lack of a native entrepreneurial movement, it is misleading to talk of the *bourgeois* essence of the elite since 1952. True enough, many of the officers hail from peasant households with medium size landholdings. Certainly many of them cannot be called sons of the "lower classes"—families owning two *feddans* or less at mid-century, let us say. But this is insufficient reason to view them as representatives of the Egyptian bourgeoisie along these lines. The concept of bourgeoisie signifies

> a body of citizens asserting their collective, as well as their individual, independence of a social system dominated by feudal power based on landholding and on the services attached to it.[27]

Now, admittedly the Free Officers spearheaded the drive to extirpate the "feudal class" (landed aristocracy) from Egypt after 1952. But does that action in itself qualify them for bourgeois status? Not at all. Furthermore, the adoption of bourgeois lifestyles, habits and tastes, while necessary for any definition of bourgeois, is not sufficient. Class corporate interests are missing; and not only this, but the essential ingredients of class: industry, commerce, the use of money, credit, markets[28]—these have not proliferated in a manner that would be required for the capitalist mode of production and a full-fledged bourgeois class. Thus, unless we change our definitions, would it not be more appropriate to talk of the neo-patrimonial, rather than of the bourgeois elite in Egypt? While due recognition must be given to capitalist development in Egypt since the mid-nineteenth century, such development must not be exaggerated. To cite G. D. H. Cole in an exceptionally lucid and relevant passage for our purpose:

> Where the bourgeoisie did not spread into the country-side but remained as an urban enclave in a feudal society, either developing

> towards a peasant society or still dominated by great landed estates there was no room for the evolution of a "middle class" on a national scale, and none, accordingly for the permeation of the whole society by the characteristically liberal values which are associated chiefly with *bourgeois* development. This was the more so because in such societies the professional and intellectual classes developed largely as servants of the state, and thus became bureaucrats rather than liberals.[29]

This extraordinary passage might well have been written with Egypt in mind. For, as we shall see, the immense powers of the President of the Republic to appoint figures to any position in public life—be it a university chancellorship, the chairmanship of an Egyptian Public Organization (*mu'assasah 'ammah*), or a cabinet post—very closely resembles the powers of a patrimonial prince. And the appointees thus constituted may appropriately be seen as loyal members of the prince's staff in the classic pattern of patrimonial rule. It now remains to examine the role of the Egyptian political elite in the country's modernization in the decades before the 1952 coup.

IV. THE MODERNIZATION PROCESS

Mention has already been made of the politically salient elites in the traditional political system of Egypt. Yet, after 1850 two other groups entered into the ranks of the Egyptian elite, regarding which scant attention has been given. These are the minorities and resident foreigners. Among the former should be listed especially the Copts (Christian descendents of the Ptolemies), but also Jews, Armenians and Greeks. The resident foreigners include Italians, French, British (who originally came to the country in the days of Khedive Isma'il and the imposition of the Debt Commission), and Syrians. The role of these "outsiders" became important in Isma'il's reign (1863-1879) because he was himself acutely interested in modernizing his country. Whatever his motivations may have been—and to a large extent he shared with his illustrious predecessor, Muhammad 'Ali, a streak of vanity—Isma'il convinced himself that he was in competition with the Western powers and the Ottoman Sultan. To his misfortune, his mismanagement of the country's finances in pursuit of his objectives forced him into fiscal arrangements with French and British financiers and investors that ultimately resulted in the loss of Egyptian autonomy.

The Syrian immigrants played some role in the country's internal trade. But perhaps their major contribution in the modernization process lay in the development of a vigorous press.[30] The impact of this relatively early development can be seen today (despite the heavy hand of the republican regime), when Egypt enjoys the most advanced and sophisticated level of journalism in the Arab world next to Lebanon.

The Coptic minority (about 7-10 percent of the population) played an important part in Egypt's politics during the first half of the twentieth century. No other minorities, after all, had members of their groups serve as Prime Minister. It is symptomatic that Be'eri felt moved to say in 1966 that "the times when the Copt, Makram 'Ubayd, was deputy prime minister have passed."[31] He might also have mentioned Butrus Ghali, another Copt who served as Prime Minister. The public image prevailed that the Copts and British worked in tandem with one another,[32] joined by the King and the Turko-Circassian aristocracy. Whether or not this image reflected the reality of pre-1952 Egypt, the nationalists thought that it was true. No better indication of the widespread feeling over this issue exists than the virtual elimination of all these groups from the leading positions of the power structure in the period since 1952.

By the time of the 1952 coup d'etat the following constituted the members of the Egyptian political elite: the King and his Court (including the land magnates); the Copts and various other ethnic and religious minorities (but excluding the Jews, it would seem); recently naturalized Egyptian citizens of French, British, Italian, Greek extraction; a small group of native entrepreneurs, led by Tal'at Harb; and the 'ulama. Muhammad 'Ali's revolution in the country's land ownership patterns has been the subject of a number of important studies which demonstrate that his major achievement was the destruction of the *iltizam* system and the Mamluk elite that serviced it.[33] In place of these tax farms, the ruler distributed vast tracts of his domain to members of his own family (the Turko-Circassian aristocracy). Subsequently, as private property in land began to be introduced after 1850 and a certain movement toward the capitalization of agriculture occurred, a new elite became entrenched in place of the old Mamluk stratum. As for the Egyptian peasants during this period of ascendancy of the land owners (say from 1875-1952), it is true that they were theoretically eligible to own land. In practice, however, it became increasingly difficult for the peasant with modest means to keep what he had and virtually impossible for the poor fallah to improve his lot. Fragmentation of family holdings and the population increase greatly exacerbated the problems faced by the Egyptian peasant.

These elite groups, then, were responsible for the modernization process in Egypt. For Cromer, Gorst, Lloyd and the British colonial administration generally, good governance comprised the essence of modernization. To them, the heart of good governance was public administration.[34] Having entrenched themselves in 1882 to ensure repayment of loans defaulted upon by the unwise Isma'il, the British attempted to regulate Egyptian affairs according to the best standards of European public and financial administration. Given this sentiment, it was only natural that the British attempted to recruit to the higher ranks of this civil service those social forces who, to paraphrase Lloyd, were *not* subordinating the claims of good administration to those of political theory. In short, the natural British allies in their endeavor were the non-indigenous forces with ties to non-Egyptian cultural values: The Copts, with their religious links to the West; the various minority groups, protected by the Capitulations; and the Turko—Circassian stratum, whose preference for good administration over political theory (Egyptian territorial patriotism and later Arab nationalism) could hardly be doubted. For, the slightest concession to the native Egyptian population—such as opening the Military Academy in 1936 to the common folk of rural Egypt—could only be interpreted as a breach in the edifice of Turko-Circassian hegemony.

British refusal to sponsor "political theory" was only one side of the coin. The other side was the steadfast denial of Egyptian aspirations for industrial development.[35] Even Gorst's Administration, which succeeded Cromer's in 1908 and was considered "liberal" in its attitude toward Egyptian nationalism, did not seek to alter the agrarian development penchant of its predecessor.[36]

Egyptian counter-elites in the early years of this century clustered around four major groupings, the *Hizb al-Watan,* or Patriotic Party, of Mustafa Kamil (d. 1908) and the *Hizb al-Ummah*, of Ahmad Lutfi al-Sayyid (d. 1963). Mention should also be made of the newspaper, *al-Mu'ayyad,* edited by Shaykh

'Ali Yusuf and forum for the conservative opposition against British rule. Finally, the *Wafd* Party of Sa'd Zaghlul (d. 1927) and Mustafa al-Nahhas (d. 1965) became the legatee of the Egyptian nationalist movement after the eclipse of the Watan and Ummah parties and *al-Mu'ayyad* around 1915. The Muslim Brotherhood, a secret society of militant fundamentalists that one may regard as the action arm of the conservative counter-elites, was founded in 1928 and soon proliferated in Egypt and other Muslim countries. The Brotherhood remains today, as it was before 1952, perhaps the most formidable opposition movement in the country.

As a general statement, it may be submitted that the leaders of these diverse movements arrayed themselves against the alien elites described above, although the Ummah Party was impressed with parliamentarianism and supported minimal cooperation with Britain. The social base of these counter-elites, and especially the Wafd leaderships, lay in rural Egypt, among the *'umdah* elements. To put it another way, the leaders of Egypt's nationalist movement came from predominantly moderate to well-to-do rural families.[37]

A small group of landowners broke rank with the aristocratic alliance with the King and British and tried to foster a modicum of industrial development. The activity of this group began in the period 1917-1922 with the creation of the Committee for Commerce and Industry, the Bank Misr, and the Federation of Egyptian Industries. These "young Turks" of the Egyptian landowning stratum were not part of the Turko-Circassian elite, since "socially they belonged to a native and relatively recent landowning and professional class from the provinces."[38] Termed the "modernist wing of the rich landowners"[39] by Abdel-Malek, it was led by Tal'at Harb and Isma'il Sidqi. The major point for our purposes is the marriage of interests between these industrialists and their organizations, on the one hand, and the dominant segment of the nationalist movement—the Wafdists—on the other. Notwithstanding the major achievements of the Misr Complex in the direction of diversification, capital development and accumulation and industrialization of the consumer goods sector, the growth of the Egyptian "bourgeoisie" remained confined to tiny enclaves through the next three decades. It certainly never amounted to "millions of families liv[ing] under economic conditions of existence that divide their mode of life, their interests and their culture from those of other classes and put them in hostile contrast to the latter" (Marx).

Issawi notes the progress of industrialization accordingly: in 1916, fifteen manufacturing enterprises were counted that employed ten or more individuals, with a total national employment of between 30,000-35,000 persons. Eleven years later total employment was 95,000, with industry and mining representing less than five percent of total output. By 1937, employment figures in establishments employing ten or more were at 155,000, with manufacturing, mining, electricity, gas and water constituting approximately eight percent of GNP. By 1952, industry accounted, at best estimate, for about ten percent of the country's GNP, whereas the employment statistics for 1947 and 1950 respectively were placed at 278,000 and 244,000.[40] Perhaps the most telling statistic of all is Issawi's implication that industry's share of gross national product moved only from five to ten percent in the space of 25 years. Such figures indicate a slow march toward eventual industrialization.

It was to a large extent in reaction against this overly slow growth that the Free Officers engineered the coup of 1952. Every indication points to the great desire of the newly entrenched military leadership to turn the corner on industrialization. Thus, in Egypt's First Five Year Plan (1959-1964) industry was slated to get "a greater share of investment than any other sector" and by 1965 "its contribution to the gross national product was expected to exceed that of agriculture."[41] Moreover, in 1966 the share of industry as a percentage of the Gross National Product was 23 percent, only five percent less than that of agriculture.[42] Nevertheless, the expected development (expected in terms of abstract logic and economic theory) of a bourgeois class has not transpired. This is basically a function of willful policy (the July 1961 nationalization laws and their subsequent variants over the next decade). Egypt has witnessed the phenomenon of the development of a new stratum of "state bureaucrats" manning the commanding heights of the economy. These Egyptian Public Organizations, Public Companies, Public Authorities, Public Agencies and the banks are all under tight state control. Consequently, even if one were to agree with Egyptian neo-Marxists that these bureaucrats are a capitalist class, their continued lack of corporate autonomy and rights from the state (which after all is employing them in Cole's sense of the term—i.e., they are "servants of the state") belie this designation. We must always revert to the question: can a capitalist class arise that has no tradition of contractual rights and independence from state authority in which to engage in economic activity?

V. THE FREE OFFICERS AND THE MODERNIZATION PROCESS

Royal rule came to an unceremonious end in Egypt when, to borrow J. C. Hurewitz's felicitous phrase, the Free Officers "rolled the well-padded dissolute [Faruq] off the throne."[43] Many issues were involved here: failure of economic development to meet the needs of the nationalist movement; the Palestine War, in which Egyptian troops generally failed to distinguish themselves, partly as a result of the Crown's dereliction in providing defective arms; deep-seated hostility to the British; political *immobilisme,* stemming from corruption, nepotism and the discrediting of Western parliamentary institutions and values.[44] But the most explosive issue was that of colonialism, with its hated symbols, the Mixed Courts, the Capitulations, the Suez Base. And if one by one the nationalist movement succeeded over the years in eliminating these institutions, this only served to inspire it to its ultimate objective of total expulsion of Britain from the country. Ironically, the nationalist movement, controlled by the Wafd, took umbrage at the British when they seemed to be siding with it against the Crown. Thus, in the famous incident of February 9, 1942, when British tanks surrounded the royal palace and forced the King to allow the Wafd to seize power in order to placate public opinion and prevent instability in wartime, Egyptian opinion was outraged. The event left a lasting impression on the minds of the young officers, notably Jamal 'Abd al-Nasir. These officers, newly matriculated from the Military Academy, apparently took a vow at this time to work against future such humiliations to "Egypt's honor" and toward the elimination of the British occupation.

The Free Officers raised the army to an unprecedented pinnacle of leadership in Egypt. The preeminence of the military in Egyptian society and politics has led Vatikiotis to assert:

> In declaring itself against 'politics,' i.e., against the existence of
> political groups in society which at least purport an alternative to
> power, the military regime had, by 1956, pre-empted all political
> activity in Egypt ... the military junta had to man an admin-
> istration which would not only permit them to govern, but which
> would also enable them to maintain effective political power over
> society. It is in meeting this requirement by recruiting their cadres
> from the armed forces that the junta gradually transformed their
> regime for the first five years into what I shall call here a
> *stratiotocracy.*[45]

Who were the Free Officers who managed to convert the
traditional political system into rule by the military in the drive
toward modernization? The sources tend to diverge somewhat
on the names, but the core group of eleven can readily enough
be identified: (1) Jamal 'Abd al-Nasir; (2) 'Abd al-Hakim 'Amir;
(3) Zakariya Muhyi al-Din; (4) 'Abd al-Latif al-Baghdadi; (5)
Kamal al-Din Husayn; (6) Khalid Muhyi al-Din; (7) Husayn
al-Shafi'i; (8) Anwar al-Sadat; (9) Hasan Ibrahim; (10) Salah
Salim; (11) Jamal Salim. These individuals comprised the
Revolutionary Command Council (RCC); and it is without
question the work of these men that transformed the traditional
patrimonial system based on the dynastic principle and rooted in
religious sanction into a neo-patrimonial system resting on
military rule embedded in the ideal of rule by native sons of the
country. Among these, 'Abd al-Nasir played the role of "ruler."
The legitimacy of his authority stemmed from both his
charismatic appeal[46] and exceptional organizational abilities. He
was particularly expert in sensing the appropriate moment to
make a political decision, although some of these decisions in
the long-run policy perspective tended to prove erroneous or
counterproductive. But his legitimacy of rule also rested in a big
way on his ejection of the British from Egypt.

Social and economic modernization, for which he stood as the
symbol to the Egyptian masses, also contributed to the legiti-
mization of his power. But one cannot help feeling that this
aspect was less significant in the mixture that ultimately comprised his appeal and acceptability. Social and economic
modernization require at least a rudimentary ideological
orientation. Yet, in the first five to eight years of the new
regime, preoccupation with the latter seemed minimal on the
part of the *Ra'is.* According to one of his most devoted

colleagues, Major Muhammad 'Abd al-Qadir Hatim:

> The method employed by the leader of the Revolution ['Abd al-Nasir] ... was one of phases, of trial and error; completing one phase, the Revolution put itself in readiness and laid down the rules of the coming phase.[47]

But if one can analyze 'Abd al-Nasir's role as the successor in a line of patrimonial princes of Egypt, one has to underscore simultaneously his attempt to give his rule a populist imprimatur. Political participation by the Egyptian masses in the Egyptian "revolution" was the symbol by which he hoped to lead Egypt on to fulfill its destiny. After the completion of the series of moves by which he and his staff rid the country of the British (the 1954 Agreement, the nationalization of the Suez Canal, the Suez War, the sequestrations of properties), the late President finally turned his attention systematically toward economic and social development. It is no accident that the First Five Year Plan began in 1959.[48]

It would not be impugning 'Abd al-Nasir's motives to say that despite his deep commitment to lead the Egyptian masses out of the endless cycle of poverty, disease and ignorance, he had no intention of surrendering his power and authority.[49] Out of the conflicts with his colleagues (leaving only two out of the original 11 Free Officers still in power by his death in September 1970), the desultory attempts to create a mass movement regime under his revolutionary auspices, the continued withholding of corporate autonomy to interest and professional groups within Egypt, we have the reign supreme of a modern absolute despot.[50] The two key differences between this neo-patrimonial prince and the Khedival princes are: (1) his profound desire to improve the lot of the Egyptian masses; (2) his commitment to rational, scientific methods and planning. Even here, though, we should recall that Muhammad 'Ali himself developed his industrial monopolies with a view to development through technology. But the Pasha's main interest in these industries was to build up a military machine so that his family could rule and withstand the European challenge.[51]

It is still too early to determine what effect 'Abd al-Nasir's death will have on the structure of patrimonialism in the country. However, it does seem as though any Egyptian leader after him must become more of a broker among the emergent interests in the country and less of a patrimonial autocrat. One may speak of an attrition of the neo-patrimonial model since September 1970, although it is probably not yet time to speak of its demise.[52] Like it or not, the industrial workers, Egyptian youth, certain Arab Socialist Union (ASU) *apparatchiki*, and some sectors of the intelligentsia will provide increasing challenges to the prince and his staff as time wears on. The prince will more and more have to prove that he deserves the right to maintain his sway. Hence, a key aspect of classic patrimonialism—unquestioned right of appropriating the rule for oneself—will increasingly be under attack.

VI. THE EGYPTIAN MILITARY ELITE

The eleven Free Officers listed above were all born within five years of each other, between 1917 and 1922. None was a Cairene by birth and only one—'Abd al-Nasir—seems to have studied there (before his military experience). Only two were born in Alexandria, Egypt's second city: Hasan Ibrahim and 'Abd al-Nasir. In brief, the Free Officers hailed from rural Egypt and were immersed in the values of the countryside. They had very little chance to acquire the political culture of the Osmanlılar stratum because of their commoner background.[53] None of the eleven was a scion of Egypt's extremely small entrepreneurial stratum. Nine of the eleven graduated together from the Military Academy in 1938, while one did so in 1939 (Ibrahim) and a second (K. Muhyi al-Din) in 1940.

Five went on to graduate from the Military Staff College in 1948 ('Abd al-Nasir, 'Amir, Baghdadi, Z. Muhyi al-Din and S. Salim), and three others respectively in 1949 (Husayn), 1950 (K. Muhyi al-Din), and 1953 (al-Shafi'i). Only two of the eleven acquired any degree of non-military higher education: K. Muhyi al-Din, who received a Bachelor's degree in Commerce in 1951; and 'Abd al-Nasir, who studied law for five months between 1936 and 1937.[54]

Beyond the eleven members of the "inner core" of the FO group stood an outer rim of eleven more. These men, not among the original founders, were: (1) Tharwat 'Ukasha; (2) Kamal al-Din Mahmud Rif'at; (3) Tawfiq 'Abd al-Fattah; (4) Muhammad Mahmud Nassar; (5) 'Abbas Radwan; (6) Fathi Rizq; (7) Husayn Zulfikar Sabri; (8) Yusif Saddiq; (9) Rashad

Mahanna; (10) 'Ali Sabri; (11) Muhammad 'Abd al-Qadir Hatim. Muhammad Najib, a senior officer whom the group advanced as its nominal leader with the hopes of securing legitimation for its coup and rule immediately following the seizure of power, was not a member of the movement.[55]

Taken collectively, the inner and outer groups of the Free Officers virtually dominated the entire society. Certainly the cabinet, the presidential bureaucracy, and the mass movement organization were all practically appanages of these men. Perhaps it is symptomatic that in the developing countries, where the level of political institutionalization is low in Huntington's sense, personal rulership of the sort exemplified by these twenty-two figures must become the "dominant form of government."[56]

An inquiry into the composition of Egyptian cabinets since 1952 demonstrates a proportionately high representation of military or former military officers. Out of ten selected cabinets between September 7, 1952 and June 19, 1967, Be'eri counted 121 officers out of a total of 274. The ratio of military to civilian ministers in these ten cabinets was 44.2 percent.[57]

These statistics do not take into account the fact that the cabinet of September 7, 1952, was subordinate to the RCC, which stood above it and consisted of officers only. Thus, the 1952 cabinet officially listed only one officer within it. Also, the percentage figure conceals the generally upward trend of military representation in the cabinet over time. Thus, Be'eri discovered very high levels of 47 percent (in 1965), 59 percent (in 1966), and 65 percent (in 1967). Using somewhat different tabulating techniques, and focusing on the 187 ministers who staffed all the Egyptian cabinets from September 7, 1952, to September, 1972, we find a total of 58 military men, a 31 percent representation ratio. This is an unusually high figure for a state whose economic development needs require advanced expertise of the order not normally to be found among military men.

Shifting attention from the cabinet to the ASU General Secretariat and the Higher Executive Committee since 1962 (the date of the ASU's creation), the military role is yet more pronounced. Of the twenty-three individuals serving on the Higher Executive Committee in three selected years, 13 were military figures, while ten were civilians. This yields a military representation ratio of 56.5 percent. The trend becomes even more pronounced if one looks at the proportion of military figures serving on the HEC for each of the three years: 1962: 64.7 percent; 1966: 100 percent; 1968: 50 percent. Since the reorganization of the ASU beginning in mid-May, 1971, the HEC has not been continued. Its membership between 1968 and 1971 remained constant.[58]

As far as military control over the General Secretariat is concerned, the only surprising trend is that, ever since the reorganization alluded to above, no military figures have sat in this organ. Of fifty-four individuals over nine years (1962-1971) who have been members of the mass movement's General Secretariat, 22 have been military figures. The military representation ratio is 40.7 percent, a figure which would be 55 percent if the period from May-December, 1971, is excluded. A yearly tabulation would reveal the following proportions of military participation in the General Secretariat: 1962: 75 percent; 1964: 61.9 percent; 1965: 56.3 percent; 1966: 60 percent; 1967 (Jan.): 56.3 percent; 1967 (Sept.): 53.3 percent; 1970: 42.9 percent; 1971: 0 percent. Exactly what the last figure portends as concerns as military participation is not clear. It may be that Sadat was determined to keep the ASU from becoming a military fiefdom or "power center" (to use a term current in Egypt) that might challenge the regime and unregenerate army officers (social reactionaries) who constitute that regime's mainstay. The successive appointments of managerial leader types (Muhammad al-Dakruri, 'Abd al-Salam Muhammad al-Zayyat and Sayyid Mar'i) as First Secretary after 1971 was greeted with contemptuous disdain by the Egyptian left. It was certain that Mar'i, scion of an *'umdah* family and a patrician type, would not create of the ASU a hotbed of counter-elites opposed to the military domination of society.

If we turn attention to the provincial governors of Egypt, it must first be noted that our data is partial. Despite this, however, strong evidence exists to allow one to assert that the military representation ratio in the governorships has consistently been near the 75 percent-80 percent range. Data collated by Dekmejian for the year 1964 reveal that 22 of the 26 governors of Egypt had military backgrounds. This yields a phenomenally high 84.6 percent proportion.[59] According to other sources, the corresponding figures for various selected years are as follows: 1960: 81 percent (firm); 1961: 75 percent (firm); 1965: 42.3 percent (at least); 1969: 45.8 percent (at least); March, 1971: 45.8 percent (at least); June, 1971: 50 percent (at least); November, 1971: 54.7 percent (at least).[60] Due to the vagaries in the coverage of biographical background of appointees to the governorship positions in the Egyptian press, it was not possible to certify for a number of cases whether or not the individuals were military or civilian figures. Even the most conservative estimate, however, that in the last decade the proportion of military officers filling governorships has been about 50 percent, would tend to indicate the theoretical potency of Vatikiotis's term, stratiotocracy. Moreover, since the governorships do seem to be the ideal instrument for the political and administrative *Gleichschaltung* of society, it is important to bear in mind the very high proportions of army officers in these ranks. The governors are perhaps the most influential members of the adminstrative staff as far as regional and local politics are concerned.

There is no doubt that, in terms of nearly every background characteristic imaginable, the post-1952 Egyptian political elite differs from the traditional elites of that country. Yet, exactly what this tells us about public policy outputs remains obscure. In other words, one may not conclude that, just because a university education, terminating in an engineering, medical or Ph.D. degree, has become standard for cabinet positions (an important segment of the political elite), a particular pattern of policy outputs exists. In fact, no correlation (and especially no *causal* correlation) may be made between such background characteristics as age, sex, education, etc., and policy. Even such an important factor as a heavy military presence in successive cabinets since 1952 does not tell us anything certain, although it may be suggestive, indeed.[61]

Surely social mobility in Egypt has improved since 1952. Individuals from groups that seldom or never hoped to rise to positions of power and influence have received the chance to do so. On certain outstanding pieces of legislation or executive decrees (for example, the Land Reform Law), it is easy to trace in broad contours the impact of the social basis of these newly participant groups on policy. For the most part, however, the specific influence of the representatives of the middle or lower strata on governmental output has not been (perhaps under present conditions *cannot* be) thus far empirically demonstrated.

Looking at the cabinets since 1952, perhaps the striking fact is the sharp decline of the military component beginning in 1968 and acclerating during the Sadat years (see Table I).

TABLE I Military Components of Egyptian Cabinets, 1952-1972

Cabinet	Military	
	N	%
7 Sept. 1952	1	6.3
8 Dec. 1952	1	5.9
18 June 1953	5	26.3
4 Oct. 1953	9	40.9
17 April 1954	11	45.8
1 Sept. 1954	12	52.1
30 June 1956	8	36.3
5 March 1958	8	38.1
7 Oct. 1958	16	48.5
17 Aug. 1961	16	51.5
19 Oct. 1961	15	51.6
29 Sept. 1962	17	47.1
24 March 1964	16	36.3
2 Oct. 1965	19	46.2
10 Sept. 1966	21	55.2
19 June 1967	19	65.4
20 March 1968	13	39.4
28 Oct. 1968	13	41.9
21 Oct. 1970	14	42.4
18 Nov. 1970	12	36.4
13-16 May 1971	10	29.4
19 Sept. 1971	11	36.6
17 Jan. 1972	7	21.2

SOURCE: For the period up to October 1968, Dekmejian, *Egypt Under Nasir*, pp. 176-77; for the remaining period, *al-Ahram*, *al-Jumhuriyah*, *al-Akhbar* and *Akhbar al-Yawm*.

In a cabinet shuffle of a minor nature on September 8, 1972, two changes were made, but these did not alter the position of the military. Even the later (October 26, 1972) dismissal of the Minister of War, Sadiq, did not disturb the military balance that existed as of January, 1972, since he was replaced by another military figure, the former chief intelligence officer, General Ahmad Isma'il.

Another significant feature of cabinet social background characteristics is related to occupational sources of recruitment. Whence is the system getting its leaders? The following data show some interest changes over time in occupation prior to cabinet appointment:

TABLE II Aggregate Count of Occupational Sources of Recruitment

1952-1968			Post Nov. 1968		
	N	%		N	%
Military	44	33.6	Military	25	30.5
Academia	30	22.9	Academia	20	24.4
Engineering	19	14.5	Engineering	1	1.2
Law	17	13.0	Law	5	6.1
Bureaucracy (Ministerial)	10	7.6	Min. Bureaucracy	10	12.2
Business-Professional	7	5.3	Econ. Bureaucracy	13	15.9
Police	2	1.5	Diplomacy	5	6.1
Diplomatic Corps	2	1.5	Syndicates	2	2.4
Total	131	100	Journalism	1	1.2
			Total	82	100

SOURCE: For 1952-1968, Dekmejian, p. 200; for 1968-1972, *al-Ahram, al-Akhbar, Akhbar al-Yawm, al-Jumhuriyah.*

The chief changes are in law (fewer since November, 1968) and the ministerial and economic (business-professional) bureaucracies (approximately 2 and 3 times as high in the later period). As for the category of "engineers" for the pre-1968 period, one assumes that these individuals were private professionals prior to co-optation into the cabinet. In the post-November, 1968 period, only one engineer turns up: Sayyid Mar'i. Yet, if one were to tabulate how many of the 82 (excluding the military technocrats) actually had obtained engineering degrees, the figure would be 16, or 19.5 percent, very close to the pre-1968 figure.

Switching the focus from an aggregate count to a detailed presentation by cabinets provides us with the following perspective:

One cannot fail to note the predominance of the military relative to the other seven categories. Since 1953, on only one occasion (March, 1964) did the other areas (specifically academics and engineering) even approach equivalence as far as proportion of membership is concerned. The most impressive instance of military domination of all the other categories was in June, 1967 (after the Six-Day War), when the military as an occupational source of recruitment registered 65.5 percent, as compared to Business-Professional (6.9 percent), Law (3.5 percent), Academia (13.8 percent), Diplomacy (3.5 percent), and Engineering (6.9 percent).

TABLE III-A Original Occupational Sources of Recruitment: Count by Individual Cabinet

Cabinet	Military		Bureaucracy-Ministerial		Business Professional		Law		Academia		Diplomacy		Engineering		Police		Total
	N	%	N	%	N	%	N	%	N	%	N	%	N	%	N	%	
7 Sept 1952	1	6.3	3	18.8	3	18.8	4	25	3	18.8	2	12.5	-	-	-	-	16
8 Dec 1952	1	5.9	3	17.7	1	5.9	5	29.4	4	23.5	2	11.8	1	5.9	-	-	17
18 June 1953	5	26.3	2	10.5	1	5.3	5	26.3	3	15.8	1	5.3	2	10.5	-	-	19
4 Oct 1953	9	40.9	1	4.6	2	9.1	4	18.2	3	13.6	1	4.6	2	9.1	-	-	22
17 April 1954	11	45.8	1	4.2	2	8.3	4	16.7	3	12.5	1	4.2	2	8.3	-	-	24
1 Sept 1954	12	52.2	1	4.4	1	4.4	4	17.4	2	8.7	1	4.4	2	8.7	-	-	23
30 June 1956	8	36.4	1	4.6	2	9.1	4	18.2	3	13.6	1	4.6	3	13.6	-	-	22
5 March 1958	8	38.1	-	-	2	9.5	3	14.3	4	19.1	1	4.8	3	14.3	-	-	21
7 Oct 1958	16	48.5	1	3	2	6.1	2	6.1	7	21.2	1	3	4	12.1	-	-	33
17 Aug 1961	16	51.6	1	3.2	2	6.5	1	3.2	5	16.1	1	3.2	5	16.1	-	-	31
19 Oct 1961	15	51.6	1	3.5	1	3.5	1	3.5	6	20.7	1	3.5	4	13.8	-	-	29
29 Sept 1962	17	47.2	3	8.3	2	5.6	1	2.8	7	19.4	1	2.8	4	11.1	1	2.8	36
24 March 1964	16	36.4	2	4.6	2	4.6	3	6.8	10	22.7	1	2.3	9	20.5	1	2.3	44
2 Oct 1965	19	46.3	2	4.9	1	2.4	2	4.9	7	17.1	1	2.4	8	19.5	1	2.4	41
10 Sept 1966	21	55.3	2	5.3	1	2.6	2	5.3	3	7.9	1	2.6	7	18.4	1	2.6	38
19 June 1967	19	65.5	-	-	2	6.9	1	3.5	4	13.8	1	3.5	2	6.9	-	-	29
20 March 1968	13	39.4	2	6.1	2	6.1	2	6.1	9	27.3	1	3	4	12.1	-	-	33
28 Oct 1968	13	41.9	2	6.5	1	3.2	2	6.5	9	29	-	-	4	12.9	-	-	31

TABLE III-B Original Occupational Sources of Recruitment, by Cabinets
November 1968 – September 1972

Cabinet	Mil		Acad		Law		MB		EB		Dipl		Synd		Eng		Total
	N	%	N	%	N	%	N	%	N	%	N	%	N	%	N	%	
21 Oct 70	14	42.5	8	24.2	3	9.1	2	6.1	4	12.1	1	3.0	0	0.0	1	3.0	33
18 Nov 70 13-16	12	36.3	8	24.2	3	9.1	3	12.1	3	9.1	1	3.0	1	3.0	1	3.0	33
May 71	10	29.4	10	29.4	4	11.8	4	8.9	5	14.7	1	2.9	1	2.9	0	0.0	34
19 Sept 71	11	36.7	6	20	3	10	3	10	3	10	2	6.7	1	3.3	1	3.3	30
17 Jan 72	7	21.2	9	27.3	2	6.1	2	6.1	8	24.2	2	6.1	1	3.0	0	0.0	33

MB = Ministerial Bureaucracy
EB = Economic Bureaucracy
Synd = Syndicates
Muhammad Hasanayn Haykal, the only cabinet minister with a journalism background, served between 26 April and 18 October 1970.

SOURCES: For 1952-1968: Dekmejian, p. 203
For 1968-1972: al-Ahram, al-Akhbar, Akhbar al-Yawm, al-Jumhuriyah.

Another significant trend is the rather sharp fall-off of the military in the two 1968 cabinets (39.4 and 41.9 percent respectively), with the slack taken up by the academics. (27.3 and 29 percent respectively). The promises of the 30 March Manifesto emphasizing technology explain this partial eclipse of the military's role. Also, student demonstrations in February and unrest over Egypt's defeat by Israel, the incompetence of the senior military commanders during the war, and the seemingly light sentences handed out to those tried by the regime fed into the decision-making that led to this drop. Since 1968, we have already noted, the role of the military declined, reaching its nadir with the last cabinet. The academic field continued strong throughout the post-1968 period, as did, relatively speaking, the ministerial and economic bureaucracies. In the future, it will no doubt be the academics and the technical specialists from the ministries and the public sector of the economy who will dominate the administrative staff. The question will be: is there any chance, in view of this development, for an evolution toward corporate autonomy and civic rights? The key to the question may well be in the hands of the free professional interest-type groups (the bar association, the medical society, the journalists' guild, and so on). To date, these second echelon elites have been administratively regulated by the government, and their political roles seem confined to mobilization; they may also be a restraining force against excesses by the regime. The Council of State has apparently played this kind of part in the past at the risk of inciting a purge in the judicial ranks (a not unknown phenomenon in Egypt). In general, we are at a severe handicap in lacking data on the role of the interest-type groups in Egyptian society and their impact on public policy.

VII. THE MILITARY ELITE AND THE OPPOSITION

The Free Officers' drive toward modernization resulted in the defeat, one by one, of the pre-1952 elites: (1) the King and his Court; (2) the landowners; (3) the Wafd national leadership; (4) the religious conservatives. The isolation of the first three groups has already been mentioned. As far as the post-1952 religious opposition to modernization is concerned, the regime has been content with administratively hamstringing it. This was not the Free Officers' original intention, since they clearly excluded the

Muslim Brotherhood from their January 1953 decree abolishing all political parties. Furthermore, a number of the Free Officers had evolved close ties with the Brotherhood—notably 'Amir, al-Shafi'i, Sadat, Husayn.[62]

In many ways, the story of the religious elite's opposition to social and political modernization can only be understood by grasping the issues involved in the debates by Muhammad 'Abduh (d. 1905) and his two disciples: Muhammad Rashid Rida' (d. 1935) and Shaykh 'Ali 'Abd al-Raziq (d. 1966). The public policy area perhaps most affected in this pre-1952 struggle to define the role of Islam vis-à-vis science and the modern world was education.

At the risk of gross oversimplification, it may be said that 'Abduh's important introduction of his concept of "Universal Reason" is the crucial aspect of the modernist-conservative debate within the religious movement. 'Abduh's ambiguity on the question should not obscure the fact that he regarded human reason as a powerful tool in the development of a society that wishes to maintain its Muslim spiritual values.[63] Rida' and the *Manar* group of fundamentalists appear to have fought a losing rear-guard action, in retrospect, against increasingly liberal interpretations of 'Abduh's Universal Reason doctrine during the twenties and thirties. 'Abd al-Raziq's book, *al-Islam wa Usul al-Hukm (Islam and The Principles of Government)* seems to have had a major impact on intellectuals in Egypt when it first appeared in 1925. When major figures such as Taha Husayn rallied to the side of the modernists, it seemed to force the issue in their favor.[64] This work essentially raised the question of whether or not Islamic government was possible and was at least implicitly inspired by the question of the role of reason in man's organization of his political affairs. According to 'Abd al-Raziq, enlightened self-interest rather than religion ought to motivate the efforts of men in the creation of their governments. As for Taha Husayn, his book, published in 1938, entitled *Mustaqbal al-Thaqafah fi Misr (The Future of Culture in Egypt)*, explicitly pleaded for the adoption of Western philosophy, modes of thought, educational methods, and so on.

It may be safe to suppose that the technical education obtained by the Free Officers in their military studies at least indirectly reflected the more open interpretation of 'Abduh's teachings. In any event, no modern military organization with an eye to professionalism and professionalization could exclude the intrusions of modern weapons technology, engineering and mathematics. These sciences, more than others, seemed to liberate thought from its traditional roots.

To suppose this, however, is not to insist on the arrant secularism of the Free Officers. These men were still bound to rural Egypt and its values.[65] On the other hand, it is a mistake to assert that they were reactionaries for whom religion provided a conveniently myopic view of society that only served to obscure the interests of that society.

Thus, the Free Officers had reason to pause in 1953 when they began outlawing political groups. The Brotherhood to them represented the real people of Egypt. Since they themselves were the trustees of the masses in the revolution, how could they crack down on the organization? Apart from that, its opposition potential must have provided a sobering image of an imamist counter-coup somewhat akin to the Sudanese Mahdist revolt in the nineteenth century.

Yet, the Brotherhood itself finally resolved the issue when it organized an assassination attempt against 'Abd al-Nasir in October 1954. From that moment on, the regime employed administrative methods (police, judicial and constitutional) to keep the influence of the 'ulama isolated in their bastion, al-Azhar. Even in their citadel, the learned men of the religious law are under close supervision by the Ministry for Awqaf and Azhar Affairs. Furthermore, the Ministry of Higher Education has close watch over the religious elite through the Rector of al-Azhar University, who is an appointee of the President, in consultation with the Minister.

In addition to these reversals, the Brotherhood failed in its effort to have Islam declared as the state religion in the two constitutions of 1956 and 1964. This changed in 1971, which is symptomatic of the regime's drift to the right under Sadat. In any case, it would be a mistake to equate the 'ulama with the Brotherhood. Thus, it is hard to know how its influence as an underground organization filters through to the organs of power. Representation of the 'ulama is somewhat tenuous and has not always been ensured. The ultimate indignity may have been when Kamal al-Din Mahmud Rif'at, a major socialist ideologue of the regime, had the Awqaf and Azhar Affairs portfolio in the 1960s.

The Egyptian left has never enjoyed the political autonomy it has wished from the government. The string of defeats for them is depressingly long, starting with the Kafr al-Dawwar execution of two laborers in 1952. Major anti-communist campaigns were under way in 1954, 1959-61 and 1971. The Egyptian left has primarily had to rest content to have its members in second echelon elite positions, especially in the media. However, beginning in 1964, when a "vanguard organization" (*tanzim tali'i*) was set up within the ASU (as sanctioned by the Charter of National Action), a change began to be noted.[66] In the wake of the events of May, 1971, and the leftist challenge to Sadat, this organization was dissolved and its leaders placed on trial.[67]

Of the 22 Free Officers, only one (Khalid Muhyi al-Din, the "Red Major") has really been accepted by the international leftist organizations as one of their own. Since joining an attempted coup against his comrades in 1954, he has never enjoyed significant political power. Both 'Ali Sabri and Rif'at may be termed "house leftists," a term indicating that their ideological orientation never was strong enough to lead them to challenge the military elite.

If the ASU has been the preserve of any one individual, that person is 'Ali Sabri, its Secretary-General between 1965 and 1967 and consistently a member of the Higher Executive Committee. Sabri, and to a lesser extent, his successor, 'Abd al-Muhsin Abu al-Nur, sought to make the ASU into a potent political party manned by cadres devoted to "scientific socialism" in Egypt. In short, they attempted to convert the mass movement into a disciplined Leninist-type of organization run on the model of the "organizational weapon."

Debates were particularly sharp in 1966-1969 over the intended nature of the ASU in the Charter (1962)—a sort of party program—and in the minds of the military. The debates were highlighted by a series of expository and analytical articles by 'Ali Sabri in *al-Jumhuriyah* during the winter and spring of 1966-67.[68] Apart from the nature of the ASU, the debates examined its relationship to other institutions of the state, its objectives, and so on.

The left opposition, in their second echelon elite positions in *al-Jumhuriyah*, *al-Tali'ah*, *al-Akhbar*, and *Rawz al-Yusuf*, together with the handful of top elite leftists (Sabri, Dawud, Abu al-Nur, Rif'at), naturally tried to interpret the questions raised to the advantage of their cause. They regarded the ASU as the supreme popular authority, rather than the National Assembly (parliament), because the latter seemed to them to be the preserve of the "petit bourgeois" and "bourgeois" (national capital) elements. They opposed the codification of an organic law for Egypt in view of their belief in the ongoing nature of the revolution. To codify would be to imply the termination of that phenomenon. The left preferred to allow ad hoc revisions to the constitution as the gains of social development were registered by the regime. In this, of course, they were employing the Marxist-Leninist interpretation of law's role in society. Law here is seen as an instrument of the revolution rather than as an enduring set of prescriptions according to which men organize their affairs.[69]

The military elite has to date successfully fended off these thrusts by the left against its dominant position in society. Although hard data would be invaluable to help demonstrate the point, it does seem that the regime has always identified with the rural middle sectors at least implicitly. Hence, when state projects in rural Egypt suddenly find part of their funds siphoned off by local officials and programs on cooperatives commandeered by the more prosperous peasants, the regime seems lethargic in its reaction. It sometimes has been rumored that high regime authorities (such as 'Abd al-Hakim 'Amir, Shams al-Din Badran, Salah Nasr) have been implicated in the conspicuous consumption for which patrimonial rulers have been famous. This kind of an easy, sumptuous life is anathema to the left. Occasionally, a scandal may become an international cause célèbre, as in the Kamshish affair of 1966. Here, the murder of an ASU *aktiv,* caused by an incommoded landholding family, caused an uproar. The regime's response was to create a "defeudalization committee" to extend the revolution further into the countryside. The appointment of 'Amir as chairman of the committee must have been greeted with mirthful derision by the ASU cadres in view of that figure's apparent hostility to defeudalization.

The "bourgeois" or "petit bourgeois" elements with which the regime appears to identify are located in the upper peripheries of categories whose participation in the "alliance of the popular working forces" (ASU) is officially sanctioned: peasants, workers, intellectuals, military, and national capitalists.

Consequently, if the definition of peasant is one who owns less than 25 faddans and tills the soil himself, it is the group owning 10-25 faddans that seems to dominate, with regime acquiescence, the seats allocated by Egypt's socialism for the peasantry in the organs of power (e.g., the Central Committee of the ASU, the People's Assembly, etc.). Similarly, the regime appears to look the other way when individuals who may actually be proprietors or labor bosses with minimal proletarian consciousness purport to represent the workers while they in fact guarantee a voice for their own special positions.

IX. CONCLUSIONS: CRISES IN MODERNIZATION

In reviewing the politics of Egypt since 1952 several themes have stood out concerning the place of the political elite in the dynamics of modernization. The Free Officers who seized power in 1952 put an end to an era when they, to paraphrase Lenin, smashed the state machinery of the landed magnates. Having destroyed this traditional elite group, extirpated the influence of colonial forces and tamed the elements of domestic religious fundamentalism by hitching them to the military's own wagon of social reform, the army has nevertheless encountered major problems. We have not been able to deal with all of them here. There is, first of all, the conflict with Israel. Second, there are issues associated with Egypt's interaction with the other members of the Middle East subordinate international system.

Among the problems of modernization that the stratiotocracy has had to face in the last two decades are those identified as "crises of political development."[70] Among these are, notably, legitimacy of authority and the continuing impact of tradition upon the modernization process. The conclusion that Egyptian politics can best be analyzed in terms of neo-patrimonialism can perhaps be more earthily summed up in the expression: "plus ça change, plus c'est la même chose." And yet, this interpretation by itself would be inadequate in view of the regime's interest in, and commitment to, technology and development. This is strikingly different from the Ottoman sultans and other defensive modernizers who limited the application of modern technology to the military and administrative fields.

The Free Officers have confronted the various crises of modernization (such as identity, legitimacy, participation, capacity, and distribution) in a number of ways. They seem to have decided that Egypt's identity can best be nurtured in interaction with Arab nationalism but never totally merged with it. Since 'Abd al-Nasir's death, the significance of Arabism to Egypt's destiny appears to have become more conjectural than ever. Within this framework, an alleged "scientific socialism" has been adopted, but it is curiously bereft of the substance of that concept: class struggle, dictatorship of the proletariat; the elitist party; total restructuring of economic *distribution* as well as of institutions and their control. The essential reason for this anomaly is that the military elite itself cannot withstand the application of these concepts. The stratiotocrats of Egypt have tried to some extent to merge with "Uncle Hamzah" (the symbol of Egypt's good hearted fallah) by the deft manipulation of symbols and expressions, but they have never really succeeded in erasing the elite-mass gap.

Egypt's identity in the modern world is a function of reformist Islam, a cooperativist ethic (for which the religion is asserted to provide a crucial filip), a technocratic orientation, and an anti-colonialist nationalism. These are overlain with a patina of praetorianism that has resulted in military corporatism. Two Soviet journalists, engaging in a post-mortem of Egypt's politics on the morrow of the June War defeat, speculated that the country was under the domination of an "officer business class with check books and bank accounts." They noted with ironic understatement:

> Eventually, the shift of military cadres from the army into the governmental and economic apparatus turned into a kind of constantly operating factor ... [as] the government frequently appealed to the army to help put this or that state office in order.[71]

Maxime Rodinson, the well-known Marxist Oriental scholar, has put it more bluntly in terming the Free Officers' political effort "a reactionary and dictatorial line."[72] This ongoing military intervention in politics since 1952 is becoming less and less viable and acceptable. What appeared to be neo-patrimonialism under 'Abd al-Nasir may indeed be transforming itself into that extreme of patrimonialism that Weber termed sultanistic behavior, hence, neo-sultanism. The key factor may now be precisely that of legitimacy.

Of course the members of the stratiotocracy have the advantage of being Egyptian. Beyond that, for years legitimacy was anchored in 'Abd al-Nasir's charisma, among other things. After 1967, routinization—which had been setting in in a latent way after 1962 (Yemen) anyway—took place in a noticeable manner. Since 1970, the greatest display of potency of the charismatic phenomenon was 'Abd al-Nasir's death and funeral. The post 'Abd al-Nasir system has not had the advantage of a charismatic leadership and has to that extent suffered in its quest for legitimacy. It is worth noting, however, that classic patrimonialism did not require charismatic features in rulership.

The ASU has constituted the chief vehicle for mass political participation in Egypt. This is not the proper place to investigate the politics of mass participation in Egypt, but it may be noted that, having purposefully chosen a rationalist, elitist model of rule and modernization from above, the military has been unable to achieve meaningful participation.[73] In consequence, political integration in society has been weak and political mobilization artificial. This is basically due to the unwillingness of the military elite to permit the evolution of professional political cadres.

The capacity to implement policy is an empirical question that cannot be answered without some knowledge of the proceedings of cabinet meetings and so on. From time to time there have been public indications that the regime's capacity has been strained beyond the breaking point. Thus, when the Second Five Year Plan (1965-1969) ran into difficulties early on and had to be drastically revised, one gained a fleeting impression of the enormous difficulties facing the Egyptian political system (problems, it is fair to note, that would loom very large for any regime). On the positive side, the military elite has demonstrated their capacity to deal with disease, poverty, and educational development. If one interprets capacity in the sense of penetration by government in order to contain and maintain, it may be deduced that high levels of capacity have been demonstrated. However, capacity should also be defined in terms of the ability to implement difficult tasks for development. It would not be unfair to say that the military elite has suffered serious reversals in the attempt to apply the Charter of National Action (1962). The thousands of faddans of land obtained from the elimination of the aristocracy have not, as was hoped, had the major effect of creating a self-sufficient small holder stratum in Egypt.

Instead, contrary to paragraphs 23 and 24 of the September, 1952 Agrarian Reform Law, "fragmentation ... of landed property into holdings of less than five faddans" *has* occurred. The reform's basic success has been to increase the holdings of formerly poor peasants, on the average from 0.8 to 1.1 faddans. This increase of 0.3 faddans is, unfortunately for Egypt, not enough to make a difference. Furthermore, the reform regrettably has failed to convert formerly landless peasants into owners, and the latter are increasing in proportion to the total population of rural Egypt.[74]

Finally, Egypt has been suffering from a crisis of confidence. In many ways, the individuals serving on the administrative staff are exceptional for their intelligence and their motivation for achievement. In examining the biographies of some of them, one comes away feeling that they embody a kind of Renaissance-man ideal. However, for reasons already discussed, the energies and capabilities of these persons seem to have been sublimated in the interests of compliance. Rodinson has belittled the authority of cabinet ministers by terming them little better than "commissioners" of the military.[75] This term indicates that the non-military members of the Egyptian political elite are a service bureaucracy. The distribution of authority to them, however, is always conditioned on loyal service to the state. But rather than serving the state militarily, as in the traditional service states of history (e.g., under Peter the Great of Russia), it is technical and managerial proficiency that must be tendered. For the rest, we agree with Binder that the relationship of the service bureaucracy (the administrative staff) to *society* is very much in the tradition of imperial officials of the historical empires: they administer as though their respective domains of activity were fiefdoms. Referring to Egypt, he notes that it is difficult for state and economic bureaucrats to emulate the rational model of administration in the West, given entirely different social settings. "The consequence," he writes,

> insofar as bureaucrats relax into traditional ways is that modern style organizations may become mutants of other traditional, feudalistic structures. Certainly in Egypt something of the sort has occurred in certain governmental enterprises.[76]

As noted previously, with the passage of time the military elite will be called upon to distribute authority and power with mounting insistence. Its typical response has been to fall back on highly centralized, bureaucratic rule. In doing so, it has followed time-honored Egyptian practice. But the question is to what extent the patrimonial model, with its modern variations, can be maintained without stimulating deep-seated forces for radical change in a manner never countenanced by the Free Officers when they first seized power: a revolution from below—whether militant fundamentalist, or radical leftist—that would join the Egyptian masses in a national movement for the first time.

NOTES

1. Karl Wittfogel, *Oriental Despotism* (New Haven: Yale University Press, 1957).

2. Charles Issawi, *Egypt in Revolution* (London: Oxford University Press, 1963), pp. 5-6, dates supplied. In this regard Jean Lacouture feels compelled to title Part I of his biography of 'Abd al-Nasir: "Né de l'Egypte." See his *Nasser* (Paris: Editions du Seuil, 1971).

3. Leonard Binder, "Egypt: The Integrative Revolution," in *Political Culture and Political Development*, ed. Lucian Pye and Sidney Verba (Princeton, N.J.: Princeton University Press, 1965), p. 399.

4. See the fine discussion by Serif Mardin, "Power, Civil Society and Culture in the Ottoman Empire," *Comparative Studies in Society and History* 11, 3 (June, 1969): 258-81.

5. Stanford J. Shaw, "The Ottoman View of the Balkans," in *The Balkans in Transition*, ed. by Charles Jelavich and Barbara Jelavich (Berkeley and Los Angeles: University of California Press, 1962), p. 56.

6. This stratification scheme is adapted from Stanford J. Shaw, "Landholding and Land Tax Revenues in Ottoman Egypt," in *The Political and Social History of Modern Egypt*, ed. P. M. Holt (London: Oxford University Press, 1968), pp. 91-103.

7. Bernard Lewis, *The Emergence of Modern Turkey* (London: Oxford University Press, 1961), p. 35.

8. For the view that the national economy has not comprised the primary unit of development in the Muslim World (cf. the West), and implicitly therefore failed to develop market and credit institutions, see C.A.O. van Nieuwenhuijze, "Social Aspects of Economic Development in the Arab States," in *Cross-Cultural Studies* (The Hague: Mouton & Co., 1963), p. 229.

9. P. M. Holt, "The Pattern of Egyptian Political History from 1517-1789," in *Political and Social Change*, pp. 82 ff.

10. Eduardo Archetti, Egil Fossum and Per Olav Reinton, "Agrarian Structure and Peasant Autonomy," *The Journal of Peace Research* (Oslo), 3 (1970): 188. The three dimensions have been quoted verbatim. Referring to the idea of vertical market, the authors state: "The peasant is introduced on the vertical market through the demand for food and cash crops on the national or international [cf. local or regional, involving horizontal exchanges] scale. This relationship becomes direct when the producer does not market his products through the landlord." Such direct relationship, the authors note, undermines the domination exercised by the landlord over the peasant. For an Egyptian Marxist's thesis that such patterns are now beginning to unfold in Egypt, see Dr. Rif'at al-Sa'id, "al-Tabaqah al-Wusta wa Dawruha fi al-Mujtama' al-Misri" [The Middle Class and its Role in Egyptian Society], *al-Tali'ah*, 8, 3 (March, 1972): 63.

11. Shaw, "Landholding and Land-tax Revenues," p. 99 stresses the inalienability of the peasant's land and his legal right to relinquish it; Gabriel Baer, however, explicitly declares that the peasants—at least in lower Egypt—had "no property rights to the land they tilled." See Baer, "The Dissolution of the Village Community," in *Studies in the Social History of Modern Egypt* (Chicago: University of Chicago Press, 1969), pp. 19-20. See also in Baer's support J.N.D. Anderson, "Law Reform in Egypt," in *Political and Social Change*, p. 210. Shaw is perhaps referring to the common practice, rather than to legal right. Even then, the village *'umdah* appears to have had the authority to decide how a deceased *fallah*'s land ought to be distributed. In brief, the fallah's rights to the land were not at all clear-cut and in no case comprised contractually guaranteed ownership.

12. Baer, "The Dissolution," in *Studies*, p. 17.

13. H. A. Winkler, *Bauern zwischen Wasser und Wüste* (Stuttgart, 1934), pp. 136, 140. Cited in *Ibid.*, p. 28. Translation supplied.

14. Berque, "Sur la structure sociale de quelques villages égyptiens," *Annales Economies-Sociétés-Civilisations*, 1955. Cited in *Ibid.*, p. 29. Translation supplied.

15. H. H. Ayrout, *Fellahs* (Cairo, 1942), p. 111. Cited in *Idem*. Translation supplied.

16. Ayrout, *The Egyptian Peasant* (Boston: Beacon Press, 1963), p. 113. Immediately preceding this citation, noting that the village will unite in extreme moments of danger to save its existence, he observes: "Thus, the village, united against the world, is divided against itself, and confidence and mistrust live side by side." *Idem.*

17. Nada Tomiche, "Notes sur al hiérarchie social en Egypte à l'époque de Muhammad 'Ali," in *Political and Social Change*, p. 254. She quotes Clot Bey: "They [the 'ulama] now have little influence and *exercise no action on the government . . .*" Emphasis and translation supplied.

18. Ibid., p. 256.

19. See the important, if somewhat obscurely written, contribution by the Dutch scholar C.A.O. van Nieuwenhuijze, *Social Stratification and the Middle East* (Leiden: E. J. Brill, 1965), p. 9. A composite, discontinuous society is, as he puts it, "only integrated insofar as it converges upon a

core [under which] the entire society is subsumed." Politics in such societies are a facet of the interplay of non-class groupings, such as families, kinship tribes and the like.

20. Ibrahim 'Amir, *Al-'Ard wa al-Fallah wa al-Mas'alah al-Zira'iyyah fi Misr* [Land, The Peasant and the Agrarian Question in Egypt] (Cairo, 1938, and two later editions). Note that Marx never considered the possibility of patrimonialism as a possible historical stage in which status honor, not class, provides the distinguishing feature and motive force of historical development.

21. Gabriel Baer, *A History of Land Ownership in Modern Egypt* (London: Oxford University Press, 1962), pp. 292, 221. Marx's pessimism over the role of the peasants in human development ("the idiocy of rural life!") rested in his belief that peasant relations are "strictly local," that the "identity of their interests begets no unity, no national union and no political organization"; peasants "cannot represent themselves, they must be represented." Cited by Lloyd Rudolph, "The Modernity of Tradition: The Democratic Incarnation of Caste in India," *The American Political Science Review* 59, 4 (Dec., 1965), p. 975.

22. Baer, "Submissiveness and Revolt of the Fallah," in *Studies*, p. 103.

23. Baer, *Population and Society in the Arab East* (London: Routledge and Kegan Paul, 1964), p. 174.

24. Tomiche, "Notes," p. 254; Afaf Loutfi el-Sayed, "The Role of the 'Ulama in Egypt During the Early Nineteenth Century," *Political and Social Change*, p. 266; Gamal el-Din el-Shayyal, "Some Aspects of Intellectual and Social Life in Eighteenth Century Egypt," *Ibid.*, p. 122.

25. Lloyd and Suzanne Rudolph, *The Modernity of Tradition* (Chicago: University of Chicago Press, 1967). Also the issue of *Daedalus* entitled "Post Traditional Societies," 102, 1 (Winter, 1973).

26. Manfred Halpern, *The Politics of Social Change in the Middle East and North Africa* (Princeton: Princeton University Press, 1963); Leonard Binder, "Egypt: The Integrative Revolution"; Eliezar Be'eri, *Army Officers in Arab Politics and Society* (New York: Praeger, 1970); Anouar Abdel-Malek, *Egypt: Military Society*, Tr. Charles Lam Markmann (New York: Random House, 1968); Benno Sternberg-Sarel, "Révolution par le haut dans les campagnes de l'Egypte," *Les Temps Modernes* 24, 274 (April, 1969): 1772-1802; Eric Rouleau, *Le Monde*, 8 April 1970. The Soviets have also gotten into this act. See I. P. Beliaev and Ye. M. Primakov, *Za Rubezhom*, 27 (30 June-6 July 1967), where the pair talk of the "military bourgeoisie." For two recent attempts to apply the concept of class to the Middle East consult Manfred Halpern, "Toward a Redefinition of the Revolutionary Situation," in *National Liberation*, eds. Norman Miller and Roderick Aya, (New York: Free Press, 1971), pp. 14-47 and James A. Bill, "Class Analysis and the Dialectics of Modernization in the Middle East," *International Journal of Middle East Studies* 3, 4 (Oct., 1972): 417-34. Halpern defines class as an aggregate of individuals with a common attitude toward social change. This is far too vague and broad a definition in this writer's view. Bill defines class more closely, but he seems to end up with what I have preferred to call a stratum, social force, or status group. On p. 424 he defines class as the "largest aggregates

of individuals united by similar modes of employment and possessing similar power positions to preserve, modify or transform relationships among such aggregates." He finds the following "classes" (read strata or status groups) in the Middle East: (1) the ruling class; (2) the bureaucratic middle class; (3) the bourgeois middle class; (4) the cleric middle class; (5) the traditional working class; (6) the peasant class; (7) the nomadic class. In the last analysis, my quarrel with these definitions is not one of mere semantics, since in my view their approach neglects or seriously underestimates the force of patrimonialism.

27. G. D. H. Cole, *Studies in Class Structure* (London: Routledge & Kegan Paul, 1955), pp. 90 ff.

28. For Weber, class considerations were operative only when individuals share "a specific causal component of their life's chances ... [a component] represented exclusively by *economic* interests in the possession of goods and opportunities for income ... under the conditions of the commodity or labor markets." Max Weber, "Class, Status and Party," in *From Max Weber*, ed. Hans H. Gerth and C. Wright Mills (New York: Oxford University Press, 1946), p. 180. Emphasis supplied. On the development of the commodity and labor markets and the impact of these on social and economic structure in Western Europe see the classic work by Karl Polanyi, *The Great Transformation* (New York: Farrar and Rinehart, 1944). Focusing strictly on the labor market, Hoselitz notes: "A labor market which functions upon the well-known principle of free markets, in general, is characteristic of a highly developed economy, one in which complex processes of economic organization have been elaborated and in which industry and large-scale enterprise, as well as urbanization and the growth of the secondary and tertiary sectors of production have become characteristic features of the social landscape." Hoselitz further reminds us that the existence of a commodity market is no guarantee for that of a labor market. The latter requires contractual relations and the meeting of entrepreneur with the free laborer offering his labor for sale. See Bert F. Hoselitz, "The Development of a Labor Market in the Process of Economic Growth," in *Transactions of the Fifth World Congress of Sociology* II (Louvain, Belgium: International Sociological Association, 1962), pp. 56-57. These comments show, it is felt, that on the grounds of the absence of a bona fide labor market alone, Egypt may be disqualified from the designation of substantial industrial and capitalist development and attainment: hence, of possessing a bourgeoisie.

29. Cole, *Studies in Class Structure*, p. 92.

30. For the major work on the press consult Ibraham 'Amir, *Tatawwur al-Sahafah al-Misriyah* [The Evolution of the Egyptian Press], 3rd. ed. (Cairo: Dar al-Tawakul, 1953).

31. Be'eri, p. 426.

32. George A. L. (Lord) Lloyd, *Egypt Since Cromer, I* (New York: Howard A. Fertig, 1970), p. 73 on British preferences for Butros Ghali and the latter's pro-British actions and views. Book first published in 1933.

33. Notably Baer, *A History*; Helen A. B. Rivlin, *The Agricultural Policies of Muhammad 'Ali in Egypt* (Cambridge, Mass.: Harvard University

Press, 1961); and Ahmad Ahmad Hitta, *Ta'rikh al-Zira'ah al-Misriyah fi 'Ahd Muhammad 'Ali* [The History of Egyptian Agriculture Under Muhammad 'Ali] (Cairo, 1950); also Abd el-Malek, *Egypt*; and 'Amir, *Al-'Ard wa al-Fallah*.

34. Lord Lloyd, British High Commissioner from 1925-1929, summed it up well: "Law and order, internal peace and quietness, and impartial justice ... there is really only one article of belief upon which we can confidently depend—that good administration is the first requirement to be fulfilled, and that all other questions are subordinate to it." And earlier: "More and more clearly the conclusion seems to emerge that the real danger to those countries which have come under our control arises when the claims of good administration are subordinated to the claims of political theory." Lloyd, *Egypt Since Cromer, II*, p. 358; also p. 5.

35. The British "have not only not succeeded in building up a single manufacturing industry, but have effectually killed whatever possibility there had been for one." T. Rothstein, *Egypt's Ruin* (London, 1910), cited in Hassan el-Saaty, "Changes in the Industrial Organization of Egypt," *Transactions of the Third World Congress of Sociology, II* (London: Hereford Times, 1956), p. 11.

36. Lloyd, *Egypt Since Cromer*, I, pp. 67-68.

37. For the political and ideological currents of this period, consult Marcel Colombe, *L'Evolution de l'Egypte, 1924-1952* (Paris: G. P. Maisonneuve, 1951); Nadav Safran, *Egypt in Search of Political Community* (Cambridge, Mass.: Harvard University Press, 1961); Jamal Muhammad Ahmad, *The Intellectual Origins of Egyptian Nationalism* (London: Oxford University Press, 1960); Malcolm H. Kerr, *Islamic Reform* (Berkeley: University of California Press, 1966); Albert Hourani, *Arabic Thought in the Liberal Age* (London: Oxford University Press, 1962), pp. 132-244, 324-340.

38. P. J. Vatikiotis, *The Modern History of Egypt* (New York: Praeger, 1969), p. 252.

39. Abdel-Malek, *Egypt*, p. 10.

40. Issawi, *Egypt in Revolution*, pp. 43-45. Issawi, moreover, feels that the employment figures for the post World War II period are inflated and realistically need to be revised downward. Saaty, on the other hand, lists 307,443 "factory" workers and 474,832 "industrial establishment" (a looser term) workers for 1951. See Saaty, "Changes in the Industrial Organization," p. 16. The semi-official *al-Ahram*, 11 August 1962, declared that Egypt in that year had 1.25 million "industrial workers in 66,000 industrial establishments." This figure is exaggerated, one suspects, although it does indicate the upward trend in the figures.

41. Issawi, *The Economic History of the Middle East, 1800-1914* (Chicago: University of Chicago Press, 1966), p. 453.

42. Issawi, "Growth and Structural Change in the Middle East," *The Middle East Journal* 25, 3 (Summer, 1971): 316.

43. J. C. Hurewitz, *Middle East Politics: The Military Dimension* (New York: Praeger, 1969), p. 124.

44. Cromer, *Modern Egypt* (New York: Macmillan, 1950), II, pp. 123,

564 protests that Britain was only interested in "the trusteeship of the masses" and "stable government." Lloyd, *Egypt Since Cromer*, II, p. 360, says the British "deliberately stimulated the growth of democratic ideas and methods." It has already been noted that Lloyd himself warned against encouraging "political theory" among the Egyptians. Hence, it is odd to find him declaring that it was British practice to do otherwise. Withal, Cromer's caveat that the Europeans "not inquire too minutely into the acts of [the Egyptian] government so much as to ensure its stability" went unheeded. And Egyptian liberals, especially the Ummah group, took this British encouragement of democratic ideas and methods seriously.

45. Vatikiotis, "Some Political Consequences of the 1952 Revolution in Egypt," in *Political and Social Change*, pp. 369-70.

46. ,Dekmejian, *Egypt Under Nasir* (Albany, N.Y.: SUNY Press, 1971), is especially impressed with the charismatic phenomenon. On the whole, it is tempting to overuse it, as witness 'Abd al-Nasir's dilemma described below.

47. Hatim, *Qadiyah al-Thawrah fi sab' Sanawat* (Cairo, 1959), cited in Be'eri, p. 93. The poverty of the regime's philosophy, so to speak, has been raised countless times, even by 'Abd al-Nasir. For one important contribution, see Malcolm H. Kerr, "Arab Radical Notions of Democracy," *St. Anthony's Papers* No. 16 (Middle Eastern Affairs, No. 3) (London: Chatto and Windus, 1963), pp. 9-40.

48. Apart from the six broad general principles of the revolution, which were aimed at ridding Egypt of colonialism, imperialism, poverty and social injustice, the major social plan of the Free Officers was the Agrarian Reform Law of September 1952. From that date until 1957, economic planning seems to have proceeded in the absence of ideological commitment. The creation of the Ministry of Industry in 1956 seemed to be a token of the change beginning in the regime's thinking on this issue. But the spectacular diplomatic and propaganda victories that accrued to 'Abd al-Nasir in the mid-fifties seemed enough to keep the heady atmosphere in its rarified state forever. The late President therefore was rudely surprised at the sullen and wordless reception accorded his speech before 100,000 at an Alexandria rally in celebration of the Fifth Anniversary of the Revolution. He had no more charismatic displays to present, no more surprises or miracles. On 5 December 1957 the regime's ideological orientation began to stiffen when he announced his idea of "a socialist, democratic and cooperative society, free from political, social and economic exploitation." Keith Wheelock, *Nasser's New Egypt* (New York: Praeger, 1960), pp. 64, 69.

49. Ibid., p. 73 in reference to the atrophy of local government under 'Abd al-Nasir's heavy hand.

50. Consider the sentiments of anonymous but presumably informed and aware Egyptians to an incredulous American reporter after 'Abd al-Nasir's death: "['Abd al-Nasir] ruined Egypt. He destroyed all of our democratic institutions and brought back the despotism of the Mamluks." Cited in Edward R. F. Sheehan, "The Real Sadat and the Demythologized Nasser," *The New York Times*, 18 July 1971, IV, p. 35.

51. Charles Issawi, "Egypt Since 1800: A Study in Lop-sided Development," *Journal of Economic History* (1961): 7.

52. The following are instances of the attrition alluded to. On September 28, 1970 (immediately following 'Abd al-Nasir's death) three former Free Officers sought unsuccessfully to persuade Sadat to diffuse political power and encourage democratic expression. In October, Sadat received only 90 percent of the vote in the plebiscite to determine his acceptability as President to the masses. This contrasted to the 99.9 percent routinely registered by his predecessor. Students demonstrated against Sadat in January, February and April 1972. All were serious incidents. Industrial workers struck in August 1971 and March 1972. In May 1971 Sadat had to overcome an "anti-party" coup against him within the ASU. The three Free Officers above-mentioned resumed their earnest attempt to decentralize power when he sought their aid. A military coup was attempted against Sadat on May 25, 1972 by troops and officers of the "special forces," motivated by their rancor against the do-nothing Soviet military advisors and personnel stationed in the country. In view of Sadat's eviction of the Soviets on July 18, 1972 and his indication upon that occasion that the presence of the Soviets had caused him internal difficulties, this rumored episode has an air of reality about it. See *al-Nahar* (Beirut), 2 August 1972. According to the Paris paper, *France-Soir*, July 24, 1972, 89 Air Force officers unceremoniously visited Sadat at his headquarters on the night of July 12 and insisted that he dismiss the Soviets. Incident cited in *Arab Report and Record*, 16-31 July 1972. In December, January and February, 1972-1973, Sadat encountered challenges from a variety of sectors of society, including the omnipresent students, the workers, and conservative military forces. The latter may have been overwrought over more than the relationship with the Soviet Union and the stalled confrontation with Israel, inasmuch as one Western reporter has interpreted the Sadat ambition "clearly [to be] to take the military out of politics." See Henry Tanner, *The New York Times*, 4 Dec. 1972. However, Sadat has also paid tribute to and shown consideration for his military officers, including special gifts "of a thousand pounds apiece." See Joseph Kraft, "Letter from Cairo," *The New Yorker*, 10 February 1973, p. 78. Symptomatic of Sadat's recent difficulties has been the outspoken criticisms of the People's Assembly against the Prime Minister's domestic programs (*The New York Times*, 15 Dec. 1972) and the Egyptian Press Syndicate's call for an abolition of censorship (*Ibid.*, 18 December, 1972).

53. Sternberg-Sarel, "Révolution par le haut," p. 1773, describes them as "petit-bourgeois . . . religious, reactionary, individualists—attached to the past." On p. 1779, speaking of their "middle management image" of the Egyptian village as taught them in the Military Academy, the author asserts that this image was superimposed on an antecedent image "impregnated with religion and patriarchal spirit."

54. Vatikiotis, *The Egyptian Army in Politics* (Bloomington, Indiana: University of Indiana Press, 1961), pp. 48-49.

55. Abdel-Malek, *Egypt*, pp. 211-212.

56. Guenther Roth, "Personal Rulership, Patrimonialism and Empire-

Building in the New States," *World Politics* 20, 2 (January, 1968): 196. He adds: ". . . some of these new states may not be states at all but merely private governments of those powerful enough to rule." *Idem.*

57. Be'eri, *Army Officers*, Table between pp. 28-29. NB, Be'eri's figures involve counting an individual each time he appeared in a particular cabinet; an individual holding more than one portfolio in a given cabinet was counted only once.

58. Sources: *The Middle East Journal*, 22, 1-2 (Winter-Spring, 1963): 140. *The Middle East Record*, III, 1967 (Tel Aviv: Israel Universities Press, 1971), p. 536; *al-Ahram*, 20 October, 1968.

59. Sources: Al Ittihad al-Ishtiraki al-'Arabi, *al-Kitab al-Sanawi* (Cairo: Dar Matabi' al-Sha'b, 1964, 1965, 1967), pp. 84, 29-30, 63 respectively; also, United Arab Republic, Ministry of National Guidance, *Arab Political Encyclopaedia: Documents and Notes* (Cairo: Documentation Research Center, July-December 1965), p. 97; *The Middle East Record*, III, pp. 536, 578; *al-Akhbar*, 25 July 1970; *Le Monde*, 19 May 1971; *al-Ahram*, 12 August 1971; Dekmejian, *Egypt under Nasir*, p. 222.

60. Sources: *The Middle East Record*, I, II, 1960, 1961 (Tel Aviv: Israel Universities Press, 1961, 1962), pp. 496-497 and 596 respectively; United States Embassy, *Directory of United Arab Republic Personages* (Cairo: mimeo, January, 1966), p. 46; *al-Ahram al-Iqtisadi*, Special Issue, "Dalil al-Mu'assasat," (June, 1969), p. 17; selective issues of *al-Ahram; al-Jumhuriyah; Le Monde; Arab Report and Record, al-Musawwar; Rawz al-Yusuf,* etc.

61. For an important empirical study correlating the strength of the military in political systems to modernization (economic and social), and finding that the military is generally either a non- or anti-modernizing force, see Eric A. Nordlinger, "Soldiers in Mufti," *The American Political Science Review* (December, 1970): 1131-1148. It would be intriguing to take the three years of 1965, 1966 and 1967, with the three successive cabinets containing 47 percent, 59 percent and 65 percent military officials respectively, and correlate this strength with public policy outputs in education, investment, rate of growth of GNP/capita, and other areas.

62. Abdel-Malek, *Egypt*, pp. 210-211.

63. See Safran, *Egypt in Search*, pp. 62-75.

64. Hourani, *Arabic Thought*, pp. 183 ff.

65. Revealingly, President Sadat at one juncture affirmed his regime's commitment to such values in a speech to the People's Assembly, 20 May 1971. He asked for a permanent constitution "rooted in the soil and customs of Egypt and founded on the message of faith . . . maintain(ing) moral values against this horrible wave of materialism . . . reflect(ing) the customs and traditions of the Egyptian village. . . ." *Le Monde*, 22 May 1971.

66. *al-Ahram*, 7 August 1966 covered 'Abd al-Nasir's discussion with Egyptian students the day before, during which he revealed the existence of the vanguard organization. It was seemingly organized by Sabri and Farid 'Abd al-Karim Basyuni, Secretary of the Jizah Governorate ASU Organization.

67. For a list of the leaders of the dissolved vanguard organization, see *al-Ahram*, 23 August, 1971.

68. The paper was made the official organ of the ASU on 23 December 1966.

69. On the debates, see *The Middle East Record*, III, (Tel Aviv: Israel Universities Press, 1971), p. 529 ff.

70. Leonard Binder et. al., *Crises in Political Development* (Princeton: Princeton University Press, 1971).

71. I. P. Beliaev and Ye. M. Primakov, *Za Rubezhom*, 27 (30 June-6 July 1967), cited in *Current Digest of the Soviet Press* 19, 26 (July 19, 1967), pp. 6-8.

72. Maxime Rodinson, "The Political System," in *Egypt Since the Revolution*, ed. P. J. Vatikiotis (New York: Praeger, 1968), p. 96.

73. See my "Political Participation in a Military Society: The ASU in Egypt," delivered at the 5th MESA Conference, New Albany Hotel, Denver, Colorado, 11-13 November, 1971.

74. Gabriel Baer, "New Data on the Egyptian Land Reform," *New Outlook* (Tel Aviv), X, 3 (March-April, 1967), pp. 26-30.

75. Rodinson, "The Political System," p. 94.

76. Leonard Binder, "National Integration and Political Development," *The American Political Science Review* 58, 3 (September, 1964), p. 628.

BIBLIOGRAPHY

Abdel-Malek, Anouar. *Egypt: Military Society.* Translated by C. L. Markmann. New York: Random House, 1968.

Baer, Gabriel. *A History of Landownership in Modern Egypt.* London: Oxford University Press, 1962.

_____ *Studies in the Social History of Modern Egypt.* Chicago, Illinois: University of Chicago Press, 1969.

Be'eri, Eliezer. *Army Officers in Arab Politics and Society.* New York: Praeger, 1970.

Berque, Jacques. *Egypt: Imperialism and Revolution.* London: Faber and Faber, 1972.

Binder, Leonard. "Egypt: The Integrative Revolution." In *Political Culture and Political Development*, edited by Lucian Pye and Sidney Verba. Princeton: Princeton University Press, 1965.

_____ "Political Recruitment and Political Participation in Egypt." In *Political Parties and Political Development*, edited by Joseph LaPalombara and Myron Weiner. Princeton, N.J.: Princeton University Press, 1966.

_____ *The Ideological Revolution in the Middle East.* New York: Wiley, 1964.

Dekmejian, R. H. *Egypt Under Nasir.* Albany, N.Y.: State University of New York Press, 1971.

Holt, P. M., ed. *Political and Social Change in Modern Egypt.* London: Oxford University Press, 1968.

Hussein, Mahmoud. *Class Conflict in Egypt: 1945-1970.* New York: Monthly Review Press, 1974.

Issawi, Charles. *Egypt in Revolution.* London: Oxford University Press, 1963.

Kerr, Malcolm H. *Islamic Reform.* Berkeley and Los Angeles, California: University of California Press, 1966.

_____ "Egypt." In *Education and Political Development*, edited by James S. Coleman. Princeton, N.J.: Princeton University Press, 1965.

Lacouture, Jean and Lacouture, Simonne. *Egypt in Transition.* London: Methuen, 1958.

Mitchell, Richard. *The Society of Muslim Brothers.* London: Oxford University Press, 1974.

Perlmutter, Amos. *Egypt: Praetorian State.* New York: E. P. Dulton and Co., 1973.

Safran, Nadav. *Egypt in Search of Political Community.* Cambridge, Mass.: Harvard University Press, 1961.

Vatikiotis, P. J., ed. *Egypt Since the Revolution.* New York: Praeger, 1968.

_____ *The Egyptian Army in Politics.* Bloomington, Ind.: Indiana University Press, 1961.

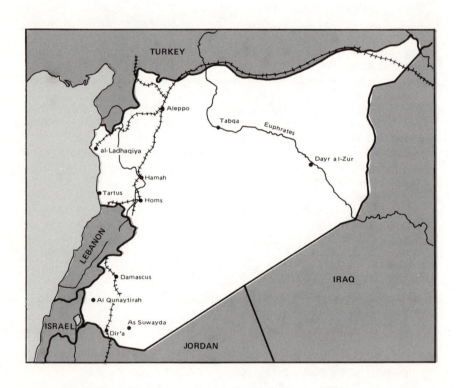

3

Syria:
Downfall of a Traditional Elite

Michael H. Van Dusen

I. THE TWENTIETH CENTURY SYRIAN EXPERIENCE

The Syrian Case The most significant political fact of twentieth century Syrian history and politics has been the complete social, economic and political ruin of the traditional Syrian political elite and the evolution of a new elite. That fact in itself does not necessarily imply any corresponding development of new institutions or political procedures which encourage increased participation in the political process. It does distinguish Syria from some of its Middle East neighbors, particularly Lebanon and, to a lesser degree, Iraq. In Iraq, vestiges of a traditional elite exercising political power the way it had for centuries were still visible in the mid-1960s; the erosion of that elite's power came more slowly than in Syria.

Syria's experience since the evolution of a nationalist movement on the eve of World War I offers a useful case study of both elite behavior and change in a society undergoing rapid social change. After a long and uncompromising struggle for independence and now after close to thirty years of national sovereignty, new dimensions of that struggle and its aftermath can be examined in proper perspective. At independence in 1946, Syria's future offered much promise: economically it was richer, and politically it seemed more organized and advanced than many other Asian and African countries still under colonial rule at the time. Then, as now, Syria was representative of the mainstream of political currents in the Arab world; as such, it provides an excellent, if in some respects unique microcosm of a traditional Arab society confronting the challenges of modernization.

The hopes and expectations which Syria's independence aroused, however, soon foundered. The democratic programs of those traditional politicians who helped guide Syria out of a twenty-year French mandate faltered: within three years after independence, the government was shown to be unable to cope with such domestic problems as corruption, inefficiency, and inflation, and regional issues such as the future of Palestine. As occurred in so many developing countries, corruption, inept and ineffective regional and international policies, and incoherent domestic programs helped discredit Syria's parliamentary institutions and drew the army into the political arena. The 1947 elections, the role Syria did (or did not) play in the 1948 Palestine War, and the succession of bickering and deadlocked cabinets frustrated aspirations associated with independence from the beginning.

The role that the military has played in Syria since 1946 is obviously a crucial aspect of this case study.[1] Indeed, post-independence Syria cannot be understood without special attention to the army: three older officers tied to the traditional elite—Husni al-Za'im, Sami al-Hinnawi and Adib al-Shishakli—successively dominated the political scene from 1949 to 1954; younger and newer elements in the military played a decisive role in the return to parliamentary government in 1954 and again in 1961 as well as in the move to unite with Egypt in 1958; and officers of the new elite brought the Ba'th Party to power in 1963 and committed that party to a new political and social orientation in 1966 and, then again, in 1970. Even this brief resume indicates that those in khaki have been significant political actors since independence and are likely to remain important for years to come. In Iraq, the traditional elite, which had a far more salient military element, had helped gain nominal independence for that country in 1932, over a decade before Syrian independence. Moreover, the power of the traditional Iraqi elite was not threatened until nearly a decade after the military first took power in Syria in 1949.

Unlike many other Middle Eastern states whose achievement of independence can be clearly defined in time, Syria gradually acquired greater responsibility and authority over its own affairs over a period of years. The last French soldiers left in 1945 and the country was officially declared independent in 1946; yet the French had committed themselves to Syrian independence as early as 1943. The significance of this is that other more precise events of the same era had a greater impact on Syrian political development than did the actual achievement of independence—the 1948 Palestine War and the first military coup (in 1949) being the most important. In fact, many political events and trends in Syrian politics since the late 1940s relate to or emanate from the events of 1948 and 1949 rather than from the achievement of independence.

Geopolitical Factors Four fundamental geopolitical factors have helped determine the context in which the political process has operated in Syria. Some of these characteristics are unique to Syria and others are common to several Arab societies, but all form an essential background to discussion of Syrian political elites. These factors are: a strong sense of regionalism; the changing territorial frame of reference for Syrian nationalism; the importance of sub-and supra-national political loyalties; and the minorities which form a majority in certain regions of Syria.

The traditional self-sufficiency—socially, economically and politically—of several regional centers throughout Syria has served to strengthen the influence of parochial loyalties on national politics and to decentralize many developmental issues. Syrian society is composed of nine such regional centers: each usually includes one city of at least fifty thousand people, several large towns and scores of villages strewn in outlying areas, and each traditionally had an agricultural base for self-sufficiency. In the south, there are four: Qunaytara, Suwayda' (or the Jabal Duruz area), Dir'a and Damascus. There are three in the more densely populated northwest which combine plains and mountain regions: Hama, Hums and al-Ladhaqiya. Aleppo in the north is second only to Damascus in importance and size. Dayr al-Zur, the commercial center of the rich farm lands in the Jazira region north of the Euphrates River, serves a regional function for the large, sparsely populated northeast of Syria. Discussion of Syrian cities, past and present, usually focuses on the four major and most heavily populated centers: Ladhaqiya, Hama, Aleppo and Damascus.

In Iraq, Mosul, Sulaymaniya, Basra and Baghdad are, to name only the largest, very important political centers for Iraqi politics. But the geographical unity in Iraq, strengthened by the proximity of all these centers to the Tigris and Euphrates Rivers, does not have a natural counterpart in Syria. No city or region in Iraq can be considered as important a focal point as Baghdad, but in Syria, Aleppo and Damascus have both had traditional geopolitical significance: both were once important city-states, and because of the lack of cohesive Syrian identity, a strong feeling of regional loyalties in one part of the country reinforces that same attitude in other areas. Thus, traditional regional perspectives remain.

A second geopolitical factor involves the ambiguity of the very definition of what constitutes Syria. To be specific, pre-World War I Syria, pre-World War II Syria, and post-independence Syria are three different political and geographic entities. This means that the political activism and awareness of a young nationalist growing up before 1918, after 1920, or after 1946, would likely have a different political frame of reference and would take different forms in each of the three "Syrias." As a province of the Ottoman Empire before World War I, Syria included Jordan, what was then Palestine and most of Lebanon. The British and French division of these territories after World War I generated the Greater Syria Plan, an effort by Syrian nationalists to regain Palestine (including Jordan) and Lebanon. During the interwar period, under the French Mandate, Syria was coupled with Lebanon and, for a time, the province of Iskandarun (Alexandretta), which was ceded to Turkey in 1939. When reference is made to pre-independence Syria in this chapter, it will be understood as that area and portion of the population which became part of independent Syria.

What constitutes Syria is also a political question: more than most other Asian and African countries, Syria has been the object of forces, both Arab and international, which have tried to mold their own kind of Syrian entity. Although little will be said about these forces or pressures here, they remain a constant factor in Syrian politics whether they are real or perceived. The Arab-Israeli conflict, in particular, has been a constant factor influencing elites in Syria, but it is beyond the scope of this chapter. If Syrian nationalism as such exists at all, it has meaning as a defense mechanism against some of these forces, like the Arab-Israeli conflict, for instance.

A comparison with Syria's neighbors is again instructive. Turkish, Iraqi and Lebanese nationalisms, regardless of any irredentist claims, are anchored in a basic geographical frame of reference. Modern Syrian nationalism and the Syrian state, on the other hand, are tied to two very different political and geographical entities. The Anatolian, Tigris-Euphrates or coastal Phoenician referents are as precise as the concept of Syria is vague and diffuse.

Strong regionalism in Syria and the contradictions between Syrian nationalism and Syrian territory have led to a third geopolitical factor of significance. Syrian political consciousness has, both before and after independence, focussed on either supra- or sub-national loyalties precisely because the many truncations of Syria since the turn of the century have stifled the development of any cohesive or definable nationalism or loyalty to post-1946 Syria. At once pan-Arab, Ba'th, Greater Syria and Palestinian slogans have been espoused alongside local and regional causes in one area or another in Syria. Thus, in the Syrian perspective, borders are artificial lines and Arab identity means more than Syrian identity. But without a middle level loyalty to the state, local parochial politics can be transformed into national politics, giving regional political issues and elites national importance.

Extra-territorial political consciousness also exists in Lebanon and Iraq, but alongside a strong and competing, and at times dominant, Lebanese or Iraqi nationalism. This is not intended to minimize the Arab identity of Iraqis or Lebanese but to indicate that for Syrians, there is no comparable, strong identification with the state of Syria to counterbalance it.

A fourth geopolitical feature of Syria reflects the social mosaic of the country. Ethnic and religious divisions in Syrian society are, on the whole, less pronounced than elsewhere in Asia and Africa: well over eighty percent of the population of some six million is Sunni Muslim. However, what often makes minorities important in developing countries is not their numbers, nor necessarily their geographical distribution, but rather the existence of a minority consciousness that can be or is used for political reasons.

Some of Syria's ethnic and religious minorities—the Kurds, Armenians, Circassians, Yazidis, Shi'i Muslims and Christians—are dispersed throughout the country and have never been politically important as individual groups. Other compact minorities are both more numerous and significant. Three must be mentioned:

the 'Alawis in the Ladhaqiya region, the Duruz in the Jabal Duruz area of southern Syria, and the Isma'ilis in three or four towns in the vicinity of Hama. All three of these Islamic minority sects are products of fundamental religious and political schisms dating far back in Muslim history. The Duruz are the most distinct because they are more independent of orthodox Islam than the others. Two of these groups, the 'Alawis and the Duruz form a majority in their respective regions which also happen to be the least developed provinces of the country. Regional loyalties in these two areas were strengthened by the traditional Ottoman *millet* pattern of ethnic differentiation as well as policies of the French mandate authorities which emphasized regionalism. Social and geographical distribution within these two areas is also noteworthy. Whereas the traditional elite of the Jabal Duruz was entirely Duruz, that of the coastal Ladhaqiya region was both 'Alawi and Sunni; this fact helps to explain the greater social cohesion of the minority in Southern Syria than in Ladhaqiya.

Development and Change Most members of an elite express a certain priority of desired goals for their society; often the impact of independence radically re-orders these priorities. The dilemmas of development—those decisions that have to be made concerning the distribution of limited financial and human resources—are such that this process is rarely coherent in times of rapid social change or in highly politicized societies. Because of social and political vagaries, development can involve many stops and starts and many radical policy shifts which, using Western performance indicators like the capital-output ratio and gross national product, seem to retard growth.

In Syria, there has been both rapid social change and economic development since independence. The shift from a basically capitalist economy in the 1940s and 1950s to a trial and error form of socialism in the 1960s and 1970s, however, has meant extensive planning and many false starts. This transformation occurred at a time of intense political conflict between the traditional Syrian political elite and a new elite. This was also a period during which the Syrian economy developed without large inputs of foreign capital, one of the few non-oil systems able to do so.

Against this background, both continuity and change in

development strategy is discernible. Continuity can be seen in the big development projects that continue to spur the economy. A British consulting firm, Alexander Gibb and Sons, delineated shortly after independence those projects that would both stimulate economic development and utilize Syria's resources most efficiently. Since the late 1940s, Syrian planners and politicians of all persuasions have relied on this spadework. The three most important projects which were absorbing so many resources and so much energy as the 1970s began—the Euphrates Dam, the Ladhaqiya-Jazira railroad and the Tartus port south of Ladhaqiya—were all envisaged in the 1940s. With less political conflict, these projects might have been started earlier, but politicians had not delineated nor agreed on the major priorities of development.

Change can clearly be seen in the style and approach to the problems of development; this change only reflects elite conflict. The tremendous expansion of the agricultural sector—the most important and erratic sector of the economy—during the early years of independence was accomplished almost entirely by private domestic capital. When this extension reached a plateau in the middle 1950s, it became apparent to many Syrians, particularly those seeking to undermine the traditional elite, that future development would depend more on intensification than on expansion of cultivable lands and on a greater role for the government in providing the infrastructure for this intensification.

The social models Syrian leaders sought to emulate have also changed. Since independence in Syria, as elsewhere in the Arab world, elites have tended to conceive of westernization as synonymous with modernization. For them, to be modern was to be European and the first step in that direction was to establish institutional structures similar to those in Europe. More recently, members of the new Syrian elite have drawn a distinction between westernization and modernization. Arab models of development and those of Eastern Europe became important reference points. In particular, the Egyptian Revolution inspired many Syrians before the Syrian-Egyptian union of 1958-1961. In the 1960s, other Arab economic models have had a certain attraction and Syrian leaders have sought to improve the economy by developing an oil industry. Much of the attraction of other Arab and East European models reflected the fact that the level of attainment through those models was more within the reach of Syria than, say, a French or Western model. For some Syrians, the more practical approach to development is to emulate those schemes that can be implemented relatively quickly and easily.

These economic changes must be put in juxtaposition to the major political alterations since independence. Those alterations revolve mainly around the transformation of the Syrian political elite. Three aspects of political change will dominate this chapter. First, the most significant political actor of the new Syrian elite is the army officer; it is important to observe that in Syria, he was not a salient member of the traditional political elite. Second, a direct result of the politicization of the officer corps after independence was the political ruin of the traditional elite which had played dominant social, economic and political roles throughout the country. And third, the paradox of Syrian independence is that the major political weapon of the traditional elites in confrontation with the new, emerging elite was the mobilization of segments of the rural and peasant population. This process of seeking to bring the disenfranchised into politics was initiated not by members of a new elite but by an important second echelon traditional elite with less wealth, owning less land, and less access to traditional sources of power than the leading elements or families. In time, however, a new elite did evolve from alliances between peasantry and elements of this second echelon elite. This situation did not automatically mean increased participation for formerly disenfranchised groups in the political process nor did it bring significant benefits to Syria's majority, the peasantry. Nevertheless, political change did occur.

II. THE TRADITIONAL SYRIAN POLITICAL ELITE

Nature The traditional Syrian political elite, or the segment of the Syrian populace which had the potential to exercise political and economic influence in Syria until the 1960s and which dominated the political system until the mid-1950s, can be usefully characterized in several ways. It was a male-dominated, largely Sunni Muslim, well educated and usually wealthy elite. To a large extent, it was involved in non-military careers. Kinship often determined elite status. It was drawn almost completely from some fifty families who had dominated the economic, political and social life of each region of the area that became Syria in 1946 over a period of several generations or even centuries. It was an upper class by virtue of its wealth and extensive landownership. In each region or city, one could clearly identify those local families who were members of this closed, fifty-family circle. For example, in Hums, it was the Atasi family; in Hama, the Kaylanis, the Barazis and the 'Azms; in Damascus, the Mardams and the 'Azms, among others; in Ladhaqiya, the 'Abbas clan; in Aleppo, the Kikhyas and the Qudsis to name only two; in Dayr al-Zur, the Shallashes and the al-Sayyids; and so on. The predictability of elite membership on the basis of name was a fundamentally important characteristic of this predominant element of the traditional Syrian elite.

A second group, or counter-elite, consisted of families with less wealth, less land, and less influence, but with increasing access to the institutions of secondary and higher education requisite for elite status. Working within established political procedures, these families began challenging the upper stratum of fifty families after Syria achieved independence. They were more heterogeneous in composition than those whom they challenged. Some were Sunni, middle-class political novitiates seeking positions of influence either in regional centers or nationally; a few were army officers who sought political power; others were non-Sunnis, particularly in Damascus, seeking recognition in a modern, diversified society where non-Muslims could play a role. Again, in each region this group was small and finite and could clearly be identified: in Hama, it was the Hawranis and Mulqis; and in Damascus, the Tu'mas, Bakdashes and the Baytars, to name only a few.

Higher education, often outside Syria, was usually a harbinger of elite status prior to independence. In the period before World War I, thousands of Syrians were educated in Istanbul. For an Arab in a province of the Ottoman Empire such as Syria or Iraq, two channels of upward mobility were available—the civil service and the military—and both involved schooling in Istanbul, the hub of the Empire. The advantage of attending the civil service school was the prospect of political influence in the provinces while the military route offered free education in, and transportation to, Istanbul. It was not strange, then, that beginning in the

1850s, more men in Iraq than Syria opted for the military because of the greater distances involved and the less well developed commercial and agricultural centers. Conversely, the civil service was preferred by a majority of the sons of the "club of fifty families."

Even at this early juncture, a military career was more appealing to Muslims outside the leading circle of families than it was to the traditional, upper-class political elite. Career opportunities for these men from the second echelon opened up as World War I approached and as the Ottoman Empire's need for more military personnel intensified.

The rise of Arabism and Arab and Syrian nationalism in this century had an enormous impact on Syrians with traditional elite status. Prior to 1914, however, very few Syrian officers became members of the secret Arab nationalist military society, al-'Ahd, an association dominated by Iraqis; however, more Syrians were involved in civilian nationalist societies. Consequently, the Syrian military contribution to the 1916 Faysal revolt was not sizable in the officer category.

Once in Damascus, King Faysal sought to reconstruct his army with a slightly increased role for Syrians. But with the collapse of his government, the Arab defeat at Maysalun, and the inception of the French mandate in 1920, this army, the core of the nationalist movement, disbanded. All Iraqis and many Syrians left the country, refusing to stay in a French-administered Syria.

One important outgrowth of the Syrian nationalist movement during the mandate was the demise of any active military component in the nationalist movement in Syria. Those segments of the traditional elite which were to struggle in various ways for independence from the French were almost entirely civilian. A few paramilitary organizations were to surface during the mandate, particularly in the 1930s, but the non-military orientations of those striving for independence remained predominant. This contrasts with other Arab states where the military was an important component of the traditional elite and where it played a key role in independence struggles. This is not to suggest that the nationalists seeking independence were not militant in that demand nor that they refrained from use of military tactics; many did use violence. But, to become an officer in a French army of local levies was to serve French interests and no good nationalist could do that. By independence, fewer than 200 officers were serving in this army.[2]

Non-military educational opportunities, however, did broaden and become more varied during the mandate. Instead of going to Istanbul, Syrians chose the universities of Europe and the United States in addition to the universities of Beirut and, to a lesser degree, Damascus. Non-Muslim, middle-class elements, particularly, were attracted to European education, having been effectively denied mobility through the Istanbul schools.

If family name, *mülkiye* or university education, and non-military character were three important parameters defining the traditional elite, a fourth was wealth. Financial wealth—in terms of land or money—was the most important source of political power in Syria until the 1950s. With some wealth, a Syrian was guaranteed elite status and political power; without it, such status was difficult to achieve.

Throughout Syria landownership was the traditional source of wealth and power, although in the nineteenth and twentieth centuries commercial and trading interests were developed by several Damascene and Aleppian families. Prominent religious families, usually wealthy, were also important members of the traditional elite by birthright. In many areas of the country, particularly the fertile and crowded Hums-Hama region, well over ninety percent of the land was owned by a very small fraction of the population.[3]

Whereas the upper circle of the traditional elite was largely involved in landownership, those families outside the "club" but with requisite education tended to develop commercial sources of power because most cultivable land was already in the hands of others. This counter-elite was increasingly frustrated in its desire for a share of the political and economic status the upper circle had so long considered its own preserve. Through the ballot box, as well as other legal and illegal means, this quasi-middle-class elite sought to maximize its power even if it had to be done at the expense of others.

Some of this group joined the small army created by the French. The older officers who ruled Syria from 1949 to 1954 were from these middle-level families. But the commercial interests of this group were most evident. In Damascus, for instance, the families that became involved in trading and commerce were often Christian. They often lived in the Maydan quarter where there were no members of the upper echelon. Few Christians had large land holdings. In another quarter of the city, the Kurdish Hayy al-Akrad, families also used small business to forge a solid economic and political position. In Hama, families like the Hawranis, while married into leading families, had smaller land holdings and therefore took on other pursuits such as teaching, law and commerce in order to build a base for political involvement.

In distinguishing the traditional Syrian socio-economic and political elites from those in Iraq and Lebanon, several points can be made. First, in all three countries, regional and city level ties and power bases were a major source of national power, but in Syria those regional centers were more varied and independent. Second, the traditional elite in Iraq had a crucially important military wing which was a major source of power for King Faysal when he went to Iraq in the 1920s. Third, the Lebanese elite, like that in Syria, was clearly definable by name and by connections but in Lebanon, the role of those middle-level families seeking to challenge the exclusive rule of the upper stratum has been minimized by the complex mosaic of communal forces that needs to be balanced if the government is to function at all.

Development of the Elite The brief Faysal interlude after World War I, when he declared an independent nationalist monarchy in Damascus, was an important milestone in the development of the Syrian nationalist movement. In the long run, however, it provided only faint memories of a bygone era. For many Syrians who overtly or covertly joined Arab nationalist societies with many of the same goals as the Young Turk Movement, the Faysal interlude was a dream come true. Its sudden and quick end and the establishment of the French mandate disillusioned and embittered most nationalists, leaving the movement in flux.

The traditional elite's response to the arrival of the French offers an excellent insight into the kinds of intra-elite conflict that formed the basis of elite interaction until well into the independence period. Several groups should be delineated. There were those who believed that much of what the French did was good for Syria and for their own vested interests. Some 'Alawis of the Ladhaqiya area, for instance, were given a greater voice in their own affairs than they had ever enjoyed before. Others approved of the French attempts to instill *la culture générale* through education in a society which members of the elite thought had suffered too long from what they called the deprivations of the Ottoman Empire. Opposed to this group were those who had deserted or left the Ottoman Army during World War I to join King Faysal. Some left Syria when the French came, going to Transjordan or Iraq to seek temporary refuge. A few even sought to return to Syria leading, helping, or participating in the numerous revolts against the French which erupted frequently during the mandate, particularly in the early and middle 1920s.

Some of those nationalists who remained in Syria sought publicly and privately to undermine French authority. Every region of Syria had its representative of the traditional elite who served as a symbolic, and occasionally vocal, rallying point for local nationalist sentiments with the emphasis often on the first rather than the second adjective. In Aleppo, there was Ibrahim Hananu and in the Duruz region the Atrashs, while in the Ladhaqiya region it was Salih al-'Ali among others. In each case, an admixture of vested local interests, specific grievances against the French, and nationalist sentiments catapulted minor issues into causes for major uprisings. But in each case, the local struggle was just that and no more: no cohesive Syrian nationalist movement emerged.

There were also those who sought to organize a nationalist movement through political associations or paramilitary groups. 'Abd al-Rahman Shahbandar and Tawfiq al-Shishakli were two leaders of such efforts. Their movement, however, never became truly national in scope although the *Kutla Wataniya* (National Bloc) proved able to unite important segments of the upper class. On another tangent were a group of paramilitary organizations which were inspired by the militaristic nationalist movements developed during the 1930s in Italy and Germany. Fakhri al-Barudi, for example, sought to organize an increasingly vocal middle-class youth demanding both independence and participation in political processes.

The overwhelming majority of the elite remained between the two poles—between overt and enthusiastic support for the French and open rebellion, between those who considered France's interests their own and those, particularly in Ladhaqiya, Aleppo and Jabal Duruz, who advocated armed conflict against the French. There were Syrian leaders who thought France would negotiate and give Syria independence, or at least gradually acknowledge a local authority. This group waited and refrained from action. There were also those families who sought to keep on good terms with both extremes. They infiltrated all major political movements: one son would be an ardent nationalist while another would serve the French either in the small army of local levies, *Les Troupes Spéciales du Levant*, or in the bureaucracy. In general, the upper class, for the most part, was involved in a holding operation seeking to maximize its position and preserve its options for the expected new independence period.

Those who sought an end to the mandate through political compromise were burned several times by the vagaries of French politics. The Blum Government in the late 1930s, for example, and the Free French-Vichy split frustrated many Syrians seeking autonomy through evolutionary approaches. Yet, all French groups found it difficult to accept the concept of independence for Syria. Those Syrians seeking a revolution in Syria were, however, no more successful during this period. In fact, it was as much world politics and the crumbling position of France during the Second World War that led to Syrian independence as it was any uncompromising or unified Syrian nationalist movement. Although the Syrians never really accepted the French and French achievements in Syria were very few, it was the dire need of the Free French for Syrian acceptance that led to the French announcement of Syria's independence in 1943 and the actual achievement of independence three years later.

Despite all their differences during the mandate, members of the upper- and middle-echelon elites who had been politically active before independence were able to convene in a national parliament and proclaim a republic in 1946. While the National Bloc was probably the best known and largest nationalist group in Parliament, it was by no means the only organized faction. Local, influential and vested interest members of the traditional elite in each region of Syria sought to cope with the problems of independence the same way they coped with their local political struggles and problems. The political broker and bargaining technique of resolving differences between competing factions of the various ruling families was designed to maintain and legitimize the traditional elite's power base, but it worked imperfectly at the national level.

Already at independence, elements of the middle-level elite were striving to gain at the ballot box, through a potpourri of political, militant, and psychological tactics, what they could not acquire in direct confrontation with the established political aristocracy, namely a share of political power. Many salient middle-class groups were represented in Parliament immediately after independence but their power base remained insignificant until the 1950s.

The pushes and pulls, the stresses and strains of the traditional elite's political interplay could have remained on the central stage of Syrian politics for many decades, as it has in Lebanon, had it not been for the Palestine War of 1948. At once, that war between the Arab states and Israel confirmed for a majority of Syrians, rightly or wrongly, the emptiness of the traditional political responses of this elite and its inability to cope with the problems of Syrian independence.

The club of fifty families had its chance, so to speak, from 1946 to 1949, a short period and a time of acute crisis. As had been the case during the mandate and throughout the period of the evolution of Syrian nationalism, concerted action was not possible. The Syrian response to events in 1948 was to let everyone do his own thing; the result was a curious mixture of supra-national and sub-national political motivations. From across the land and from every region and representing every influential family, disorganized groups of volunteers, each loyal to some Syrian political grouping, converged on Palestine often in the hope that somehow, through their participation, political gain in their own hometowns could be achieved.[4]

It was the inability to cope with the many problems facing Syria that gave credibility to a direct political challenge to the ruling families by non-'club,' middle-class, politically motivated elements even though these middle-class groups had also participated in the fiascoes of the early independence period. The history of Syria from 1949 to the early 1960s involves, in the main, a struggle between these two salient elites—the political brokers of the older, more wealthy families and those new politically ambitious elements with specific programs seeking to undermine the exclusive power of the older brokers. Through this conflict, certain perspectives can be gained on how the traditional elite exercised power and how conflict and change occurred in independent Syria. Concurrent with this conflict and, in some respects, an outgrowth of the traditional elite's approach to social problems and the issue of participation, came the development of a third, entirely new elite.

Political Frame of Reference The traditional concept of politics in Syria and the premises on which the traditional elite exercised power and sought support involved political loyalty based largely, if not solely, on ascriptive ties of family, economic dependence, and proximity of religious persuasion. Political parties became important and support of the "people" or "masses" was sought, but both were symbols for manipulation rather than vehicles for increased participation. Schooled in Western political concepts of democracy and socialism, almost all members of the traditional elite advocated Western style institutions to the degree that they were compatible with their traditional ways of exercising political power and preserving their vested interests. Throughout the 1940s and 1950s, political organizations were founded and championed to promote a relatively few numbers of careers. And when the leaders died or changed affiliations, organizations could fold as quickly as they were founded.

Over two-thirds of Syria's population is involved in agriculture: for Syria's political institutions to be representative, the peasantry and townspeople should appropriately be considered an important element in the political process. In practice, peasant causes were supported by politicians of the traditional elite but were rarely advanced. Politicians spoke about land reform, improving conditions of tenant farmers and promoting the interests of the poor, but the Parliament did little. Most politicians merely relied on the traditional dependence of villagers in outlying areas on the city markets and those who owned the markets. If the peasantry was in fact dependent, the politicians, as landowners and city merchants, would be able to maintain a high degree of control over a majority of Syrians.

Invariably, regional or sub-national politics dominated the national political scene. It is significant that the traditional elite was never able to develop a cohesive or national political institution. Most parties and professional associations were limited to one city or region. Most Damascus-based politicians and professionals had not seen much of the Syrian countryside and most Syrians did not relate to Damascus except through their regional center. Some parties did come closer to achieving national recognition and support and there were important differences in emphasis between the traditional, dominant political brokers and those challenging them. It was in the degree of national support and in their programmatic orientations that these traditional political organizations in Syria could be differentiated.

The National Bloc was probably, as mentioned above, the most significant political organization of the nationalist groups striving for independence. But the Bloc never succeeded in establishing any clear leadership role or legitimizing its claim to represent an important or major thread of the Syrian nationalist movement. This lack of controlling position was not so much the fault of the party leadership, as it was the strength of other parties and individuals with stronger regional bases. A few examples are illustrative of this point.

First, the People's Party, *Hizb al-Sha'b* played an extremely important role in Aleppo. Although its support was not as widespread as that of the National Bloc, it remained, as a political institution, as important as the National Bloc because it dominated the politics of Syria's second largest center (in the opinion of some, the largest). The National Bloc's representation throughout the country meant little in terms of national political power if it had no single strong political hub.

Second, important clans in parts of Syria stayed on the fringes of party politics in order to insure political flexibility and maximize their roles. The Atrashs in the Duruz area of Suwayda', the leaders of the Atasi family in Hums and important members of the al-'Azm in particular, entered the political scene with impressive local support but often no clear party affiliation. They were willing to join any party provided they could bring their followers with them; but they would never have joined merely as ordinary members. The crucial roles played by Hashim al-Atasi and Khalid al-'Azm during the first decade of independence were far more impressive than the positions gained by parties with far wider support.

Third, the politics of the traditional elite of Hama can be viewed as a microcosm of all of Syria. The traditional mode of bargaining and conflict resolution of the Kaylani, Barazi and al-'Azm families had enabled those clans to maintain control over that fertile region for many decades. This exclusive role was first threatened and then destroyed in the independence period, however. Although in 1946 most Syrian parties, including the *Ikhwan al-Muslimin* (The Muslim Brotherhood), a religious party, had extremely loyal local supporters in Hama, the power and influence of all these groups was so compromised by local conflict after 1946 that by the time the local contingent of political leaders arrived in Damascus to perform national functions they had little to offer; they remained committed to and preoccupied with local political and social problems.

Almost all members of the traditional elite and their political organizations were dedicated to the Western concept of democracy and to a free enterprise system. This was natural because they knew how such a system worked and they knew that such a system tended to reinforce their own political roles. Their political philosophies were dominated by theories of change filtering down from the elite and of the elite's role in educating the masses. Their international political orientation was almost exclusively toward the West in general and France and the United States in particular. The preference of the latter two states usually reflected the locale or orientation of higher education. In short, the political frame of reference of the vast majority of the traditional elite was dominated by one question: how does the elite preserve its role, cope with the problems of social and economic development, and create new elite elements to succeed it. The concept of participation in the political process—the need for political development—was outside the frame of reference of this elite. If there was a plea for broadening leadership or extending the base of the party or a politician's appeal, it meant bringing brothers or friends or confidants into a political machine. They expected a passive or conservative role for the peasantry—a role the Lebanese peasantry performed and the Lebanese political elite sought and was able to encourage.

The political novitiates of the counter-elite were not, however, content with the exclusive political role the sons of Syria's wealthiest families had carved out for themselves. They used their limited wealth and access to education to seek, through the espousal of socialism and calls for social justice, to broaden the political structure enough for their own participation in leadership roles because they were not content with secondary roles serving their traditional masters. In the process of inter-elite conflict, the traditional elite's position was compromised, threatened and finally destroyed.

Several of the more significant political movements of the independence era were initiated and led by such challengers. An examination of four movements—the *Hizb al-Qawmi al-Suri al-Itjtima'i* (Syrian Socialist National Party or the SSNP), the Ba'th Party, the Arab Liberation Movement, and Akram al-Hawrani's political movements—will show both similarities and differences with other traditional political movements. Like the older political organizations, none of these four was truly national in scope during the first two decades of independence. The SSNP was able to pick up a large local following in the Ladhaqiya region but it was never able to penetrate the Sunni Muslim heartland beyond the coastal mountains. Akram al-Hawrani, in the course of a long and at times violent political career, was involved with several political organizations, including for a time the Ba'th Party and the SSNP, but he always remained dedicated primarily to the political situation in his own Hama region. He did acquire some support elsewhere in Syria but it was small in scope and temporary in nature.

Both the Arab Liberation Movement and the Ba'th Party were sincere attempts to construct national parties, broaden popular participation, and avoid the temptations of so many Syrian political organizations to base themselves solely on local, parochial issues. The Arab Liberation Movement was the creation of middle-class army officers whose leader, Adib al-Shishakli, was a neighbor of Akram al-Hawrani in Hama. This movement initially enjoyed widespread support in 1953 but it was based almost exclusively on a single man and a handful of his supporters: the whole effort collapsed with al-Shishakli's political demise and subsequent exile in 1954. His supporters took their political fortunes elsewhere. The organization did not become a cohesive national political force. Nevertheless, in some places, like Dir'a close to the Jordanian border, the party's cell was highly organized and effective, and there was, perhaps for the first time in Syria, participation by several peasant groups.

The Ba'th Party had a bigger and more diversified organization, and a stronger commitment to socialism and to social and economic change. By the end of the 1940s, the party had important cells throughout the country but it was the cells—not the party—that were politically influential. Moreover, one cell differed from another both in policy and in scope. The Dayr al-Zur and Ladhaqiya cells are cases in point. In Dayr al-Zur, Jalal al-Sayyid, a fairly wealthy, well known and popular member of the traditional elite, organized a cell. However, he played down the party's socialist platform, because he felt that socialism would not be popular with segments of the elite whose support was essential. In Ladhaqiya, a middle-class doctor named Wahib al-Ghanim organized another cell on a completely different premise. He stressed the fundamental importance of socialism in the party's platform. The party's success, in his view, depended largely on the participation of politically disenfranchised Syrians—in particular the peasantry who make up a majority of the population.

In each case, the local cell made important decisions about the operation of the Ba'th Party in its area. In effect, there were at once seven or eight parties, instead of one. In the 1950s when the party was relatively weak, such distinctions were somewhat academic. But in the 1960s when the Ba'th Party came to power and there was a need to weld a cohesive, national movement, these differences within and among regions became significant. Nevertheless, in the 1940s and 1950s, Ba'th Party members were motivated by economic and social inequities at the local level.

Even the Syrian Communist Party displayed the same type of strong local or parochial orientation. Khalid Bakdash, the middle-class leader of the Kurdish community in the al-Akrad quarter in Damascus, was Secretary-General of the party and a vast majority of the party's support in the 1940s and 1950s came from his Kurdish neighbors. The party also had middle-class support in Hama.

But given the similarities in organization, in nature of support and in the ascriptive factors involved in political expression by a majority of Syrians, there are important differences between the older, traditional parties and those organizations representing counter-elite interests. All of the new parties had defined programs, policy goals, and a definite cell structure which at times were secret. While goals and programs might change, the existence of systematic procedures within parties for policy considerations was novel to Syrian political activity. The cell structure itself evolved primarily from the situation and nature of the support of these parties. Because their very organization was considered by the "club of fifty families" to be a threat, cells were necessary to protect some followers from economic retribution and to develop greater support. These organizations were very popular with the youth and students immediately after independence and during the 1950s, and many of the organizers were themselves teachers. The relationship of teacher to student—the *halqa* or traditional circle of students around a professor—often developed into party cells.

This support was mainly from middle-class youth and/or from the lowest socio-economic group to whom secondary education was available. This latter group, which became increasingly important during the 1950s as educational institutions multiplied, formed the core of a wholly new Syrian political elite which took power in the 1960s. The *halqas* and cells of the SSNP and the Ba'th in particular date from the late 1940s. It was also at that time that many future army officers were, while secondary students, attracted to these organizations. It was possible, though illegal, for them to maintain party contacts while in their military careers because of the cell structure.

In the process of the development of these parties, the style of politics changed. The older, established parties sought support on the basis of social, regional, and economic loyalties, but with the newer organizations, appeals were also made to attract new people to political participation, in particular, the sons of families with access to secondary education, for the first time. In two cases, in Hama and in Ladhaqiya, middle-class leaders went even further and sought to forge middle-class-peasant alliances as a vehicle for challenging the traditional political brokers. What was in fact done to help the disenfranchised peasantry or ex-peasant groups was less relevant to these members of the older elites than their mobilization. For many people, the symbolism of such an alliance was more important than what changed: the simple fact that Akram al-Hawrani, for example, set up peasant grievance bureaus in Damascus where they could bring their complaints impressed many peasant groups and won him much support.

The stage for inter-elite conflict was set mostly by the uncompromising nature of the two older elites. The old families were determined that they would rule Syria; the middle-class segments were equally determined that they would play a role. This stubbornness was demonstrated after dissolution of the union with Egypt in 1961. This was to be the last chance of the traditional elite to rule Syria. But the leaders proved unable to bargain with each other, nor to provide opportunities to their political protégés who in many cases had been waiting for a chance to prove themselves for over two decades.

Elite Conflict The vulnerability of the traditional Syrian political elite to new groups seeking political power was heightened by conflict both within and between the two salient elites, the middle-class challengers and the traditional upper stratum. The sources of conflict and antagonism were social, economic, and personal. Although most were ascriptive, ideological and social motivations increasingly triggered bitter conflicts. The cumulative effect, however, was to render accommodation extremely difficult primarily because so many members of the traditional elite had personal or regional sources of power and support that enabled them to resist compromise. So from 1946 to 1963, Syria witnessed the gradual erosion of the national and eventually subnational political power of the traditional elite, not so much through the emergence of new and especially dynamic elites but rather by internal conflict.

In the years before as well as following independence, suspicion, distrust and deep-seated antagonism affected the relations among the heirs to Syria's wealth. The rivalry of cities was one important source of elite conflict. For example, Damascene families often suspected the commitment to Syria of Aleppian families: they thought that the latter had more loyalties down the Euphrates River in Iraq than across the desert in southern Syria. Aleppians, for their part, considered Damascene politicians parochial and selfish. Both groups were suspicious of the clans that dominated the Hama-Hums region, and most Syrians distrusted the 'Alawis and Duruz because they felt that the special status these minorities had enjoyed during the French mandate had produced continuing foreign ties.

As a matter of fact, cooperation with the French during the mandate was another source of conflict among members of the elite. Anyone who had dealt with the French might be considered unreliable and thus willing to betray the nationalist movement or to subvert the state. Those who sought independence through negotiations in the 1930s were just as vulnerable to attack. Differences in education also reinforced elite rivalries. In particular, French-educated and American-educated Syrians were suspicious of each other. Although those with an American education (either in the United States or at the American University of Beirut) were fewer in number, they often held positions of influence. The growing importance of English as an international language and of the United States in world politics after World War II irritated the French-oriented elite.

Two other features of elite conflict are particularly pertinent. First, although differences in ideology and socialist programs were not of paramount importance in elite conflict, ideological differences in conjunction with other antagonisms did lead to violent confrontations, particularly between the SSNP on the one hand and the Communist Party and the Ba'th Party on the other. In fact, some of those attacking the SSNP in the 1950s were themselves former members of it. Throughout the 1950s, middle-class leaders in these organizations spent as much time in conflict with each other as they did in pursuit of their goal, acquiring the right to exercise power so long denied to them. The cell structure of these parties also tended to increase the distrust between them, especially since some parties had cells in the army. Even though many members of the elite felt that the threat of reprisal from the political and economic aristocracy made cell structures for their organizations essential, this type of basic unit tended to increase rather than decrease elite tensions. An individual's public and private, overt and covert, postures were automatically assumed to be different. Again, those in one cell of a party in one region invariably did not know their fellow party members in other cells of the same party in different cities.

Salient elites in four areas of Syria dominated politics during the first two decades of independence. While the major conflicts among the traditional ruling clans of Syria involved the elites in Aleppo and Damascus, middle-level elites were most active in Hama and Ladhaqiya. This shift is not surprising because up to independence the major focal point of Syrian wealth, power and politics centered on the families of Aleppo and Damascus—the oldest and largest urban areas. But by the mid-1950s, two important middle-class-peasant alliances in Hama and Ladhaqiya had begun to develop and became personified in the Ba'th-SSNP struggle. The result was the demise of the latter and the eventual rule of the former.

Two aspects of inter-elite conflict between the middle sector and the ruling aristocracy are crucial to an understanding of post-independence Syria: first, the nature of the conflict between the two groups and their perceptions of each other; and second, the approach of each group to the largest groups outside the established political procedures—the peasantry and the ex-peasantry—those who had recently migrated to large villages and towns. In vying for the support of these lower-class, semi-deprived groups, the middle-class elite was threatening the very heart of the traditional economic and political power base of the aristocracy. Previously, the middle class had sought to maximize its strength vis-à-vis the "club of fifty families" by increasing its land and commercial holdings and seeking education. But in trying to win over support of villagers and townspeople, peasants and ex-peasants, they were challenging the socio-economic position of the traditional ruling class directly and that was their goal.

The Ba'th and SSNP, especially, sought to represent the poor and deprived and through their mobilization, to revolutionize Syria. These parties had much success in Hama and Ladhaqiya, two areas of the greatest socio-economic differentials in Syria, the fabulously wealthy alongside the humble poor. Here the ambitions of members of the middle class could easily play on the very legitimate grievances of the poor. In the Ladhaqiya area, for example, destitute tobacco farmers in the coastal hills were forced to sell their products very cheaply to a few wealthy families on the coast who were able to market that famous brand. In the Hama region, the crowded but rich farmlands were often overworked by tenant farmers as the landed aristocracy sought to maximize their yields.

Inter-elite conflict was also intensified by the marked efforts of many ambitious individuals on both sides who sought to destroy the political base of opponents rather than compromise or restrict the struggle to the ballot box or parliamentary debate. Again in Hama, the energetic efforts of Akram al-Hawrani to ruin the political and economic fortunes of the ruling, local families must be coupled with the attempts of those clans to undermine al-Hawrani's developing base of support. Elections throughout the 1940s and 1950s in Hama and else-where were indeed close and hotly contested and the outcome rarely clear-cut. But the ambitions of these elites which had been politically active since the beginning of the nationalist movement before World War I were too strong to compromise, and their followers were usually too committed to change course or allegiances quickly.

Thus, by the 1960s, the traditional and middle-level elites

were politically and economically spent. Those who had fought longest and hardest for independence were dead or dying. They had enjoyed only minimal opportunities to gain control of any Parliament since independence. Because they had never exercised real political power for any significant length of time, they did not let their own sons share their political roles. Thus, their sons, although having some elite status by name and education, were increasingly unknown, untried and unwanted by emerging and new elites. The lengthy political battles, based on policy, personal, and regional conflicts, often spilled over into regional and international politics. These battles left most traditional and middle-level elite members scarred and discredited, if not politically ruined. Nearly two political generations had come and gone and yet independent Syria was only two decades old.

III. THE NEW POLITICAL ELITE

Nature The new political elite had played minor roles in some of the political parties during the 1940s and 1950s. It emerged in positions of power and responsibility in the 1960s after the Ba'th Party came to power. This elite was dedicated primarily to the transformation of Syria through economic and social change. Its goal was the destruction of the traditional elite through nationalization, socialism, land reform and the exile of opponents. Its major instruments came to be the Ba'th Party and the army. This new elite differs in many fundamental ways from the traditional and middle-level elites, although the style of its leadership does have some similarities with them.

One fundamental difference between the new and old elites is the larger size of the new elite. The core of the new elite can be defined as simply those Syrians of the lowest socio-economic background to whom a high school education was available. The elite came from different families also: it was lower middle-class, by and large, and from more rural areas, from the towns and villages rather than the cities. At independence, Syria had fewer than twenty high schools; over a decade later there were almost two hundred.[5] The larger size of the new elite is associated directly with the increase in the number of schools. Syria's schools, both before and after independence, help define the field from which political elites emerge.

Not only did the size of the elite cohort broaden but the

kinds of professions in which those with elite status were found narrowed. Whereas the traditional elite opted for a variety of technical and non-technical professions, the salient segments of the new elite were unable to afford extensive education. Even though secondary education at government schools was available to all who could get to the few schools that existed in the large towns and cities in the late 1940s, higher education was, like so many other opportunities in Syria at that time, an almost exclusive preserve of traditional ruling clans. This meant that the careers chosen by those who could not afford a college education were those careers which afforded free higher education. In Syria, these were two: teaching and the officer corps of the armed forces. As in so many Middle Eastern countries, careers were chosen less by desires and more by what opportunities were available and to whom they were available. The backgrounds of many members of the new elite show striking similarities. Children would go to school for about nine years and then enter teacher training schools where students were paid to prepare for teaching primary school in the villages. Traditionally, these men would have left school at a young age and returned to their families in order to work the fields or join the family business. The free teacher training would make a student a breadwinner and also enable him to complete his secondary school education while teaching.

With a secondary degree, a high school teaching or military career again afforded a free education and a promising job. After independence, these two professions grew in size at very rapid rates, far more rapidly than the legal or business professions preferred by sons of the ruling clans. There were fewer than two hundred army officers in Syria in 1946. Less than four years after independence, the corps had more than doubled. The teaching corps proliferated at a similar rate.

The new Syrian elite can also be defined as largely rural and small town in terms of locale and lower middle-class and ex-peasant in origin. They were ex-peasants because they would not have had the education they did if their families had remained in the fields. Ex-peasant status usually implies a move from the remote villages to the larger towns, often extremely small in size but invariably near education and job opportunities. Often Syrians of the new elite in high government or army jobs in the 1960s were the first high school graduates from their village or in their families.

Their background, indeed, had very much of a rural orientation which should be juxtaposed with the city orientation of the traditional elites. For all elites, the regional city or center was a focal point, but for different reasons. For the new elite, the city was the link between the village or town and Damascus: people were motivated to move to the cities partially by economic need and partially by the availability of education, and therefore hopefully, mobility opportunities. The new elite appeared both more national and more parochial than the traditional elites: its concerns were both with the very large, supra-national picture in the Arab world and with the very small, self- or family-centered scene in the village. Its motivations were thus complex.

This new elite was dominated by army officers, reserve officers or teachers-turned-officers. But these officers who joined the military after independence must be differentiated from those who had been in the French army before 1946 and who had played a political role from 1949 to 1954. The older officers were both middle-class in origin and in interests: they were not oriented toward rural Syria and they were very far removed from it.

Teachers formed a second, but important, part of the new elite. Their backgrounds paralleled those of the officers and they became an important generator of social change after achievement of independence. They were often located in parts of the country totally ignored by the old elite and rarely visited by government officials. Because of their own often humble origins, they were usually able to empathize with the problems of those receiving education and they could delineate specific ways of achieving social mobility in a changing society.

Development of the New Elite The political socialization of the first cohorts of the new elite occurred in the late 1940s in Syria's high schools. Lower middle-class, ex-peasant sons were courted in the schools by several ideological parties often represented by teachers. By the early 1950s, there was not a single high school graduate who had not had some exposure to the Ba'th Party or SSNP while in school. But the process tended to perpetuate the strong sense of regionalism. The very parochial environs in which this political activity took place and the secretive nature of the parties led to a generation of Syrians who would often identify largely with such an initial political encounter.

The time frame of this new elite was very different from that of the traditional elite as the events of the late 1940s and 1950s showed. Debates within the new elite had little to do with nationalist issues. They were more concerned with the social and economic problems confronting Syria. Independence was assumed; credentials to cope with it were not. The hectic and frustrating years of early independence came as this group was preparing for or starting its careers. Corruption, defeat in the 1948 Palestine War and the inaction of the Syrian Parliament over the years as well as the poor performance of older military officers in the 1949 to 1954 period so alienated these ex-peasant groups that they chose not to work within the existing political procedures in the 1960s when they came to power.

The core of the new elite, lower middle-class officers, was to play key roles in every political and military event in Syria starting in 1954. Young officers were instrumental in removing military leaders from power in 1954, but they were frustrated by the inadequacy of the Parliament that replaced the army rule. They were also instrumental in bringing union with Egypt in 1958, only to be discouraged by the economic and political effects of that union. They then played a key role in extracting Syria from the union in 1961, only to be frustrated again by the failure of the new Parliament. Finally they were the leaders in bringing the Ba'th Party to power in 1963 and in ringing the death knell of the traditional elite in 1964 and 1965 when sweeping nationalizations and economic reorganizations undermined the props which supported that elite. Efforts to institutionalize these economic and social changes after February 1966 only confirmed the existence of a new order in Syria. And the reconciliation sought after 1970 by men like Hafiz al-Asad represent only a minor reaction to the stresses and strains of the policies of the previous years.

Thus, the pattern of development from 1954 on was one of action and reaction, of impulse and second thoughts, of hope and despair. The impact on the growth of the new elite was great. Events occurred because of its participation and yet, it had little influence over these events. There were important trends which in turn had an impact on the formation of the new elite.

The distrust of the new elite for most of the traditional

aristocracy was strong and was reciprocated. Because the core of the new elite was in khakis, a civil-military conflict surfaced. But what was interesting about the development of this new elite was the relative lack of any civil-military dichotomy in its own peer group. High school friendships and other experiences at a young age so important in the development of the new elite created bonds at a local level that could transcend professional careers.

Cohesiveness within the new elite can also be seen in its relationship with the middle-class leaders of the political organizations they initially supported. The mutual interests of both groups in the parties kept them together in the early 1950s. But that mutuality did not survive when the new elite gained positions of influence in the late 1950s and early 1960s. The middle-class leaders merely wanted their share of power in the old existing system; most members of the new elite wanted an entirely new system of political interaction, involving greater benefits and power for rural Syria and for themselves. A fundamental city-rural cleavage came to divide elites.

What remains least clear about the development of the new elite is the effect of the military careers of a salient portion of its members on its development. The tensions between groups of officers as politicians increasingly sought their support for particular causes, the assassination of some officers in the middle 1950s, the discovery of numerous plots by some officers against others, and the existence of regional and ethnic rivalries among officers—all these factors built in certain attitudes and reinforced others. Distrust on the part of many officers for most politicians was reinforced. The situation tended to encourage them to be secretive and to strike out on their own. Basically, it helped mold and mobilize a new group dedicated to the overthrow of the traditional leaders of Syria and the destruction of their social and economic power throughout the Syrian countryside: that ruination came quickly after 1963.

Political Frame of Reference The political frame of reference of the new Syrian elite was almost exclusively concerned with the problems of rural Syria: its main concern was with the extension of political activity to rural areas. Such a ruralization of politics took a variety of forms. First, the concerns, needs and aspirations of the peasantry—embodied in programs such as land reform—became major themes in government planning. Second, and perhaps more important, men with rural backgrounds were brought into the government and the parties at both the local and national levels. A third feature was the movement of thousands of peasants to the cities and large towns both to find better employment and to escape the harsher realities of rural subsistence, a move which city dwellers—particularly the traditional elites—often interpreted less as a ruralization of politics than a physical ruralization of cities.

The poverty or lack of rural development in Syria follows the pattern of most Arab countries. What distinguishes rural Syria is both the diversity in types of rural areas and the extreme isolation of some areas. It is useful to distinguish between the economic patterns of the mountain as against those of desert or plain: rural areas of Ladhaqiya, for example, are different from those of the interior. On another level, the problems of the rural mountain areas of Ladhaqiya are much more basic than those in the plain or desert areas. Cultural and infrastructural deprivation when combined with the poverty and minority status of most inhabitants made the hills of the Ladhaqiya area Syria's most underdeveloped area. Other rural areas suffer from some but not all of the problems of Ladhaqiya. In the Hama-Hums area, an excessive man:land ratio is a pressing rural problem. This contrasts sharply with the vast openness of the northeast where, in fact, there are not enough peasants to take full advantage of the supposed economic potentials.

For most villages, life after independence did not change: French officials were simply replaced by Syrian rural administrators and gendarmes. Villagers still worked the fields of absentee landowners, a tenant position which offered neither steady employment nor a guaranteed income. The bonds between landowner and peasant did not persist in Syria as they did in Lebanon because middle class-peasant alliances in Hama and Ladhaqiya, in particular, sought to end the feudal relationship by attacking all links between peasantry and the traditional ruling elites.

The dominant role of Hama and Ladhaqiya citizens in Syrian politics and the military since independence is directly related to local politics. The greater the intensity of the local political confrontation between elites, the greater the role of those areas of high political conflict in national politics.

In the mid-1960s when the new Syrian elite gained effective control of Syria through the Ba'th Party, rural issues received special attention, and by the beginning of the 1970s, these issues were well institutionalized in departments throughout the government. In listing its domestic priorities, the government at one point suggested that top priority be given to the development of a new system of social relations in Syria; this meant:

> agrarian reform cooperatives, laws of agricultural relations, participation in directing factories, increased health facilities and national medical programs, the development of education and the extension of water and light facilities.[o]

While agrarian reform had a long history in Syria, these concerns led to a complete reorientation in domestic policies. One Syrian stated that "the most important problems facing the state are concentrated in the society of the rural areas which form the majority mass base."[7] He added that the transformation of the *"Insan al-Rifi"* ('the rural being') and the creation of rapport between rural areas and the cities were crucial.[8]

For those ex-peasants who sought to represent the village revolution, the major problem of human relations in Syria was not intra-elite frictions but rather the village-capital dichotomy. In effect, the villagers came to feel that during the first two decades of Syrian independence modernization had meant the intellectual and material development of the capital and other cities while rural areas had remained traditional and poor.

The villagers' commitment to the peasant movement's middle-class leadership, however, was as tenuous as the lower middle-class, ex-peasant elite's commitment to the village was ambivalent. Many members of the new elite tended to think and act in terms of the rural conditions in their own areas: peasant uprisings in other areas were outside their frame of reference. Although ex-peasant groups continually stressed their role in this village revolution, many abandoned their association with the rural movement when they had to choose between their roles as politicians and as revolutionary leaders in the 1960s. Before the June 1967 Middle East War, for example, the new elite talked boldly of arming peasants in the south, but, in fact, these arms were collected almost as soon as they were distributed: their insecurity was as great as that of the traditional elite.

Although the new elite was involved in some of the political movements founded by middle-class members of the older elite, it is significant that the new elite in the late 1950s was also centrally involved in two short-lived organizations. They were the Syrian section of the National Union, which was created during the 1958-1961 union with Egypt and the *Quwat al-Muqawama al-Sha'biya* (Popular Resistance Forces), a paramilitary organization created in 1957 when many Syrians felt hostilities could break out at any moment with any one of five countries bordering on Syria. The Popular Resistance Forces played an important role in Syrian politics precisely because they were not tied to any one personality. Their initial leader stated that their goal was mobilization of the Syrian people for the defense of the country and for Arab unity. It is noteworthy that in the early 1960s, long after the departure of the original leadership and in a political situation far different from that of 1957, the formal structure of this paramilitary organization was still maintained in many villages throughout Syria. There are two important reasons for this fact: first, the party had always been issue-oriented rather than personality-oriented, and it stressed issues—Arab unity and national defense—on which no one could disagree; second, the party had been organized in such a way that the village cells could operate without regular directives from central headquarters. Only in the late 1960s, with the development of the Ba'th Party as the locus of political activity, has there been similar stress on the importance of responsive local cells.

The National Union Party was important not because of its village organization but because it brought into politics many Syrians who had never participated before. Although the party was short-lived and delegates were not involved in basic decision-making, the many thousand Syrian delegates to the National Assembly represented, for the most part, a new segment of Syrian society—they were more numerous, more rural, more geographically dispersed and of humbler origins than members of most other Syrian organizations. The degree of overlap between this party's membership and that of the Popular Resistance Forces remains an important question. The National Union organization could have evolved from the 1957 paramilitary organization.

The many political commitments and organizations that

involved the new elite all indicate that this group was united against the traditional elite but that intra-elite conflict was greater and more violent than it was among members of the traditional elite. The greater the in-group cohesion, the greater the likelihood that even minor differences can become major issues within the group. In a society like that of Syria where ascriptive ties and personal loyalties continue to play such a significant role, intra-group conflict is a reality despite the strength of the in-group relationship and its agreement on a broad set of societal goals.

Elite Conflict Conflict within the new Syrian political elite has been both more ideological and more personal than conflict among competing factions of the traditional elite. After the Sixth Party Congress of the Ba'th and the February 1966 coup, the new elite demonstrated a stronger ideological commitment and greater cohesion than any Syrian elite during the previous two decades of rule by traditional politicians. But this fact does not diminish the intensity of intra-group conflict.

Conflict among the salient segments of the elite, while following some of the same lines as conflict within the middle-class elite, often surfaced within very small groups or cells. Whereas intra-elite conflict in the past had revolved around inter-city variables, education, and civil-military distrust, elite tensions now took on different forms. Ideological commitments to a party or to political rule, for example, often transcended parochial loyalties and this minimized inter-region squabbles. But this fact did not prevent an increased distrust of city dwellers on the part of the rural-based, lower middle-class and ex-peasant groups.

Commitments to certain ideological programs, loyalties to decentralized party units and appeals to Syria's peasantry—all issues which caused conflict within segments of the traditional elite—were also issues that divided the new elite. But what differentiates the new from the old is the greater likelihood that such issues would split parties or causes. Different ideological commitments and different ties to local political concerns in the Ladhaqiya region, for example, were the cause of conflict between Salah Jadid and Hafiz al-Asad, two 'Alawi officers with somewhat similar backgrounds. The similarities in background and in outlook among Nur al-Din al-Atasi, Yusif al-Zu'ayyin and Ibrahim Makhus, three doctors committed to the creation of an ideologically cohesive, socialist party state, did not prevent their differences from undermining the goal they all professed; it took only a few years for their internal conflicts to jeopardize their programs. The traditional elite, it seems, had more built-in mechanisms for seeking compromises on policy and organizational matters; their domination of the country and their survival had depended on compromise and the avoidance of conflict.

Elite conflict can perhaps best be understood by a brief examination of the dominant military officer segment of the elite. The conflict focussed on four main groups, two of which were united by a common commitment and two of which were highly complex in terms of loyalty structure. The first two, the SSNP and the Damascene Officers (*Dubbat al-Shawwam*), collapsed when challenged; the first in 1955 and 1956 and the second in 1962 and 1973. The two more complex factions, a progressive conglomerate, including the Ba'th and the Unionist Group, went through a series of political confrontations in which subsections, sometimes individual cells, were discredited.

The most important intra-elite ideological conflict involved the SSNP and the Ba'th. While policy issues separated the two parties, the conflict between them fed on personal antagonisms. The conflict, which erupted following the assassination in 1955 of a middle-class, Sunni Damascene officer by an 'Alawi, was to divide much of Syrian society. There are two significant aspects of this event. The first is the reaction of young, lower middle-class officers to the assassination: ideologically motivated, non-SSNP officers throughout Syria united with Ba'th officers to eliminate whatever SSNP sympathizers were still in the army or at large in society. A lengthy trial was little concerned with the acts of individuals, the key figures in the trial being dead or in another country. Rather, the trial served to put the whole party, its philosophy, and its credibility on trial.

A second feature of the event was that various factions became involved on both sides of the dispute. It appears that ideological, personal and religious factors were all involved and were equally important. Each of these facets concerned a different combination of officers and civilians, though membership in the groups was not mutually exclusive: thus, officers found themselves allied on certain issues and opposed on others. This was characteristic of the complex loyalties that divided and united the new Syrian elite.

Many interlocking groups—Ba'th officers, other progressive party-oriented officers, "city"-oriented officers, Hama officers—all united to destroy the SSNP. This alliance caused many 'Alawi and SSNP sympathizers in the army, the two groups most closely associated with the 1955 assassination, to avoid overt political activities for several years. But it soon became evident that these groups could unite only against a common enemy. Shortly after the creation of the United Arab Republic in 1958, significant fissures among the civilians and within the army took place. The first to be eliminated were officers close to the Communist Party. Soon, however, many seeds of intra-elite conflict emerged. Three groups of officers who played important roles in Syrian politics during the 1960s were involved in changes in the army during the union: the Damascene Officers, the Ba'th officers and the Unionists, (i.e., those who wanted another union in the 1960s after the collapse of the first).

The 1958-1961 union with Egypt did much to persuade Damascene Officers to organize themselves. Inter-regional and urban-rural frictions came to the fore during the union. Damascene officers had plans to dissolve the union precisely because of its adverse effects on the capital; the center of Arab nationalism had suddenly become a provincial capital, much to the chagrin of those with interests in the city. During the post-union period, this faction continued to champion its city, but the group never won any support outside Damascus. Its several attempts to control the army after 1961 ended with its own dismissal in 1963; the group was regarded as having too many similar interests to the traditional, city-oriented elites.

The union also had an impact on the Ba'th Party. Despite the dissolution of the party during the union, it was able to reorganize and recoup its strength rapidly after 1961. Ba'th officers who had worked hard for the party since the late 1940s found the 1950s frustrating years; these frustrations culminated with the union. Their bitter disillusionment in the early months of union when many of them were transferred to such outlying areas as Asyut in Upper Egypt prompted some to form their own secretive Military Committee. This Committee was dedicated to a Ba'th revolution and was determined that the party should stay in power. Despite its name, the Committee was not concerned with military matters. Rather it sought to define the precise relationship of military officers to the party and their role in the revolution. There is no evidence that the Committee, as a unit, sought power for itself rather than the party as a whole in the pre-1963 period; only after 1963 when the Ba'th Party came to power did intra-Committee conflict lead to a more important political role for some officers of the Committee.

The exclusive nature of the Military Committee and the Ba'th officer faction inevitably led to intra-elite conflict with other groups, the largest non-Ba'th group being the Unionist—itself a collection of factions. Some wanted to reinstitute the same union, others wanted another union and still others were only committed to the general concept of Arab unity. But these groups all came into conflict with the Ba'th Party after it took power in 1963. Open conflict in the summer of 1963 led to the demise of the Unionist group and the unsuccessful attempt to avoid further intra-army conflict by the Ba'thization of the army.

Two groups were involved in intense conflict in the Syrian army between 1954 and 1963: the Ba'th officers and the Unionists. Both had support in all regions of the country and neither was associated with one individual or area. The origins of both groups were lower middle-class or ex-peasant, and based in small towns rather than large cities. This regional diversity which was lacking in both the SSNP and the Damascene Officer groups was complemented by an ideological imprecision which at once broadened support and intensified intra-group conflict. The basis for and structure of the union, the course of leadership of the socialist transformation, remained unanswered questions which these groups chose to ignore in the face of the genuine appeal of Arab unity and socialism to all of their members.

By 1963, however, external political events and elite conflict had taken their toll on the cohesion and commitment which the members of this new elite had manifested at the beginning of their careers when they initially became involved with the new ideological parties. In particular, the period of the union and its aftermath resulted in political realignments which raised other fundamental issues; these, in turn, led to further realignments. Distrust between the Sunnis and minority groups, like the 'Alawis from Ladhaqiya, became intertwined with capital-countryside tensions which had been largely suppressed by the nationalism of the 1940s. It was parodoxical, in a sense, that regional integration in the form of the United Arab Republic proved to be dysfunctional for national integration efforts in Syria. The failure of the union thus led to a reaffirmation of many parochial interests.

IV. INTER-ELITE PERSPECTIVE: SOME CONCLUSIONS

There are elements of both continuity and change in the composition and behavior of the two echelons of traditional and new Syrian political elites. Most of the differences are evident in the nature of the elites and in their political commitments. Most of the similarities among the three groups can be seen in their political behavior and their attitudes toward popular participation in political processes.

Rooted in city or town life, the small, traditional elite had gained position and status in Syrian society by virtue of its socio-economic background, its relative monopoly of education before 1946 and its proximity to the nationalist movement which started to develop just prior to World War I. The second echelon of this elite was less wealthy, owned less lands, had more varied educational background and was able to gain some political recognition by both traditional and political means. On every count, the third group, the new elite, was different from both of the others. It was larger, rooted in the small towns and villages, and was involved in petty bureaucratic work, small agriculture and business, or menial managerial work for the wealthy landowners. It has been defined above as the lowest socio-economic group to whom secondary education has been available since independence. Whereas the traditional elites sought to enter politics from a variety of professions involving law, commerce, business, and agri-business, the new elite came to the political scene from the military and the teaching professions, the only two professions which offered upward mobility at independence.

There were also differences in the political commitments of these elites. The traditional elite's commitments tended to be based more on ascriptive loyalties of regionalism, social and economic ties, and religion, and less on ideological issues. The second, or intermediate, elite, of middle-class background, shared these commitments with its more traditional counterpart. While its ideological commitments to socialism in particular were well articulated, those commitments were based on local issues or concerns of local cells.

The bases of the new elite's political commitments were much more complex. Vague but emphatic concerns for social justice meant different things to different segments of the elite. For some, the basis of commitment to a political cause was merely revenge against the traditional elite, often its representatives in their place of upbringing. For others, it was less negative and more oriented toward rural development. For some 'Alawis and Duruz, ascriptive ties to community were paramount political considerations while others from the same regions and communities showed a more general commitment to political and social change. The greater complexity of the new elite's political commitments represents a distinct change from the more simple and singular concerns of the traditional elites.

Such differences and changes are less clearly identifiable in an examination of the political performance and actions of the three groups. While obvious differences exist in the traditional elite's strong vested interest in parliamentary rule and the new elite's commitment to single party rule (albeit party rule on the terms of those leading the government at a specific time), such distinctions are less apparent in their approach to the issue of political participation. Both elites show a strong tendency to try to lead what they believe to be "the popular will" rather than to follow it. Programs and policies have often been made on the basis of what the leaders think the "people" want rather than on what might be known objectively about popular wishes. Legitimacy is something acquired by Syrian politicians through actions at the top of the political structure rather than through broad support across the country. Political parties and movements, new and old, do not seek articulation of views by followers: support of a cause usually implies more formal ties of party membership than ties based on active participation in a political process.

Political participation for elites, then, meant intra-elite discussions rather than broad-based participation by the citizenry. But mere size of elite can be one indicator of change because even though decision-making may still be centralized, more people are participating. The Ba'th Party Congresses of the 1960s represent the largest and most heated interchanges in Syria since independence even though party membership remained a very small fraction of those with elite status in Syria.

To perceive change, it is essential to examine closely all three periods of Syrian independence: 1946 to 1954 when traditional elites had complete control over the political system; 1954 to 1965 when traditional and new elites were in constant competition and conflict with each other; and the period since 1965 in which the new elite has dominated politics. Outwardly, the parliamentary and praetorian procedures of the traditional elites in the first and second periods contrast only slightly with the attempts at one party rule since the middle and late 1960s. In both cases, a relatively small group has ruled the country. Membership in the transformed Ba'th Party of the late 1960s, while larger and broader than membership in many earlier political parties, only offered to lower middle-class and ex-peasant members of the new elite what other, traditional parties once offered to small middle- and upper-class, city-based elites.

Change can be seen more clearly under the surface. Political actions of the traditional elite in the first and second periods were dedicated to the premise of continued domination of the political system. However, the nationalizations of 1965 and subsequent attempts to organize a new and rigorous economic and social system implies the total ruination of the traditional elite's power base. Evidence of the new elite's commitment to this goal can be seen throughout the 1954 to 1965 period of inter-elite conflict, although systematic efforts at implementation came only in the middle 1960s as the younger, more rural-based groups in the Ba'th Party took over from more traditional, middle- class leadership. In the process, the social and economic fabric of Syria was transformed. More recent attempts at reconciliation have been designed less to reconcile the traditional elements to the new course than to stabilize and institutionalize the new programs. Thus, the real and the only revolution in Syria since independence has been the transformation of the salient political elites. It is perhaps truer of Syria than almost any other country of the Arab Middle East that after independence the lowest socio-economic groups receiving secondary education began to achieve elite status. It is also true that the new elite in Syria does not and cannot make an appeal on the basis of nationalism: its political frame of reference is totally removed from the pre-1946 Syrian nationalist experience.

The elites of Iraq and Lebanon offer an interesting comparison. While the military establishment in Iraq became a vehicle for social mobility for lower middle-class elements after 1936 as well as continuing to offer a career for members of the traditional elite, Iraqi nationalism was a very important issue in the development of the new elite which emerged in the late 1960s. The 1941 revolt against the British and the Iraqi monarchy, which lasted until 1958, offered continuing symbols on which nationalists could play and debate. The strong xenophobia in Syria toward almost all outsiders, and not a cohesive nationalist movement, remained one issue on which most Syrians agreed. The Arab-Israeli conflict strengthened that xenophobia throughout the 1960s and early 1970s. As in Iraq, local nationalism also remained crucial for the Lebanese elite.

The political experience in Iraq and Lebanon has also differed because of longstanding ties between the military elite and salient political elites and because the lower socio-economic groups did not achieve elite status the way they did in Syria. The perspective from Syria is that elite change which might have taken place over several generations, as it did in Lebanon, occurred in only two decades because of the coincidence of rapid social and economic change and because of intense inter- and intra-elite conflict.

NOTES

1. Four of the better general studies on post-independence Syria in English are: Tabitha Petran, *Syria*. (New York: Praeger, 1972); Itamar Rabinovich, *Syria Under the Ba'th, 1963-66: The Army-Party Symbiosis* (Jerusalem: Israel Universities Press, 1972); Patrick Seale, *The Struggle for Syria: A Study of Post-War Arab Politics, 1945-1958* (London: Oxford University Press, 1965); and Gordon H. Torrey, *Syrian Politics and the Military, 1945-1958* (Columbus: Ohio State University Press, 1964).

2. See République Française. Ministère des Affaires Etrangère. *Rapport sur la situation de la Syrie et du Liban, 1924-1937* (Paris); and *Revue des Troupes du Levant* (Beirut).

3. Torrey, *Syrian Politics*, 420.

4. For a discussion of some of the activities in 1948, see: Patrick Seale, *The Struggle for Syria*; Muhammad Khalid Mataraji, *Ma'a Atbaluna fi Filastin*. (Beirut: n.p.), 1954; and *al-Ba'th*, no. 233, May 4, 1948.

5. See Syrian Embassy, Washington, D.C. "A Brief Outline of the Educational System in the Syrian Arab Republic." 1962. (mimeographed).

6. *Jaysh al-Sha'b* (Damascus), no. 922 (February 23, 1970), 8.

7. Muhammad al-Tall, *al-Mujtama' al-'Arabi al-Suri fi al-Dawla al-Haditha*. (Damascus: al-Matba'a al-Ta'awuniya, 1967), p. 19.

8. Ibid., p. 21.

BIBLIOGRAPHY

Dawn, C. Ernest. "The Rise of Arabism in Syria." *Middle East Journal* 16, 2 (1962): 145-64.

Koury, Enver M. *The Patterns of Mass Movements in Arab Revolutionary-Progressive States*. The Hague: Mouton, 1970.

Longrigg, S. H. *Syria and Lebanon under the French Mandate*. London: Oxford University Press, 1958.

Macintyre, R. R. "The Arab Ba'th Socialist Party: Ideology, Politics, Sociology and Organization." Ph.D. dissertation, Australian National University, 1969.

Petran, Tabitha. *Syria*. New York: Praeger, 1972.

Rabinovich, Itamar. *Syria under the Ba'th, 1963-66: The Army-Party Symbiosis*. Jerusalem: Israel Universities Press, 1972.

Rondot, Pierre. "Tendances particularistes et tendances unitaires en Syrie." *Orient* 2, 1 (1958): 135-48.

Saab, Edouard. *La Syrie ou la révolution dans la rancoeur*. Paris: Julliard, 1968.

Seale, Patrick. *The Struggle for Syria: A Study of Post-War Arab Politics, 1945-58*. London: Oxford University Press, 1965.

al-Tall, Muhammad. *al-Mujtama' al-'Arabi al-Suri fi al-Dawla al-Haditha*. Damascus: al-Matba'a al-Ta'awuniya, 1967.

Torrey, Gordon H. *Syrian Politics and the Military, 1945-58*. Columbus, Ohio: Ohio State University Press, 1964.

Van Dusen, Michael H. "Political Integration and Regionalism in Syria." *Middle East Journal* 26, 2 (1972): 123-36.

Winder, R. Bayly. "Syrian Deputies and Cabinet Ministers, 1919-59." *Middle East Journal* 16, 4 and 17, 1 (1962-3): 407-29, 35-54.

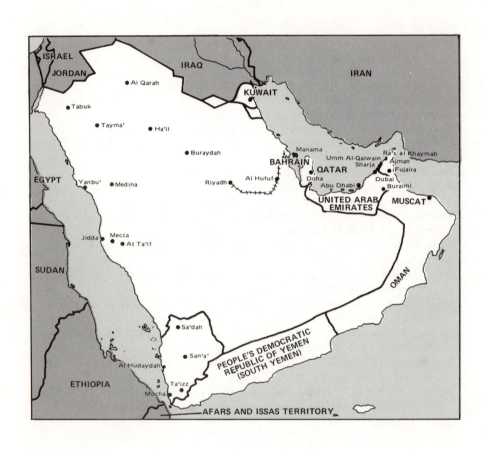

4

Saudi Arabia:
Survival of Traditional Elites
Manfred W. Wenner

THE ARABIAN PENINSULA

The Arabic name for the Arabian Peninsula, "the island of the Arabs" (*Jazirat al-Arab*), implies the past and present differentiation of this geographical subdivision of the Middle East from surrounding territories. Beginning in pre-historic times, the natural frontier which the desert regions on the northern edge of the Peninsula create provided both a physical and cultural barrier between the population of the Peninsula itself and the residents of the "Fertile Crescent" region which encompasses the eastern shore of the Mediterranean, the southern flank of Turkey and geographical Mesopotamia. Despite evidence that the Arabian Peninsula may have been the original "home" of a number of Semitic peoples who left their mark on the ancient and medieval worlds (e.g., the Nabataeans), essential and permanent differences remained between lifesyltes and the political, economic, and social concerns of the residents of the Peninsula and those outside it.

It can be argued that the geographical differences between the Peninsula and the rest of the Middle East, as well as within the Peninsula itself, determined in large measure the "political" distinctions still relevant to an understanding of the Peninsula's current role in the larger region of which it is a part. Geographically, the Peninsula can be divided into a number of relatively clearly differentiated parts:

(1) the mountainous southwest, comprising the region of Asir (part of Saudi Arabia) and the two modern states of Yemen and the Peoples Democratic Republic of Yemen (usually known as South Yemen). Although the mountain chain which runs along the western (Red Sea) coast of the Peninsula is an obvious feature of the entire Peninsula, it is not until the highlands of Asir that these mountains achieve sufficient height to markedly affect agricultural and residential patterns. In central Yemen, there are numerous peaks with heights of over 11,000 feet. Until the coming of Islam, these mountainous regions provided the climatic and geographically distinct background to a series of empires which, though linguistically related to the population of northern Arabia, had few political connections with it. The population of this area has engaged in organized agricultural activity for thousands of years, and has for the most part lived in towns and cities with organized, structured social and economic differentiation and stratification;

(2) the mountainous southeast, comprising the area from the Musandam Peninsula around the coast to Dhofar, that is, largely the territory of the modern state of Oman (formerly Muscat and Oman). Once again, the climatic characteristics of this region permitted sedentary agricultural activity which may also go back more than 3000 years.

Of more than passing importance for these two regions is the continuing tendency for their inaccessible mountain fastnesses to become the center for divergent and anti-orthodox, religio-political ideologies and movements. Shortly after the rise of Islam, both regions became the refuge for adherents of alternative interpretations of Islamic theology and ideology, for instance, the Zaydis in the southwest, and the Kharijites (Ibadites) in the southeast. These deserve mention at this point because they continue as the basis for socio-political systems which are at variance with the remainder of the Peninsula;

(3) the relatively fertile western Red Sea fringe, from the Gulf of Aqaba south to the mountains of Asir—the Hijaz. Connected economically with the pre-Islamic empires of southwestern Arabia by the land trade routes which passed through this area (and extended up into Palestine), the population of this area has traditionally been trade-oriented, and therefore substantially more cognizant of the rest of the world and its concerns. This orientation was enhanced by the founding of Islam, which made

two of its cities—Mecca and Medina—major foci of a religion which numbered its adherents in the millions, and among whom, whether they were Chinese, Indian, Indonesian, African, or of other extraction, there existed the religious injunction to visit these centers (the pilgrimage);

(4) the largely desert regions of the interior—the Najd— comprising the Rub' al-Khali (the Empty Quarter), the great desert of the south which extends to the mountainous fringes of the southeast, south, and southwest; the Nafud, the desert of the north, and the Dahm, a crescent-shaped connecting desert in the east. Linguistic evidence indicates that it was the population of this central region which was the first to label itself "Arab" (which apparently originally meant simply nomad). Though some of the plateaus and larger oases within this region permit settled cultivation, the population here has through the ages been predominantly nomadic in its lifestyle;

(5) the eastern fringes of the Peninsula, comprising both ancient trading and commercial centers such as Bahrain (located about 15 miles off the coast in the Persian/Arab Gulf) and the geographically isolated but distinct settlements (some with apparent histories of more than 3000 years) of Kuwait, coastal Qatar, and the present-day United Arab Emirates (the former Trucial Coast).

Historically, these five regions of the Peninsula developed rather differently. Their geographical distinctiveness led to separate socio-political orientations which, at first, the pene-tration of the European powers did little to change, for the Portuguese, Dutch, and English occupations and economic activities during the seventeenth to the nineteenth centuries produced no permanent or lasting alterations in these traditional orientations, interests and lifestyles.

With certain minor exceptions, the Arabian Peninsula has been at least nominally Muslim since shortly after the appearance of Islam. This is not to suggest that the Peninsula has not experienced significant conflicts due to varying interpretations of the Islamic doctrines, much less that all these regions have populations which show the same dedication or strength of adherence to these doctrines. In fact, the interpretations of the basic elements of Islam have varied widely, and the people of some areas of the Peninsula today show no more than a nominal acceptance or understanding of Islam.

Demographically, the population of the Peninsula is rather more varied than one might be led to expect by its relative isolation from many of the politico-military events which deeply affected other portions of the Middle East (e.g., there are few of the linguistic and religious minorities found, for example, in the Fertile Crescent region). Many of these distinctions, however, are only comprehensible within the context of the tribal (or segmented) nature of the society. For example, a major distinction among Arabs which is still of some social significance (though its political role is now marginal) is that between 'Adnani ("northern") and Qahtani ("southern") Arabs; the latter, claiming to be the "pure" Arab, regard the 'Adnani as a "derived" Arab and therefore significantly lower in status and prestige.[1] It is of interest, therefore, to note that some anthropological and lay observers claim to be able to visually distinguish the indigenous population of the southern regions of the Peninsula from the physical type which predominates in the northern areas and the Fertile Crescent—though little scientific evidence which would support this difference on the basis of objective physiological or genetic characteristics exists.

In the Peninsula, as in so many other places in the Middle East, it is difficult to clearly distinguish between groups which adopted an alternative interpretation of Islamic doctrines as a means of preserving their distinctiveness (usually based upon pre-Islamic differences from the majority), and those groups which adopted an alternative interpretation and as a result were relatively isolated from the majority, and in turn developed (sometimes only marginally) different physical, social, or linguistic characteristics as a *consequence* of their exclusivism.

At the same time, however, the *political* distinctions between the peripheral states of the Peninsula and the contemporary state of Saudi Arabia are quite real and relatively easy to locate in space and time. While it may be argued that many of the distinct political entities found today upon a map of the Peninsula are the artificial creation of the intervention of the European powers (e.g., the United Arab Emirates, whose distinctive identity may be traced back to the intervention of the British Government on the Gulf's pirate activities in the nineteenth century), one may just as legitimately argue that the distinctive status and lifestyles of the populations of the Yemeni highlands and the Bahrain archipelago have in large measure been the result of an entirely different historical experience reflecting different geographical circumstances.

In ethnographic terms, then, a division of the Arabian Peninsula would result in the following breakdown: (1) the largely 'Adnani population of the Hijaz, the Najd, the Empty Quarter, the eastern regions of the Peninsula, and most of the presently existing peripheral states; (2) the Qahtani population of the mountainous southwest; (3) the mixed Arab populations of the coastal lowlands, the mountainous southeast, and the Bahrain archipelago, (these mixtures are the result of extensive slavery in the past, as well as the lengthy trading history of the Gulf region); and, (4) the population of certain relatively isolated portions of the southern coast and the island of Socotra: the Mahri peoples, concerning whose origins there is little agreement at the present time.

Although there is some evidence that portions of the Arabian Peninsula provided a rich souce of certain minerals in the ancient world (e.g., gold in northern Hijaz and copper in the region of the Buraimi Oasis), the first penetration of the Peninsula and its fringes was not primarily for the purpose of exploiting known natural resources. The first European forays and colonial operations were largely for the purpose of establishing "factories," i.e., sales outlets for European products in exchange for whatever local products might be marketable in the European nations (e.g., coffee from Yemen, pearls from Bahrain). Other motives for European penetration and arrogation of sovereignty over areas of the Peninsula were the result of intra- and inter-European power rivalries and the wish to "establish a presence" in the event future developments required such presences (e.g., the British occupation of Aden during the period of Egyptian expansion into the Peninsula), or the protection of trade routes (especially true of British activity in the Gulf region).

In other words, it may be said fairly that the Arabian Peninsula as a whole did not raise in the European powers the same degree of concupiscence which other areas in the Middle East, Asia, and Africa succeeded in doing. In the aftermath of World War I, when the Mandates over the Fertile Crescent/ Levant nations were considered a prize by the winners, the Arabian Peninsula was largely left to its own devices. Yemen was permitted to declare itself an independent nation; one finds little if any interest in Muscat and Oman and most of the other peripheral states, and the intra-Arab frictions and disputes in central Arabia remained remarkably free of direct European manipulation or interest.

It was, in fact, not until the discovery of oil in the Arabian Peninsula that we may begin to speak of an extensive and active Western interest in the affairs of the Peninsula. Once World War I had demonstrated the economic and military advantages of oil as a source of energy, interest in the Middle East outside of Iran began to increase—but only in direct proportion to the likelihood of finding commercially exploitable sources of petroleum. In fact, the Eastern and General Syndicate, the first concessionaire in the Gulf region, had considerable difficulty in convincing the oil companies even to consider sending technical personnel to the region in order to evaluate the possibilities of finding such sources.

SAUDI ARABIA

Much of the present and future of the Peninsula as a whole depends upon what happens in Saudi Arabia. It dwarfs its neighbors—aptly named the peripheral states—by its vastness, the variety of its natural resources, the size of its population, its economic potential, and the political influence which it has exerted in the past, the present, and is likely to exercise in the future. It occupies about four-fifths of the Peninsula, an area equal to approximately one-third of the continental United States. Its sheer size and its own political history, on the other hand, also result in problems: substantial provincial variations in population, economic characteristics, as well as administrative organization and relative power, heightened by transportation difficulties and communications barriers. The Hijaz, for example, is predominant in religious, social, and commercial matters; the Najd is politically predominant, due to its association with the House of Sa'ud, the Wahhabi faith, and the political weight of the tribes; the Eastern Province dominates the economic life of the country because of its oil deposits, while Asir has distinct agricultural advantages vis-à-vis the remainder of the Kingdom. Last but definitely not least, Saudi Arabia has a religio-political tradition which is more deeply ingrained in the fabric of the society than is the case in most if not all of the peripheral states.

Because the rise of the contemporary state of Saudi Arabia is so intimately connected with a religious movement which arose in central Arabia in the eighteenth century it is essential to briefly review this history. In the 1740s, Muhammed ibn Abd al-Wahhab of Najd began preaching a puritanical form of Islam which included a return to the fundamentals of the faith as it had existed in the seventh century. Expelled from his home town, Muhammed Abd al-Wahhab found refuge with the ruler of the town of Dariya, the Amir Muhammed ibn Sa'ud—the founder of the present ruling dynasty. Ibn Sa'ud embraced the doctrines and used them to attract a large Beduin following which became fanatical in its support of what became known as the Wahhabi movement. By marshalling this support, the Amir was able to capture Riyadh, and, by the time of his death (1765) establish his supremacy throughout Najd by a web of conquests, marriages and alliances. His descendants were able to continue the expansion of the House of Sa'ud: by the first decade of the nineteenth century they had captured Mecca, Medina, Asir, Yemen, the Hijaz, and most of the remainder of the Peninsula as well as parts of Syria and Iraq. Inevitably, the Ottoman Empire reacted to this threat and with the assistance of the Viceroy of Egypt, succeeded in crushing the first Saudi-Wahhabi Empire by the end of the next decade. This expansion of Egyptian power in the Peninsula resulted in the British campaign to establish a presence there through the signing of a large number of protectorate treaties with the fringe states. The history of nineteenth century Arabia, like much of European history, consists of an unedifying series of violent personal, familial, regional and national conflicts and therefore need not concern us in detail. Suffice it to say that by the end of the century, the remnants of the Saudi dynasty were forced to flee to Kuwait while a Wahhabi tribal shaikh of the Shammar tribes, Muhammad ibn Rashid, established himself as the major political figure in central Arabia.[2]

In exile, the next leader of the House of Sa'ud began his campaign to re-establish the family. Abd al-Aziz ibn Sa'ud (usually known as Ibn Sa'ud), beginning with the takeover of Riyadh in 1902, succeeded in re-establishing a Saudi foothold in Najd. By 1906, he was in control of Najd; by 1913 he had taken al-Hasa Province (now the Eastern Province); Asir fell in 1920, and Hijaz in 1925. Though Ibn Sa'ud was crowned King of the Hijaz and Najd and its Dependencies in Riyadh in 1927, full consolidation of the realm took considerable additional effort during the next three years. Major resistance to the House of Sa'ud may be said to have been decisively eliminated by early 1930, and in September of 1932, the reunited realm was renamed the Kingdom of Saudi Arabia.

The early Saudi rulers introduced a new concept to central Arabia as a part of their conquests: territorial organization. They built moated garrisons outside the towns which they captured, and in large and small towns alike installed officials loyal to the precepts of the Wahhabi version of Islam. District governors were appointed to collect taxes as well as to recruit additional soldiers for the campaigns. Rule was highly centralized; indeed all important decisions were personally made by the Amir.

In the early years of the twentieth century, when Abd al-Aziz ibn Sa'ud began his campaigns to reassert the dominance of the House of Sa'ud over central Arabia, a major factor in his success was the fact that the title of *imam* (religious leader) of the Wahhabis had remained in the family. This position enabled Ibn Sa'ud to establish a large-scale political organization, for it made it both legitimate and possible for him to dispatch Wahhabi "missionaries" to the tribes, obtain a measure of support and adherence to his programs, and obedience to commands which he issued.

One of the most significant of these commands was the decision to encourage the settlement of Beduin tribesmen in agricultural communities which were founded on and governed by Wahhabi precepts. His pilot project, begun in 1912 in the northern Najd, was successful in settling some 10,000 Mutayr nomads into a community. Within a few years, such settlements numbered over 60 and sheltered some 40,000 former nomads. The movement became known as the *Ikhwan* (the Brethren), and had as its aim the welding of all true believers regardless of their tribal affiliation into a larger whole. By 1916, the Ikhwan movement in Najd had spread to such an extent that Ibn Sa'ud was compelled to assume direct personal control over it or face a serious threat to his rule. He ordered all the tribes to join the Ikhwan and pay the *zakat* (alms tax) to him as Imam. In addition, he required that the tribal shaikhs attend schools of religious instruction (in Riyadh), upon the completion of which the shaikh was frequently invited to remain in attendance upon Ibn Sa'ud in Riyadh. He thus succeeded in keeping most of them under close supervision to ensure their loyalty and obedience. Other orders called for an end to blood feuds within the brotherhood, in part accomplished by emphasizing the exclusive nature of the Ikhwan and the need for mutual assistance and cooperation in the face of the outside threats which the movement encountered and had to overcome. Ibn Sa'ud in effect created a highly-motivated, highly-trained, loyal armed force numbering about 25,000 men which could be mobilized, it was said, within four days, although no more than about 5000 were usually called upon for active duty.

With the elimination of intertribal raiding and feuding, and an almost unbroken record of martial successes, however, the Ikhwan sought to extend their doctrine outside what had become the post-World War I frontiers of Najd; specifically, on different occasions they moved into Transjordan and Iraq. By the early 1930s, the Ikhwan had served their purpose; gradually the settlements were abandoned; the veterans were pensioned off or transferred to the regular army which Ibn Sa'ud was beginning to organize along more modern lines.

Despite the importance of religion in the establishment of the state of Saudi Arabia within the frontiers of today, it is important to emphasize that tribal organization, tribal values and norms, and the political "weight" of the tribes within the context of Arabian society remained intact in the new order. They were all simply required to operate within the religious order; and socio-political relationships were to be based upon the tie of (Wahhabi) Islam rather than on kinship.

It is this characteristic of twentieth century Saudi Arabia which makes it literally impossible to suggest that nationalism, as it is understood in the social science literature, may be found in that country. Although the House of Sa'ud undertook some major changes in the administrative framework for the governance of the tribes and its vast new possessions (for instance, organization of the Kingdom on a territorial basis), and despite the fact that the acceptance of the spiritual authority of Ibn Sa'ud made the majority of the population aware of vaguely belonging to some larger community, it remains wholly inappropriate to suggest that a modern, political loyalty had emerged or developed, despite the Western predilection for associating territorial bases of governance with "nationalism." It would be far more accurate to say that, despite substantial innovations, the House of Sa'ud had re-emphasized the traditionally Islamic view that there is no (theoretical) separation of "church" and "state."

Even prior to its establishment in its current form, Saudi Arabia has been accurately described by one authority as a "patriarchal desert state."[3] In other words, no political authority which has ever ruled in central Arabia has been an urban-based imperial state as were all other larger political entities with which we are familiar in this region of the world. The traditional elites in central Arabia have based their leadership upon customary, hereditary, and religious bases and not upon their effective control of major urban centers where the political, economic, and social standards and life of the whole are set or elaborated.

The role of religion in Saudi Arabia resembles nothing more than the role of religion in the traditional Islamic state: one finds the co-existence of urban centers and tribal regions, where the former are in effect garrisons (e.g., the Ikhwan settlements), centers of trade and commerce (e.g., Jidda) and Muslim instruction and piety (e.g., Mecca and Medina). Although there is in addition an administrative center (generally the seat of the ruling family—in this case, Riyadh) from which authoritative decisions flow, this center does not fully control the rest of the society either in a territorial or a qualitative sense. That is to say, there are territorial limitations upon the effectiveness of the central authority based upon the ability of tribal rulers to resist this authority, and qualitative limitations based upon the influence and authority of the 'ulama (religious scholars) and the consultative rights of the leaders of major tribes and confederations.

Nevertheless, and it is important to realize this, the society remains a *single* politico-religious unit. Although, as will be noted below, the rule of Ibn Sa'ud and his son Faysal has changed aspects of the society and its organization, the essential bases remain the traditional ones enumerated above: custom, heredity, and religion. It must also be recognized that the traditional value system continues to have immediate significance to the overwhelming majority of the populace.

More than any other of the Islamic nations, and more than any other Arab nation Saudi Arabia has retained the essential elements of a value system, a set of behavior patterns for both elite and mass alike, and a political system which is in most respects an anacronism in the modern world. This, of course, does not preclude the analysis of Saudi Arabia within one or more of the frameworks which have been proposed for the analysis of "development," "modernization," or the role of elites in producing, furthering, or implementing different kinds of "change." Although the political elites—in the Western sense—are often indistinguishable from the religious, the social, and even the economic elites, one may fairly suggest that Saudi Arabia presents us with a "textbook" example of a "modernizing autocracy."

Saudi Arabia, for example, "exhibits profound internal solidarity based upon . . . religion, by means of which support is retained for the political leader, the king who makes claims on the members of the system and controls them."[4] Indeed, it fulfills all five of the suggested characteristics: (1) hierarchical authority patterns; (2) exclusivism (based upon Wahhabi Islam); (3) strategic flexibility (especially with regard to its ability to utilize rational behavior patterns in the administration of the nation's petroleum resources); (4) unitarianism (very little willingness or ability to delegate decision-making power to regional authorities of any kind); (5) neo-traditionalism.

Before expanding further on how one may categorize Saudi Arabia for purposes of analysis, it remains essential to obtain a clear understanding of the traditional bases of authority and the role of the tribes. Alone among the major Arab nations, the bulk of Saudi Arabia's population lives according to traditional tribal organization patterns. Of its roughly 6 million people, approximately 15 percent live in villages and an additional 20 percent live in the major urban areas (Riyadh, Medina, Jidda, etc.).[5] There are about 100 major tribes in the country with a membership of over 1000 persons, and kinship remains the major principle according to which these tribes are organized. They are pastoral and unsettled, that is, they migrate almost continuously with their camels, sheep and goats in the search for water and grazing areas. The tribe remains a basically autonomous political entity which demands loyalty from its members; indeed, it is widely recognized by both government and tribe alike that governmental laws and regulations which are applicable in villages, towns and cities are not necessarily relevant nor applicable to the tribes. In addition, inter- as well as intra-tribal relationships are largely governed by tribal law, consisting of accepted customs and precedents. Authority patterns are hierarchical; political power and prerogatives tend to be concentrated in the hands of the particular family from which the shaikh is traditionally selected. Nevertheless, there are institutionalized restraints or checks upon the arbitrary exercise of these powers: (a) the tribal council, which is composed of the senior members, (b) the subordinate position of the shaikh to the paramount shaikh (of the main tribe), and (c) custom.

In keeping with the largely traditional nature of the Saudi political system, it is important to note that essentially the same framework to provide restraints upon the arbitrary exercise of power exists at the "national" level. In other words, the paramount political authority in the Kingdom, the King, is subject to basically the same restrictions; it is both expected and accepted that the King will consult with members of the royal family, the paramount shaikhs of politically significant tribes, confederations, and geographical regions; that he will consult with the 'ulama in order to assess religious sentiment, and that in general no radical break with previous custom or tradition will be undertaken without precisely such consultation and a thorough "testing" of the socio-political currents within the country.

As indicated above, the rise of the House of Sa'ud and the establishment of the Saudi state in the 1920s did little to change these basic arrangements except to inject a stronger Islamic element into the amalgam than had heretofore been the case. The social relationships which arise within such a framework are a complex sliding scale (in terms of proximity and kinship) and not, as is frequently supposed, a simple dichotomy between the in-group (within which all relationships exist) and all out-groups (with which there are no relations). The tribesman recognizes a series of superimposed "in" and "out" groups with obligations that are graduated and enforced (and enforceable) according to the context. Distinctions between persons and groups may be based upon a large number of characteristics or factors: relationship to an eponymous ancestor, kinship (immediate), social status (often associated with the performance of a particular task within a larger framework, as is the case with the Sulabah), and so on.

Within such a context, there was, until recently, no inkling of the bases of personal and group identification as these are understood in the West: the territorial "nation-state." Western criteria for the assigning of a person or group were incomprehensible and irrelevant. In order to understand the broadly political framework in which change is, in fact, taking place in Saudi Arabia, it is essential that these differences be continually kept in mind.

It is possible to date the beginnings of change in the traditional patterns outlined above quite easily: the interest in Saudi Arabia by Westerners because of its potential petroleum deposits. Although this interest goes back to the early 1920s, when Major Frank Holmes obtained a concession of 30,000 square miles in al-Hasa, it was not until the discovery of oil deposits on the island of Bahrain in 1932 that Saudi Arabia became a focus for determined oil prospecting (the original concession had lapsed for lack of interest). Negotiations with Ibn Sa'ud resulted in a concession agreement in 1933, at which time the concession was assigned to the California Arabian Oil Company (CASOC), owned by Standard Oil of California. Although some small oil deposits were discovered earlier, it was not until 1937 that a real commercially exploitable well was drilled. Nevertheless, the Texas Oil Company (Texaco) had been brought in so as to provide additional marketing facilities, and later Standard Oil of New Jersey and Socony-Vacuum (Standard Oil of New York, now known as Mobil) joined the consortium, renamed the Arabian American Oil Company (Aramco) in 1944.[6]

It is in association with the expansion of the oil extracting industry and its hundreds of ancillary activities that the changes which Saudi Arabia has experienced since then must be considered. Some indication of the stupendous impact which the petroleum industry has had upon Saudi Arabia may be gained from the following table of production of the major concessionaires and revenue derived from them. Among other things, one may readily see how significant Aramco operations have been, and still are, in the economic life of the Kingdom.

TABLE I

Year	ARAMCO Production[1]	Revenues		GETTY OIL (USA)	ARABIAN OIL (Japan)
1938	1,357	$ 3.2	million	--	--
1946	164,229	10.4	"	--	--
1950	546,703	56.7	"	--	--
1955	965,041	338.2	"	$ 2.6 million	--
1960	1,247,140	312.8	"	18.4 "	$ 2.5 million
1963	1,629,018	418.6[2]	"	23.0 "	13.6 "
1967	2,597,563	859.4	"	17.8 "	31.8 "
1969	2,994,824	895.1	"	15.2 "	37.1 "
1970	3,548,865	1,088.4	"	17.2	40.3 "
1971	4,769,863	1,866.4	"	78.5	
1972	5,773,395	2,667.9	"	101.4	
1973	7,345,000	5,700(est.)		175 (est.)	
1974	8,500,000(est.)	20-25,000 (est.)"			

NOTES: 1) Production is in average barrels per day (bbl/day).

2) Not including extras; special additional payments as a result of changes in the calculation of royalties and taxes were paid in 1963 ($152.5 million), 1965 ($46.0 million), 1966 ($29.4 million), and 1967 ($29.3 million). All but the 1963 figures given above include these extra payments.

SOURCES: *Aramco Handbook* (Zonen-Haarlem, Netherlands: Joh. Eschede, 1960);

Aramco Handbook (Zonen-Haarlem, Netherlands: Joh. Eschede, 1968; rev. ed.);

British Petroleum, Ltd., *Statistical Review of World Oil Industry 1972* (London: Baynard Press, 1973);

Arab Report and Record (London), Issues of 15-28 February 1971, p. 115; 16-31 May 1972, p. 263; and 1-15 June 1973, p. 257;

Saudi Arabian Monetary Agency Annual 1389-1390 AH (1970), (N.p., 1971), p. 88.

As should be obvious, the growth and development of the petroleum industry, with its worldwide distribution and marketing concerns, the technological expertise and sophisticated materials-handling equipment which it requires, and the vast range of ancillary and related tasks which it must undertake for successful operation in an environment as inhospitable as that of the Gulf region, required large numbers of specialized personnel not available in what was clearly an "underdeveloped" country. It should not, therefore, be surprising that Aramco employed thousands of American and other non-Arab nationals in the primary exploitation area from the very outset of operations—in field operations (drillers, etc.), support (medical, housing, etc.), administrative (accounting, etc.) and management. Table II provides a summary of the nationality of Aramco employees at different levels over a two-decade span.

TABLE II

Country Year:	1949	1954	1959	1967
Americans	2,201 (10.7%)	3,141 (10.6%)	2,464 (11.8%)	1,284 (10.6%)
Other Nationals	3,087 (15.9%)	4,535 (15.4%)	2,111 (10.1%)	976 (8.1%)
Saudi Arabs (Skilled & Semiskilled)	6,932 (33.6%)	14,208 (48.1%)	13,421 (64.4%)	9,813 (81.3%)
Saudi Arabs (Unskilled)	8,379 (40.7%)	7,650 (25.9%)	2,837 (13.6%)	Not Available

SOURCES: *Aramco Handbook*, 1960, pp. 161, 211; *Aramco Handbook*, Rev. Ed., 1968, O. 156.

Although the percentage of American employees, overwhelmingly in the higher management levels, has not altered appreciably, the percentage of Saudi nationals who are skilled or semiskilled (including lower management levels) has increased remarkably, providing a rough indicator of the rapid spread of modern skills among the Saudi population associated with the country's major industry and source of revenue.

On the other hand, this does not accurately reflect all aspects of the Saudi economy, much less of the government. Aramco as well as other modern corporations within Saudi Arabia have for long been dependent upon the nationals of other countries for the many skills which require at least a secondary education: for example, medical personnel from India, accountants from Pakistan, teachers from Jordan and Egypt, and translators from Lebanon, with various middle-level administrative positions filled by Palestinians.

Indeed, the spectacular increase in governmental revenues and expenditures within the last decade has resulted in an ever-increasing dependence upon foreign nationals. Although the official Saudi statistics on the number of foreign workers in the country was in 1969 placed at 45,796,[7] other observers have estimated the total at 30,000 in 1965,[8] 300,000 in 1970,[9] and 700,000 in late 1972[10]—a staggering increase of over 2300 percent in less than a decade! In addition, it is widely agreed that Saudi Arabia has become dependent upon Yemeni nationals in the heavy labor portion of the economy, that is, the modern industries and construction.

The significance of this, however, is not so much that many of these individuals, along with their Saudi counterparts, constitute a new class in the Saudi social framework, that is, an industrial working class,[11] or that many of them may be grouped with the "new middle class"[12] which has also appeared on the Saudi scene and will be treated below, but rather that their influence has so far been exceedingly small—at least in the social and political spheres.

Foreign observers are inclined to view this situation as a volatile one and speculate on how long a confrontation between a society and government simultaneously committed to the ideals of traditional Islamic society and the development of a modern and technologically sophisticated economy can continue. In fact, one may attribute the stability of the government and the society to a relatively short list of characteristics. (1) There is no evidence of a clear relationship between dependence on foreign labor and expertise and political instability; a roughly equivalent situation exists in many of the Gulf states, and in Kuwait nearly 52 percent of the total population is of foreign origin. (2) The continuing rapid economic growth rate of the country—in excess of 10 percent per annum, has resulted in an expanding bureaucratic apparatus which has been able to absorb newly-graduated and Western-educated Saudis in positions of sufficient prestige and status while simultaneously retaining and even adding foreign nationals where their skills are required. (3) There exist next to no opportunities for public discussion of change in the existing social and political framework; since organizations for political, social, and economic action or cooperation (for example, labor unions, clubs, a free press and other media, etc.) are either forbidden or actively discouraged, there is little opportunity for any concerted and organized planning for bringing about rapid or radical change. (4) The overwhelming portion of the population which is directly affected by and feels the "claustrophobic atmosphere of the country" is in a position to seek release of whatever social (entertainment, sexual, etc.) frustrations accumulate by short-term departures from the country; for example, in 1972, $144 million was spent on travel and personal transportation out of Saudi Arabia.[13] (5) The overwhelming majority of the population supports the present arrangements; briefly, one may suggest that the rural and tribal population remains committed to the ideals of Saudi Wahhabi Islam, due to the fact that (a) westernization of local and regional nobles and tribal leaders has barely begun, thereby creating no great disparity between the lifestyles of this rural elite and their subjects, and (b) an established pattern for the expression of discontent among this population continues to exist, that is, the expression of preferences is sufficiently institutionalized and accepted that it does not appear as dangerous opposition to the government. The average Saudi continues to expect that he may deal directly with the King and/or his Ministers in the search for "justice," while the King and his family accept that they must and should deal with such grievances on an individual and personal level as frequently as possible. At the same time, the resources of the modernized sector are sufficiently great that the mass of the educated population is absorbed into positions reasonably appropriate to their skills and, more importantly, their status expectations, thereby in effect "buying off" much if not all the latent dissatisfaction which may exist with the socially restrictive nature of the society and government.

In fact, of course, the growing sophistication of the economy is putting tremendous strains on the existing framework. The tradition of personal patriarchal government which permits the average Saudi to continue in his expectations of personal approaches to the King appears stretched very near the breaking point. At the same time, there is the awareness on the part of the growing "new middle class" that this increasing sophistication and complexity requires, in turn, an increasing rationalization and specialization within the bureaucratic framework. The major factor in this delicate balance is, of course, the King and the Saudi family, which apparently seeks to promote economic development and a measure of social reform while at the same time depending upon the traditional elites for assistance and support.

At this point it is desirable to investigate in some detail the changes in class structure and elite composition which have taken place in Saudi Arabia as a result of the development of the petroleum industry and its immense revenues.

Prior to the "age of oil" in the kingdom, one may briefly summarize the characteristics of the traditional society as follows: (1) An "upper class" consisting of the ruler and his extended family, that is, the Āl Sa'ud; the tribal nobility, including such families as the Āl Shaykh, the Sudayri, the Ibn Jiluwi, etc.; the native landlords and landholders in major cities and towns; the high 'ulama; and the military elite. (2) A traditional "middle class" which consisted of the regular civil servants; the small independent businessmen, traders, etc.; and the lower-level Muslim "clerics." And, (3) a "lower class" which consisted of the workers in cities and towns; the nomads (Bedu); and the peasant, small farmers and landless tenants.[14]

The exploitation of oil brought an increasing complexity in Saudi government—at least in terms of organization, and the recognition of the distinctive nature of certain governmental functions and services. One may gain an impression of this process from a brief review of the founding date of various Ministries:

> 1930: Ministry of Foreign Affairs
> 1933: Ministry of Finance
> 1944: Ministry of Defense and Aviation
> 1951: Ministry of the Interior
> 1953: Ministries of Agriculture, Communications, and Education
> 1954: Ministries of Commerce and Industry, Health
> 1960s: Ministries of Information, Labor and Social Affairs
> 1970: Ministry of Justice

One should note the relationship of the founding of certain ministries to other significant dates in the country's recent past, for example, Finance and the Aramco concession, and the spate of ministries founded in the last year or so of King Ibn Sa'ud's life. Although the Council of Ministers, a formal organization established to act in an advisory capacity to Ibn Sa'ud, was created in 1952 with the present King, Faysal, as "president" (i.e., prime minister), this body did not begin to function in any effective manner until 1954; in other words, during Ibn Sa'ud's reign, power was *wholly* retained in his hands. One might also add that the increasing power of the Council during the reign of King Sa'ud (1953-1964) was due to the increasing power of Faysal, and the family's disenchantment with the profligate and ineffectual leadership of Sa'ud.

It is important to note in this connection that the Saudi family, as a collectivity concerned with maintaining its traditional position within the state, has demonstrated on a number of occasions since the death of Ibn Sa'ud that it responds to domestic pressures of various kinds and not solely to those provided by the religious notables. Perhaps the most important examples of this awareness of, and willingness to respond to, domestic situations which could provoke an altered view of the wisdom and value of retaining the Family are the decisions to grant Faysal expanded powers in 1958, and the decision to force King Sa'ud to abdicate in 1964.

Although the process of social and economic development in the Kingdom has accelerated most rapidly within the past two decades, it is nevertheless legitimate to credit the old King, Ibn Sa'ud, with taking the first steps in the direction of change. For example, over the vigorous objections of the 'ulama, he introduced the use of the automobile, modern telecommunications, and the like—that is, some of the twentieth century's technology. In addition, he was (probably painfully) aware that the escalating oil revenues could not conceivably be spent rationally without the assistance of individuals who had training and skills far different from those his "desert kingdom's" rudimentary educational system could provide. It was under his rule, then, that the first Saudis were permitted to study abroad and obtain a secular education; a very small number apparently were permitted to leave in the 1920s. It was, however, the dispatch of Saudi students to Egypt in the 1940s which provided the real breakthrough: heretofore all education had been obtained in schools of the traditional religious type, controlled by the arch-conservative Wahhabi 'ulama. Within a decade after these first students had returned (in the post-war years), the number of Saudis receiving a secular education began to increase rapidly. It was not long before they began to fill many of the new, middle-level civil service jobs which required technical expertise—as engineers, managers, teachers, and similar professional positions.

Some indication of the significance of this trend may be gained from the Government's expenditures on education since Ibn Sa'ud's death. From a budgetary item of roughly 12.5

million Saudi Riyals (SR) ($2.78 million) in 1952-53 for some 40,000 students in primary and secondary schools, educational expenditures had risen to nearly SR 665 million ($148 million) in 1970 for nearly one-half million students at all educational levels, up to and including college and university level institutions.[15]

Even here, however, one may note the dependence of the Saudis on foreigners. The Government's own statistics indicate that out of a total of 22,346 teachers at the primary and secondary level, 12,745 are of foreign origin—in 1970, these were primarily Jordanians, Palestinians, and Syrians.[16] Other sources indicate that the budgetary allocations to education have continued to increase at this astounding rate, necessitating even more imported teachers; it has been reported that in 1972 alone, Saudi Arabia recruited an additional 25,000 Egyptian teachers.[17] While the actual figure may be exaggerated, it is an indication, nevertheless, both of the détente bewteen the two countries (in 1970, Egyptians were only sixth in the list of Arab countries providing teachers), and of the continued dependence on the expertise of others for maintaining the social and economic development programs. Interestingly, Saudis outnumber foreigners as teachers only in the primary schools and in the so-called Religious Institutes; even the Colleges of Islamic Law, Arabic Language, and the Islamic University of Medina have more foreigners than Saudis on their staffs.[18]

In Saudi Arabia, then, as in other nations of the Middle East, we may document the growth of new classes and elites, perhaps the most important of which is what Manfred Halpern has called "the new middle class," the professionals: managers, technicians of various sorts, higher clerks, lawyers, scientists, teachers of secular subjects, etc. This "class" is distinguished from the older, traditional middle class by its reliance upon secular, non-traditional knowledge, and its expectation that it will obtain positions within societal structures on the basis of personal qualifications and expertise, rather than familial connections, influence, and traditional Islamic scholarship and achievement.

In the still overwhelmingly traditional governmental structure which existed in the 1950s, however, these secularly educated Saudis were only able to achieve middle-lower positions within those ministries which clearly had responsibilities in the modern sector, for example, Commerce, Health, and Communications.

The traditional upper class retained control of the upper echelons. It was in the 1960s that the first breakthroughs into the higher levels of government took place. In 1960, five ministerial positions were assigned to secularly educated commoners, four of whom were graduates of Cairo University. Perhaps the most significant step of all was the decision to assign the newly-created Ministry of Petroleum and Mineral Resources to an American-educated Najdi townsman, Abdullah Tariki.

Although the royal family continued to retain the key control agencies of government in its own hands, for instance, Foreign Affairs, Defense, Interior, Finance, and the National Guard, and for the sake of balance and in recognition of the continued power of the 'ulama assigned the Ministries of Education, Pilgrimage and Awqaf, and Justice to members of the traditional elite, the increasing influence and numbers of the secularly educated Saudis swelled from a trickle to a stream. By the early 1970s, as the following tables show, their influence had reached remarkable proportions when compared with just two decades earlier. As is perhaps obvious, however, their expertise was most in demand in those administrative structures which dealt with aspects of the society and the economy which could not reasonably employ members of the traditional elite in responsible management positions, though ultimate ministerial control might still be retained in the hands of the royal family or its immediate traditional allies (i.e., the Āl Shaykh in the administration of *shari'a* justice, though by 1970 even this had begun to change.)

Table III provides a brief summary of the educational background of upper-level Saudi civil servants in 1969.

Similarly, the following table (see Table IV) provides an indication of how important secular education has become in recent years: of 44 high-level Saudi officials in 1972, nearly 65 percent had a B.A. or above. Note also that there remain only two ministries, Defense and Justice, where secularly educated Saudis have not been assigned at least the position of Deputy Minister.

In other words, it is possible to document the rise and increasing influence of what has been called a "new middle class" among whom are to be found the predominance of rationalist, universalist and secular value systems. On the other

TABLE III Educational Background of Top Saudi Civil Servants, 1969

Ministry	Education of Ministers	Grades 2 and Higher				
		Western	Secular Arab	Traditional	Total Top Employees	Cadre Employees
Petroleum	Western	13	3	0	17	525
Agriculture	Western and Secular Arab	5	12	0	14	3,750
Education	Secular Arab	7	24	13	41	34,650
Labor	Secular Arab	0	4	7	12	2,010
Finance	Secular Arab	5	16	0	25	1,530
Information	Secular Arab	0	10	0	11	1,160
Commerce	Western and Secular Arab	9	22	2	25	490
Communications	Traditional	6	20	4	24	6,050
Pilgrimage	Traditional	0	0	5	5	670
TOTALS:		45	111	31	189	50,835

SOURCE: William Rugh, "Emergence of a New Middle Class in Saudi Arabia," *Middle East Journal* 27,1 (Winter 1973): 13.

hand, one cannot yet point in Saudi Arabia to the beginnings of a political system dominated by mass participation, populist ideologies, much less the prominent role which a modernized and rationalist military structure is often expected to play in the "drive for modernization."

There is an especially interesting anomaly: although trained and equipped by the major Western powers—primarily the United States and Great Britain—the regular armed forces of Saudi Arabia have not so far demonstrated any viable opposition to the Government. While it has been alleged that there was a plot against the regime in 1969, the treatment of the alleged participants (including the release of all 150 persons in November

TABLE IV Educational Background, Top Saudi Officials, 1972

Ministries	Minister	Deputy Ministers:
Interior	Saudi Family	Saudi Family
Defense	Saudi Family	Saudi Family
Finance	Saudi Family	BA (Cairo)
Pilgrimage	Saudi Family	BA (Cairo)
Foreign Affairs	Traditional*	BA (USA)
Education	Traditional	BA (USA)*
Communications	Traditional	BA (USA)
Justice	Traditional	Traditional
Commerce	BA (Cairo)	MA (USA)
Health	BA (Cairo)	DDS (Cairo)
Labor	BA (Cairo)	MA (USA)
Information	BA (Cairo)	BA (USA)*
Petroleum	MA (USA)	BA (USA)*
Agriculture	MA (USA)	MA (USA)

Major Agencies (Directors are Ministers of State and on Council of Ministers)		
National Guard	Traditional*	Traditional*
Central Planning Organization	MA (USA)	PhD (USA)
Petromin	PhD (USA)	BA (UK)*
General Personnel Bureau	MA (USA)	BA (USA)
Investigations Bureau	BA (Cairo)	MA (Cairo)

Major Governorates		
Mecca	Saudi Family	BA (USA)*
Riyadh	Saudi Family	BA (USA)*
Medina	Saudi Family	
Eastern Prov.	Saudi Family	

*Members of the Saudi Family listed by educational background

SOURCE: William Rugh, "Emergence of a New Middle Class in Saudi Arabia," *Middle East Journal* 27, 1 (Winter 1973): 16.

1972) has been widely interpreted as indicating that further investigations showed the original charges to have been exaggerated, and that in fact the regime does not feel threatened by its military establishment. In part, this attitude on the part of the government may be explained by the continued existence of the National Guard (the so-called "White Army"), a force of some 20,000 tribal levies which are, in effect, the King's own personal army and whose manpower resources (though not its equipment) are approximately equal to those of the regular Army and Air Force.[19] Again, in part, it might be suggested that the perquisites, training, and equipment of the regular forces have been continually updated, consequently providing no grounds for complaint along these lines. For example, though Saudi Arabia has not participated in any major foreign conflict directly since its formation, its expenditures on the military both in absolute terms (dollar equivalents) and as a percent of gross national product (GNP) have consistently been among the highest in the Middle Eastern area; only Egypt, Israel, and Jordan have maintained levels as high as those of Saudi Arabia.[20]

The remoteness of a possible revolutionary military uprising in Saudi Arabia is well summarized in the following words:

> Saudi Arabia ... is ill-adapted to revolutionary coups .... With a population less than half the size of London's scattered over an area as big as Western Europe, a successful coup would be difficult to accomplish even with an efficient central administration to direct it and a large and coherent army to enforce it. Saudi Arabia, in spite of its recent changes, has neither. Its civil power is still split into thirds, between the royal seat in Riyadh, the Foreign Ministry, diplomatic missions and commercial houses in Jeddah, and the vital oilfields in Dhahran.[21]

It was suggested earlier that perhaps the most accurate of the accepted typologies into which one may place Saudi Arabia is that of "the modernizing autocracy," a state where traditional values are not destroyed, but are instead, modified and extended. Typically, such a state is "bureaucratic," and traditional and bureaucratic loyalties coincide. There is, as should be evident at this point, some difficulty in arguing that the Saudi system is "bureaucratic" in the accepted definition of that term, though visitors to that country may be excused for making a point of how difficult it is to get the "dropsical (Saudi) bureaucracy, staffed by nepotism and Parkinson's Law, and graced with as many niceties of style and rank as the civil service of Whitehall or Washington" to *do* anything.[22]

It is essential to remember, for example, that it was as a result of the impetus of the development of the petroleum industry and the vast revenues which it provided that change came to Saudi Arabia, and *not* as a result of a direct colonial experience or heritage. Moreover, there was a conscious decision by the ruling Saudi elite to undertake the programs of economic and social reform which have altered, albeit surprisingly slowly, the relationship between the traditional elites and the "modernized" and "modernizing" elites.

This, in essence, is the contradiction of Saudi Arabia today. It has not been the intellectuals, the military, and the bureacracy which have provided the inducements and impetus for change; it has been a highly traditional, tribally-oriented, patriarchal Muslim elite which, despite an occasional seeming threat (e.g., the alleged military plot of 1969) has managed to retain almost completely undiminished control over the progress and process of change.

Saudi Arabia remains one of the most conservative and religious nations in the world—in fact, an anomaly. It remains just as difficult for an urban Lebanese, Egyptian, or Syrian, for example, as for a North American or Western European to conceive of the immense influence which the Wahhabi religious authorities—the 'ulama and its traditional allies and supporters—still retain in nearly all aspects of Saudi life. The 'ulama's "advice and consent" is still required for policy changes in such diverse areas as mass communications, education, justice, and social policy and practices (i.e., the barely diminished power of the Public Morality Committees—the "religious police") to mention some of the more important matters.

Ultimately, the final analysis of Saudi society and government, as well as of the relative position of such different elites as the royal family, the modernized military structure (as well as the National Guard), the professional middle class, the new economic elite, the small group of intellectuals in the Western sense (journalists, professors, etc.), and the many other types of elites that may be identified, depends eventually upon the individual's starting point. For those observers of Saudi Arabia's development since the death of

Ibn Sa'ud, there is substantial respect for the real as well as potentially real changes which King Faysal has brought into being since his accession to power less than a decade ago.[23]

For others, who have only recently begun to investigate the Saudi experience, the most frequent reaction is likely to be disbelief—that Saudi Arabia with its immense oil revenues has not undergone the experience of its regional cohorts. In fact, predictions of major social upheavals for Saudi Arabia have been made with astronomical frequency. The inaccuracy of these predictions has only recently led to a more concerted effort to investigate the bases for the continuity which patently exists, rather than assuming with facile ease that revolution must come eventually.

This is not to suggest, of course, that further changes will not or cannot occur—in the political, as well as the economic and social arenas. They will, and for many, they will be "revolutionary" in the broadest sense of that word. For the moment, however, it is necessary to account for the present. One may suggest, for example, that the basically conservative Saudi elite—whether traditionally or Western-educated—possesses an unusual (though probably not unique) combination of advantages. While able to count upon the traditional supports of religion and custom, it also has the incalculable benefit of nearly inexhaustible financial resources.

It is this particular combination which appears to have produced a domestic policy (consciously or unconsciously) which will result in precisely the kind of unified state which Western experience has usually relegated to a different phase of the process of modernization. An immense investment in an educational and economic infrastructure is being developed at a time when previously undreamed-of wealth seems to have produced a common interest in ensuring that this wealth remains within the current "community." As the previous history of central Arabia amply demonstrates, there are few "natural" reasons why such disparate regions as the Hijaz, the Najd, the Eastern Province, and Asir should constitute a unity. But the resources which have become available to the whole provide a clear and immediate means and motive for avoiding the fragmentation into the older component parts which might leave some of these parts without sufficient resources for their own development or an increased standard of living. Without the dynastic foundation, associated with the older and historically more significant customary and Islamic bases of authority, precisely such a fragmentation would be likely to occur.

It is, for example, of more than passing significance that the East-ern Province—the site of the petroleum deposits—remains in the hands of the Ibn Jiluwi, a powerful traditional elite related to the Saudis by countless marriages and shared historical experience.

In other words, it is probably neither possible nor legitimate to separate the continued dominance of the traditional and Islamic elites in Saudi Arabia from their continued control over what appear to be the world's largest petroleum reserves and the immense revenues which current production provides. Recent estimates of the rate at which Saudi Arabia is accumulating reserves (over $750 million per month in 1974), and of revenues from pro-duction by the end of the decade ($35 to 50 billion per annum), seem to imply that many if not all of the factors mentioned above as accounting for the surprising strength of the Saudi family's control over the pace of development will continue to operate.

It is therefore logical to conclude, perhaps not so surprisingly, that the theories and analyses of other writers with respect to the ability of royal families to substantially maintain their position in developing states must be supplemented by more far-reaching studies of the financial resources available, as well as the complex pattern of symbiotic relationships and alliances which have developed over time between the ruling dynasty and the rural and urban elites—both traditional and modern.[24]

THE PERIPHERAL STATES

The other political entities on the Peninsula are often collec-tively termed the "peripheral states," both because of their geographical locations, and because they are peripheral to Saudi Arabia in terms of their economic and political influence. In some respects, these states were nothing more than a commen-tary on developments in Saudi Arabia during the first half of the twentieth century; the relentless search for oil since World War II has recently produced some significant differences among them. As a group, they now provide some illuminating contrasts with Saudi Arabia, as well as highlighting some of the generaliza-tions made above. A brief survey of some important character-istics is provided in Table V.

The most important factor in changing the status of these states from insignificant principalities to political entities capable of wielding influence in the modern world has been the search

TABLE V The Peripheral States of the Arabian Peninsula

Country	Population (Est.)	Government (Family)	Oil/Production 1972
Yemen (San'a)	5.5 million	Republic since 1962	None
South Yemen (Aden)	1.3 million	Republic since 1967	None[1]
Kuwait	800,000	Traditional (Sabah)	Since 1949 (167.1 mmt)[2]
Oman	650,000	Traditional (Bu Sa'id)	Since 1967 (13.6 mmt)
Bahrain	225,000	Traditional (al-Khalifa)	Since 1932 (3.5 mmt)
Qatar	100,000	Traditional (al-Thani)	Since 1939 (23.3 mmt)
United Arab Emirates			
(a) Abu Dhabi	80,000	Traditional (Ibn Sultan)	Since 1958 (50.0 mmt)
(b) Dubai	85,000	Traditional (al-Maktum)	Since 1966 (7.5 mmt)
(c) Sharjah	35,000	Traditional (al-Qasimi)	Since 1973
(d) Ras al-Khaimah	28,000	Traditional (al-Qasimi)	None
(e) Fujairah	11,000	Traditional (al-Sharqi)	None
(f) Ajman	6,000	Traditional (Ibn Hamaid)	None
(g) Umm al-Qaiwain	5,000	Traditional (al-Ma'alla)	None

1) South Yemen, however, has income from the British Petroleum Refinery at Little Aden.

2) MMT = million metric tons

SOURCES: Production figures for 1972 are from *Arab Report and Record 1973* p. 196.
Population figures have been compiled and projected from a number of different sources; in all instances they are estimates wince most nations have not had a recent census which would provide an accurate picture of current conditions. For actual data, consult the *Statistical Abstract of Kuwait*, the *Handbook of Bahrain*, and the *Trucial States Development Office Census* of 1968.

for, and the discovery of, commercially exploitable petroleum deposits. For purposes of comparison, it should be noted that Abu Dhabi's oil exports in 1973 were expected to produce revenue in excess of $500 million (for a population of 80,000+).

All but two of these states are governed by a traditional ruling family; that is, a specific family which is associated with one of the status-elite tribes or confederations of the Peninsula, and has acquired (within the last two centuries) that dominant position within a relatively small community that previously engaged primarily in commercial activities (Kuwait, Bahrain, Qatar). During that time, it slowly arrogated to itself the title and powers associated with the Western concept of monarchy. None of these families (with the exception of the Sultan of Muscat in 1868–1873) had or have any claim to leadership of a particular sect of Islam.[25] They, therefore, lack the formidable association with religious authority which characterizes the House of Sa'ud. In all but one of these states, religious leaders and scholars tend to be under the influence or control of the rulers. Only in Qatar, where both the family and the population are adherents of Wahhabi Islam, is there any ideological/religious bond between the rulers and their people.

In general, the governments/families of these states represent a traditional Muslim Arab political system, wherein the ruling family's modus operandi varies from that of a collective government taking oligarchic decisions on all matters of state (Bahrain, Qatar, Kuwait), to that of a single individual autocrat with little or no interest in consultation with other members of the family, much less with other traditional elements in the power constellation: wealthy merchant families, major landholding families, the shaikhs of powerful local tribes (Abu Dhabi, Oman). As a result of their origins and path to power, some of these families regarded their embryonic state as their private domain, particularly in matters which fall outside the scope of customary law and rights, for example, mineral resources. This in turn, explains why the first reactions and policies of some of these families to the new wealth was outrageous profligacy and little concern for the public interest. Indeed, limited though Great Britain's domestic influence was in these principalities, it took great persuasion to convince some rulers at the outset to arrogate only one-third of the oil revenues to the expenses of the ruling family.

All of the states which have become oil exporters have found it necessary to permit large numbers of foreigners to take up residence in the country. As in Saudi Arabia, many of these immigrants are skilled personnel who perform vital functions in the administrative and economic arenas for the governments, the oil companies, and the myriad new commercial activities (banking, insurance, transportation, export-import, etc.) which have sprung up as a result of the oil boom. In all but one of the Gulf states the indigenous Arab population is now outnumbered by those foreign immigrants—whether as skilled, semiskilled, or unskilled labor. Overwhelmingly, these are Arabs from nearby countries (e.g. Saudi Arabia, Jordan) and Iranians, Baluchis, Pakistanis, and Indians. Foreigners do not outnumber the local population only in Bahrain where according to the 1965 Census, 79 percent of the population was of Bahraini origin. This exception can be easily explained by the fact that (1) Bahrain's production and reserves do not even remotely approach those of the others, and (2) Bahrain has had extensive educational and social development programs since the 1930s, thus allowing it to develop an indigenous educated elite capable of performing nearly all of the tasks which in the other states require foreign expertise and assistance.

In general, there is simply no place for these foreigners in the traditional pattern of social and political relationships which exist in these societies. The common attitude of the rulers has been that even foreigners of longstanding residence who have contributed significantly to the development of these states and their ruling families (e.g. H.St.J. Philby, Charles Belgrave), not to mention merchant families of foreign Arab origins, have no claims on the family or the state. Rather, they owe a debt for the privilege of residence and the opportunity for earning a livelihood.[26] Recent immigrants seem to represent the greatest threat because of their tendency to propagate modern ideas and ideologies, leading in turn to more modern views of political and economic organization and action which is seen as a potential threat against the continued domination of the state by the ruling family.

On the other hand, the experience of some of these countries suggests that the foreign element, especially when it comes from more modernized and politically sophisticated societies, frequently displays an "air of superiority" or condescension toward the original inhabitants, who then regard the immigrants with suspicion and as aliens. As a result, the foreigners frequently act as a catalyst in the development of a form of local patriotism or nationalist sentiment centered on the present ruling family. At the same time, they serve as ready scapegoats against whom grievances against the government and the family may be diverted.

The peripheral states, then, highlight the significance of extensive oil revenues in permitting traditional elites to remain in power. The two states with a republican form of government are the only ones with no current oil production and little, if any, chance of becoming major producers; they are also the states with the lowest GDP and per capita income.[27] The capacity of the states with extensive oil revenues to meet the *material* demands by their populations appears to be almost unlimited, and it would appear that they, like Saudi Arabia, may be able to create a "public" with a stake in the existing political community and even the current regime. Their authority will inevitably diminish as modern ideologies gain ground, but with the oil revenues and the ability to meet demands, it would appear that many, if not all, may be able to retain their position long enough to lay the foundations for constitutional, limited monarchy with the traditional family in that new role.

This assumes, of course, that their domestic policies for the spending of the oil revenues are reasonable, and that they develop the educational, social, and economic infrastructure which will permit them to satisfy current and expanding demands from their populations while at the same time, providing appropriate employment for those citizens who have become members of the "new middle class," as well as preparing them for greater political participation at some point in the (not-too-distant) future.

It is, then, of considerable significance that two of these Gulf states—Kuwait and Bahrain—have already laid the foundations for precisely such constitutional, limited monarchy which includes some form of popular representation in decision-making: Kuwait's Constitution was promulgated in 1962, and Bahrain's in June of 1973. This development is due to the fact that: (1) the ruling families had secular origins in trading communities; (2) these countries had more intensive rapid economic development and modernization due to their far smaller size; that is, the burgeoning oil revenues in such small communities had an immediate and far-reaching effect; and, (3) the development of a sense of "community" which centered on the ruling family was at least, in part, nurtured by the presence of large numbers of foreigners and/or an occasional foreign threat.

As a result, for the first time in the Arabian Peninsula outside the republican regimes, we find a traditional elite that has begun to more-or-less voluntarily "open up" access to the decision-making processes of government to members of the "new middle class" who are *not* members of the traditional elite or its allies and supporters. In fact, the literacy and educational requirements for suffrage promulgated so far practically limit the franchise (and eligibility for public office) to members of the "new middle class." What the long-term effects of this development will be are, of course, unknown. Current "best evidence" would seem to indicate that the traditional elite, at least in these two countries and perhaps Qatar and Dubai in the near future, have made it over the first and most important hurdle in the transition outlined above.[28]

NOTES

1. The significance of this distinction is, today, largely restricted to the tribes, who retain immensely complex status differentiations among themselves. It is, however, possible, that changed circumstances might occasion the more widespread reintroduction of such differences, as occurred in Yemen in the late 1950s and early 1960s. See M. W. Wenner, *Modern Yemen 1918-1966* (Baltimore: Johns Hopkins, 1967), p. 128.

2. H. St. John Philby, *Arabia* (New York: Charles Scribner's Sons, 1930), provides the best summary of this material.

3. George Lenczowski, Seminar on Middle Eastern Politics, University of California, Berkeley, 1960.

4. David Apter, "System, Process, and Politics of Economic Development," in *Industrialization and Society*, eds. B. F. Hoselitz and W. E. Moore (The Hague: Mouton, 1963), p. 139-140.

5. There is no agreement on the population of Saudi Arabia. The Government's Statistical Abstract carries no population figures whatever, since no official census has ever been undertaken. Since the mid-1960s, Saudi and non-Saudi estimates have generally ranged between 6 and 8 million.

6. For the history of the concessions and the development of Aramco, see: *Aramco Handbook* (Joh. Eschede, 1968; revised edition).

7. Kingdom of Saudi Arabia, *Statistical Yearbook* (Dammam, 1970), p. 209.

8. U.S. Department of the Army, *Area Handbook for Saudi Arabia*. (Prepared by the American University Foreign Area Studies, and published

by the Government Printing Office, 1966), p. 259.

9. U.S. Department of the Army, *Area Handbook for Saudi Arabia*, revised edition (1970), p. vii.

10. Robert Graham, "From Slumber to Riches: An Arabian Dream," *New Middle East* (January-February 1973): 16.

11. James Bill, "Class Analysis and the Dialectics of Modernization in the Middle East," *International Journal of Middle East Studies* 3, 4 (October 1972): 427-434.

12. Manfred Halpern, *The Politics of Social Change in the Middle East and North Africa* (Princeton University Press, 1963), Chapter 4.

13. Graham, "From Slumber to Riches," p. 17.

14. Bill, "Class Analysis and the Dialectics of Modernization."

15. Kingdom of Saudi Arabia, *The Story of Education* (Ministry of Information, 1971), p. 8-13.

16. *Ibid.*, and *Statistical Yearbook*, p. 41-77.

17. Graham, "From Slumber to Riches, " p. 18.

18. *Statistical Yearbook*, p. 41-77.

19. It should be noted that White Army leaders derive their power from their position as tribal leaders with access to the government (the Royal family) rather than from their position as officers within the White Army. George Lipsky, ed., *Saudi Arabia* (Human Relations Area Files Press, 1959), p. 102. On the military, see also *Area Handbook for Saudi Arabia.*

20. International Institute for Strategic Studies, *The Military Balance 1971-1972* (London, 1971), p. 61 and 31; and, United States Arms Control and Disarmament Agency, *World Military Expenditures (U.S.G.P.O., 1972)*, p. 22-23.

21. David Holden, *Farewell to Arabia* (Faber & Faber, 1966), p. 138.

22. Ibid., p. 122.

23. "Potentially real" refers to the immense number and variety of regulations and decrees which have been promulgated but not always implemented during the past decade in an effort to reform governmental arrangements, establish clearer lines of responsibility, promote the use of objective information in decision-making, and last but not least, set the stage for accommodations between the traditional Islamic bases of governance and the modern legal, social, and political problems which have been recognized.

24. See the immensely valuable work by John Waterbury, *The Commander of the Faithful* (Columbia University Press, 1970), p. 81-128 for an analysis of these relationships for Morocco. There are more than a few similarities to the relationships which exist in Saudi Arabia, though the latter does not have the extensive ties to the urban economic elite which Morocco exhibits.

25. The interior regions of the former state of Muscat and Oman have until recently been considered "Oman," whereas the coastal regions, governed by the Bu Sa'id Sultans, has been considered "Muscat." The interior is the domain of the Ibadi tribes, who have their own *Imam.* However, since these imams are not internationally recognized as the governors of a political entity, the generalization remains valid.

26. One exception to this generalization has been Shaikh Rashid ibn Sa'id of Dubai, who though an autocrat, was raised in the merchant community, and as a result is sympathetic to their interests, as well as conscious of the dependence of the "state" upon them and their activities. See: Frank Stoakes, "Social and Political Change in the Third World: Some Peculiarities of Oil-Producing Principalities of the Persian Gulf," in Derek Hopwood, ed., *The Arabian Peninsula* (London: Rowman and Littlefield, 1972). This is a valuable recent work on the whole Peninsula.

27. It is tempting to add that of all the states in the Peninsula, South Yemen has the greatest demographic problems as well as the fewest resources, and that for this reason it has experimented with the most thorough-going attempt at radical government in the Arab World. Yemen, on the other hand, with the greatest agricultural potential, and good prospects for commercially exploitable natural resources other than oil, ended its eight-year civil war in a compromise, a more pragmatic attempt at social reconstruction, and following less radical policies.

28. For additional information, the reader is urged to consult the *Area Handbook for the Peripheral States of the Arabian Peninsula* (Washington, D.C.: U.S.G.P.O., 1971). Prepared by Foreign Area Studies of American University and Stanford Research Institute, it is the best single compilation of recent information on these states.

BIBLIOGRAPHY

Arabian American Oil Company. *Aramco Handbook.* Edited by George Rentz. (Haarlem, Netherlands: John. Eschedé, 1968)

El-Mallakh, Ragei. *Economic Development and Regional Cooperation: Kuwait.* (Chicago: University of Chicago Press, 1968)

Holden, David. *Farewell to Arabia.* (London: Faber and Faber, 1966)

Hopwood, Derek, ed. *The Arabian Peninsula.* (London: Rowman and Littlefield, 1972)

Kelly, J. B. *Sultanate and Imamate in Oman.* (London: Oxford University Press, 1959)

Landen, Robert G. *Oman Since 1856.* (Princeton: Princeton University Press, 1967)

Lipsky, George. *Saudi Arabia.* (New Haven: HRAF Press, 1959)

Little, Tom. *South Arabia; Arena of Conflict* (New York: Praeger, Inc., 1968)

Longrigg, Stephen H. *Oil in the Middle East* (rev. ed.) (London: Oxford University Press, 1968)

Marlowe, John. *The Persian Gulf in the 20th Century.* (New York: Praeger, Inc., 1962)

Philby, H. St. J. *Arabia.* (New York: Charles Scribner's Sons, 1930)

——————. *Saudi Arabia.* (London: Geoffrey Benn, Ltd., 1955)

Sanger, Richard. *The Arabian Peninsula.* (Ithaca: Cornell University Press, 1954)

Twitchell, Karl S. *Saudi Arabia.* (rev. ed.) (Princeton: Princeton University Press, 1958)

United States. Department of the Army. *Area Handbook for Saudi Arabia.* (Washington, D.C.: U.S.G.P.O., 1971)

——————. *Area Handbook for the Peripheral States of the Arabian Peninsula.* (Washington, D.C.: U.S.G.P.O., 1971)

Wenner, Manfred W. *Modern Yemen.* (Baltimore: Johns Hopkins Press, 1967)

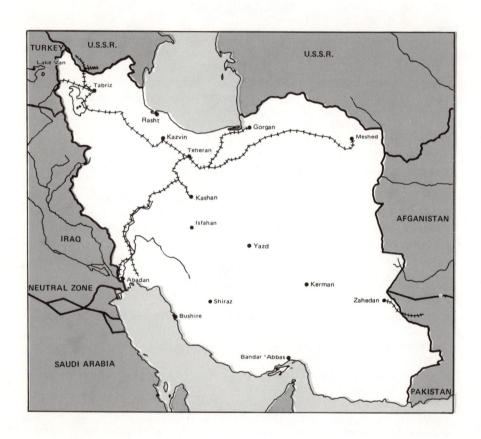

5

The Political
Elite of Iran:
A Second Stratum?

Marvin Zonis

In late 1970, an official of Iran's secret police, the State Security and Intelligence Organization (SAVAK), held a press conference in which he announced details of an alleged plot to overthrow the regime. The leader of the plot was said to be the late General Teimour Bakhtiar, formerly head of SAVAK, who had been "accidentally killed on a hunting trip" in Iraq while in the company of some Iranian visitors during the previous summer. The security official went on to describe a series of aborted operations which had been planned by the plotters to produce chaos and lead to the overthrow of the Shah. One aspect of their plans was to assassinate some 27 Iranians. The official went on to list those intended victims:

> 1. Amir Abbas Hoveyda, the Prime Minister
> 2. Ardeshir Zahedi, then Minister of Foreign Affairs, and the ex-son-in-law of the King
> 3. General Fereidun Jam, Chief of Staff of the Imperial Iranian Armed Forces
> 4. Lieutenant General Namatollah Nasiri, Director General, State Security and Intelligence Organization
> 5. General Mohammad Khatami, Commander in Chief, Imperial Iranian Air Force and a brother-in-law of the King
> 6. Assadollah Alam, Minister of the Imperial Court and a boyhood playmate of the King
> 7. General Fatollah Minbashian, Commander in Chief, Imperial Iranian Army

8. Major General Hossein Fardust, Director of the Shah's Private Intelligence Bureau and a boyhood playmate of the King

9. General Gholam Ali Oveissi, Commander in Chief, Imperial Gendarmerie

10. Major General Farssiu, Chief Military Prosecutor, actually assassinated by urban guerrillas in Tehran

11. Brigadier General Moqaddam, Deputy Director, SAVAK

12. Lieutenant General Mohsen Mobasser, Commander in Chief, National Police Forces

13. Dr. Manuchehr Eqbal, Chairman of the Board and Managing Director, National Iranian Oil Company

14. Major General Mohsen Hashemi Nejad, Commander of the Imperial Guard

15. Major General Palizba, Director, Military Intelligence

16. Major General Reza Azimi, Minister of War

17. Major General Fazlollah Homayuni, Member, Armed Forces Chief of Staff

18. Abdollah Riazi, Speaker of the Majles, the Lower House of the Iranian Parliament

19. Javad Mansur, Minister of Information

20. Parviz Khonsari, Undersecretary of the Ministry of Foreign Affairs

21. Hushang Ansary, Minister of Economy

22. Ezzatollah Yazdanpanah, Secretary General of the Iran Novin Party

23. Dr. Ayadi, personal physician to the Shah

24. Dr. Jahanshah Saleh, Senator and physician to the Royal Family

25. Rezazadeh Shafaq, Senator

26. Prof. Yahya Adl, Secretary General, Mardom Party

27. Dr. Hassan Emami, Iman Jom'eh of Tehran, the regime's "official" clergyman

The list of names was read and the press conference held because SAVAK had successfully crushed any threat to the regime and rounded up all the alleged ringleaders and participants. Whether or not the list was the creation of the security officials or was in fact found in the possession of the plotters, the list is fascinating for revealing a rather accurate assessment of the distribution of power within the society. Certainly, these are the effective and responsible wielders of power in Iran, with few notable exceptions. The most glaring exception, of course, is that of His Imperial Majesty, Mohammad Reza Shah Pahlavi, *Aryamehr*, the King of Iran, who, as ought to be clear from his impressive list of titles, is the ruler of the nation. His wife, Empress Farah, and other members of the royal family are other notable omissions. That such names are absent from the list is not to be taken as a sign of devotion on the part of the plotters but rather to the longstanding regulations which forbid any derogatory or threatening public mention of members of the royal family. But the Shah is clearly the "pivot" around whom the entire system of power and privilege in Iran revolves.[1] (In fact, the title "Pivot of the Universe" was one of the many laudatory titles of which Iranian monarchs would boast in the nineteenth century and the imagery of the sun was a metaphor frequently used to characterize the ruler and his court.)[2] There may be no metaphor other than the sun which more aptly characterizes the place of the Shah in the political system. It is by the grace of the Shah that individuals are accorded elite status through positions or activities he designates or tolerates, and wealth, whose acquisition or retention he encourages or condones. His power is in all significant respects unchallenged by the politically powerful in Iran.

In such circumstances, in fact, one may question the utility of elite studies at all. Given the concentration of power in the hands of the Shah, can elite analysis provide an understanding of politics in Iran? Or a prior question, given the distribution of power, to what extent is the Iranian political system characterized by "politics" at all? To the extent that politics is concerned with competition to acquire power for the purpose of instituting policy, politics does not, in fact, exist in Iran, for policy is set by the monarch. There are three over-arching pillars of his policy; pillars which set the boundaries for day-to-day decisions. First, preserving and strengthening his own power and that of his family is the basic criterion against which all policy is judged. Second, the Shah seeks to assure survival for the institution of the monarchy. Third, the Shah seeks to build the power of the Iranian state. Below this trinity against which all other policies must be judged is the Shah's "White Revolution" as he has labelled his reform program.[3] Originally instituted in 1963, the then six-point plan was meant to bring an end to the political disorder of 1960-1962. The plan called for land reform, nationalization of forests, the sale of shares in government-owned factories, suffrage for women, a profit sharing scheme for workers, and the creation of a Literacy Corps, whereby army draftees would serve as teachers in rural areas. The reform plan was submitted to the nation for approval, the Iranian parliament having been abrogated by the Shah. The referendum "returned" a vote of 5,589,710 in favor of the six-point plan with only 4,115 opposed! Subsequently, more programs were added to the "White Revolution"—the creation of three additional groups to work in rural areas, the Health Corps, the Extension and Developmental Corps, and Houses of Justice to settle disputes; also, the nationalization of all water resources, the "reconstruction of the country," a general development program, and an administrative and educational revolution. (These latter points were not put directly to the people for approval. The *Majles* or parliament had by then been elected and it approved each of the programs.)

That these programs constitute a "revolution from above" is argued by only the most ardent devotees of the monarch. But clearly they and the three pillars which constitute the Shah's basic interest do establish the range of permissible policy.

Not only does the monarch establish the policy which sets boundaries on decision-making for government officials, he also makes a phenomenal number of decisions regarding the day-to-day operations of the government—passing on appointments at relatively low levels of the civil and military bureaucracies, building new roads, expanding the universities, constructing factories, altering export subsidies, selling particular land owners' fields to their cultivators.[4] Given the domination of the Shah in both policy and decision-making, what then can be learned by studying the political elite? Can there be politics without basic competition over policy?

In fact, there is much that can be learned from such a study. The political elite of Iran can be thought of as the "second stratum" of the ruling class,[5] whereas the Shah himself plays a role equivalent to the political elite in other societies. The Iranian second stratum is located structurally between the Shah and the non-elite. They translate the Shah's policies and decisions into action. In the process, they do make many decisions which reflect their own wishes, at least to the extent that those are not in direct contradiction to those of the monarch. Moreover, they compete for positions within the Imperial Court, the Cabinet, the lower and upper houses of Parliament (the Majles and Senate), the civil bureaucracies, and the Armed Forces in order to acquire power. With that power comes material reward, status, control over the destinies of others, and the opportunity to play a role in the unfolding history of Iran. Politics, the process of competition for power and the results of that competition, then, do exist in Iran. But they exist within the political framework as established and constantly altered by the Shah and no opposition to that framework, nor reservations to it, nor suggestions for its change are tolerated.

One result of the very tightly regulated milieu in which Iranian political actors must operate is their frequently noted cynicism. When political competition is primarily oriented towards acquisition of the "spoils" of politics, much of the substance of political life is lost. The combination of this aspect of political competition with a steady burgeoning of oil revenues has produced an ethos of economic boom comparable to American stereotypes of a gold rush, with all the resultant extravagance, exploitation, and "carpetbagging."

The Iranian second stratum, or more conventionally, the group we shall continue to refer to as the "political elite," are crucial, and the list of twenty-seven names given out by SAVAK is a fascinating introduction to them. (Certainly the list does not contain the names of all Iranians who might be counted in the "second stratum." Any such listing of the politically powerful would be considerably longer than this one. Moreover, the list focuses on those members of the political elite who constitute the security bases of the regime. Nonetheless, the list is a useful heuristic device for organizing the study of the political elite.)

Of the 27 names mentioned, 13 are military figures, indicating the preponderance of the military in Iranian life. In a private audience with the author, the Shah of Iran mentioned that the military are not really an interesting group to study in Iran because "we in Iran have an invariable rule—the complete and unalterable separation of the armed forces from politics." While the military may have no definitive role in the influence of policy, it is certainly true that it is a crucial institution in the state both in terms of the preservation of the regime and in terms of its consumption of immense resources in the fulfillment of that role.

A second fact of political life in Iran revealed by the list is that without exception all of its occupants are members of an official elite. That is, all hold formal positions within the bureaucracies of the Iranian government and all have power for that reason. A particularly good example of this is the Iman Jom'eh of Tehran, which is an officially designated post rather like that of a chaplain for the regime. Clearly, Dr. Emami is politically important because he holds that post and not because he is a celebrated religious leader. It seems, in fact, that his appointment as Imam Jom'eh can be attributed to his relative lack of repute among the public, for as long as his power came from his reputation with the masses of Tehran, rather than solely from his official post, the regime would have less control over his activities. Thus, there are a number of religious leaders widely celebrated by the people who receive no official appointments and whose activities are closely circumscribed by the regime precisely for the reason that their links with the masses make them relatively independent of the regime and, thus, less subject to the wishes of the Shah.[6]

A third observation to make of the list is the relatively few cabinet ministers listed. Despite the constitutional centrality of the cabinet in political life, most important political events occur outside that institution. The civilian individuals on the SAVAK list tend to be the heads of institutions not represented in the cabinet but those with direct links to the Shah. The National Iranian Oil Company, the Royal Court, the political parties, the Houses of Parliament are such institutions. Certainly, a "legalistic" or "constitutional" analysis of the Iranian system of government could produce an organizational chart which showed a hierarchy of institutions and individuals, each responsible and reporting to the next higher level, eventually relating to a cabinet and houses of Parliament and the Shah. But a more apt description of the Iranian system would be that of the sun around which revolve men and organizations mostly in direct contact with the Shah, facilitating his direct control of the administrative apparatus.

The list suggests other facts about the contemporary political elite. For one, they come overwhelmingly from the capital city—21 of the 27 were born in Tehran, a remarkably high percentage considering that after three decades of explosive population growth, Tehran still contains but ten percent of the population of Iran. The fact that the political elite or, more narrowly defined, the second stratum have been born in Tehran reveals several important phenomena of politics in Iran. This is a highly centralized political system. The country is dominated by the capital to an extent greater than virtually any other Middle Eastern society.

The ethnic, racial, and linguistic diversity of Iran is but little represented by the political elite. While reliable figures are difficult to come by, it is estimated that half the population of Iran speaks as a native tongue a language other than Persian.[7] But these minorities tend not to live in Tehran, but rather all along the perimeters of the country. The Tehran-based elite represent the Persian speaking half of the population. This is a matter of concern to the regime because of periodic centrifugal threats to Iran's geographical unity. Hostile foreign countries or indigenous enemies of the regime seek support by attempting to create or mobilize nationalist sentiment among Turkish speaking Iranians in the northwest, Kurds in the west, Arabs in the southwest, and Baluchis in the southeast, bordering Pakistan.

Yet another salient fact of politics in Iran is the extent to which the narrow geographic base of the elite is both a reflection of and a contributor towards the hereditary nature of elite status. Many of the present political elite are sons of former members of the political elite. For a country which has witnessed in the twentieth century major foreign invasions and occupations, a constitutional revolution, a change of dynasties, and nearly successful coups d'etat, the continuity of personnel is very high. However, two processes are altering the hereditary transmission of elite status in Iran. There has been an appreciable expansion in the size of the Government's bureaucracies with the result that the demand for individuals to occupy positions with formally designated political power has been far greater than the number of offspring of the existing elite. Second, the Shah and his second stratum have imposed new standards of recruitment to high office. In an effort to maximize the developmental effectiveness of the bureaucracy and also to increase its legitimacy, standards of formal education have been imposed for appointment. The initial effect of such a criterion was to put the scions of the elite into a more competitive position since they had been largely able to monopolize access to institutions of higher learning. But with the spread of secondary schooling and the opening of the universities of Iran to the children of the middle and lower middle classes, new groups are able to claim formal skills previously restricted to the elite. Given the ideology of the regime for recruitment to positions carrying considerable political power which stresses only skills and loyalty, and with greater demand for personnel, the children of non-elites have found their way in appreciable numbers to the higher reaches of the Iranian bureaucracy in recent years.

Thus, unlike other elites, who have held power across generations or through great political turmoil,[8] the Iranian elite is characterized by high levels of formal education. Among the twenty-seven on the list are thirteen graduates of the Tehran War College, four with B.A. degrees, two with law degrees, four who are M.D.'s while three have Doctorates or Ph.D. degrees. In short, the elite of Iran can be characterized as highly educated men (the recruitment of women being restricted largely to a few basically show parliamentarians). Moreover, as Iran begins the transition to a system dominated by a "skill elite," the children of the present elite remain in a highly advantageous but certainly no longer monopolistic position by dint of their having acquired technical expertise through formal education.[9]

The list also suggests the particular links which members of the elite have to the "sun" of the Iranian system. Two from the list are boyhood friends of the monarch, one is his brother-in-law. Three perform medical services for the king or prominent families. The rest of the list are trusted civil servants most of whom have held a large number of different posts in a variety of bureaucratic organizations, demonstrating thereby the prerequisite for high administrative responsibility—a conclusive demonstration of trustworthiness to support the established distribution of power in Iran, the rules of the game, and the "code" of the regime.

By examining those individuals marked for assassination in the most publicly discussed alleged coup in two decades, we have sought to understand the nature of the contemporary elite. For the twenty-seven intended victims, while somewhat over-representing the security forces of Iran, are essentially typical of that elite. Together with the Shah of Iran, their interactions within the framework of a political culture or code constitute the essence of politics in Iran.

Certain components of the political culture, a stress on the necessity to preserve and strengthen the Pahlavi dynasty, maintain the ideology of the monarchical institution, and build state power, have already been mentioned. In addition, central components of the political culture stem from contemporary inter-national realities. One is the burgeoning demand for oil which has resulted in sharply higher foreign exchange earnings for Iran and the increased importance of the Persian Gulf as the principal route for the export of Middle Eastern oil. A third con-temporary reality is that Iran is the greatest military power in the region, a fact which influences the actions of the Shah and the elite as well as foreign governments towards Iran.

There are, as well, historical phenomena which are important influences on the political elite. One set of these stems from Iran's foreign relations. Since the introduction of European powers as major actors in the contemporary Middle East, beginning with Napoleon's invasion of Egypt in 1798, Iran has never been party to any direct colonial experiences.[10] Unlike most of the Middle East, Iran was never subject to the direct control of a foreign, usually European, power. Again, unlike the Turkish Republic, which constituted the core of the Ottoman Empire, Iran never had the experience of ruling over other lands. This is not to suggest that until relatively recently Iran was free of any involvement with other powers. In fact, in the nineteenth century both Great Britain and Russia had immense influence over the affairs of the Royal Court and at different periods in the twentieth century Great Britain, Russia, Germany and the United States have had immense influence over domestic political affairs. Certainly, the United States must still be con-sidered an important force within Iranian domestic politics. Nonetheless, the influence which these foreign governments have been able to exert is considerably less than and qualitatively different from the situation which prevailed in so much of the Middle East which was subject to a direct colonial experience.

Several important benefits accrue to Iran as a result of her having avoided the status of a colony of a Western power. For one thing, the myth of Iranian independence was perpetuated. In addition to the existing repertoire of beliefs and codes was a notion that Iran is virtually unique given its ability to avoid control by foreign powers. This, after all, was no mean feat. Throughout much of the last two centuries Iran was hemmed in by powerful outside forces. Great Britain has been the dominant colonial power around Iran's frontiers—along the Persian Gulf, in present-day Kuwait and Iraq, and in Pakistan, then part of the British colony of India, and also in Afghanistan, titularly independent, but actually heavily influenced by British policy. To the north, Iran was subject to direct pressures from Russia whose rulers have had a historical interest in control of its southern neighbor. Iran's strength in warding off the attempts of these countries to increase their control and even to physically occupy Iran has contributed to the national feeling of uniqueness. While this sense is a valuable basis for the construction of national unity and the preservation of Iranian nationhood, it serves to hinder Iranian efforts to participate, as an equal, with her neighbors in the Middle East.

A second set of benefits which Iran derived from her avoidance of colonial status was the valuable experience gained in diplomacy and bargaining. Certainly, no one has ever considered the Iranians deficient in this regard, the domination of Iranian cities by a large bazaar section being a symbolic representation of the importance of bargaining in Iranian culture.[11] Two centuries of practice in dealing with unfriendly and more powerful neighbors must be considered most valuable experience for the further development of this aspect of the Iranian genius. It was the considerable skill of Iranian monarchs and politicians which made it possible for her to preserve at least nominal independence through the nineteenth and twentieth centuries while so many other Asian and Middle Eastern societies were falling under Imperial domination. One of the principal means by which Iran avoided that status was to play off one colonial power against the other for as long as possible and then to seek a new player—a third international power—to intervene and "save" it from either of the two if Iran's balancing act began to fail. Thus for much of the nineteenth century Iran played off Great Britain and Russia, turning to Germany as a countervailing force late in the century. With Germany's defeat in World War I and the withdrawal of the Russians from active involvement in Iran following the Bolshevik Revolution, Iran sought to balance Great Britain's influence and interests by acquiring the friendship of the United States. After World War II, and the more active intervention of the Soviet Union in Iranian affairs through their support for the establishment of the so-called "People's" Republics of Mahabad and Azarbaijan, Iran turned once again to the United States for backing and "salvation" from the Soviets. (Or to put it differently, but equally accurately, the regime sought American aid to perpetuate itself from the challenge of Soviet external and indigenous pressures.) Following a period of unparalleled American influence, Iran turned, in the early 1960s, to Russia and Britain as a way of extricating itself from too close and direct involvement with the United States. This itself was an indication of the new self-confidence of the regime, and an accurate appraisal of its power after it had put down, in the first half of 1963, tribal uprisings and major urban rioting with much loss of life.

Considerable advantages have accrued to Iran from having avoided colonial status. Certainly a sense of national pride from that rare achievement is a major contributor to Iranian successes at "nation-building" which have been so startling in the last decade. Nonetheless, it would be a gross misstatement to suggest that only positive results have followed from Iran's success at maintaining at least nominal independence. In fact, Iran has lost much in the process. For one thing, Iran never had direct experience with a "benevolent" administrative structure which could serve as a model for creation of indigenous bureaucracies, nor were there models of individual bureaucrats devoted to the fulfillment of their official duties.

More importantly, perhaps, Iran never gained the experience of having a palpable enemy with tangible symbols of that enemy's control. There was never, then, the rallying point for national aspirations that independence or anti-colonial struggles provided other nations. Myths of national unification or bases of national identity failed to develop. The Iranians did not develop a sense of the concept of Iranian citizenship. Rather, as is the case today, people were considered "subjects" of the monarch. In fact there is no word in the Iranian language for citizenship in the Western sense. The Iranian word used for that concept is tābi'iyat which has as its root the Arabic word meaning "follower" or "dependent." But the notion of "participant," which would have been fostered by an independence struggle, is missing. The political relations with foreign powers in the nineteenth and twentieth centuries fostered instead the notion of a political game occurring among the elites and foreign powers with the vast majority of the population serving as dependent subjects.

An additional factor adversely affecting Iranian politics was the fact that the elite game of politics vis-à-vis foreign powers was highly divisive. There is an Iranian expression which relates to this outcome, an expression which is frequently advanced to explain unexpected political events—*ab zire kah*—"water under the straw." That is, while one sees the barn floor covered with straw, water is flowing continually underneath, so that when the walls of the barn collapse, one need not be surprised. The allusion here is that while Iran managed to avoid a direct colonial situation, a number of foreign powers could boast great influence over domestic events in Iran. There were certainly parts of the country which were always more nearly under the control of foreign powers than under the control of the monarch in Tehran. The British, for example, made annual cash payments to tribal leaders in the southern parts of Iran in order to insure the safety of the British-owned pipeline in that region. The Russians, on the other hand, by dint of their staffing the officer corps of the Iranian-financed Cossack brigade were able to exert major influence on the capital by the operations of that military force. Numerous other examples of foreign penetration of indigenous institutions might be mentioned. But they all lead to one inescapable conclusion. At least to the time of Reza Shah, many of the major indigenous political actors of Iran were beholden to or implicated in advancing the interests of foreign powers.

Clearly, those Iranian political figures did not view themselves as acting contrary to the interests of Iran. It is not necessarily the case that they were so doing, but the results were to give foreign powers a great amount of influence over Iranian events. (Like so many other developments within Iran, it has been argued that one of the principal effects of the reforms of Reza Shah and his son, the present ruler of Iran, Mohammad Reza Shah Pahlavi, has been not to eliminate patterns from earlier Iranian history but to alter their form. That is, foreign powers, it is frequently alleged, still have a great deal of influence in Iranian politics but that influence has been centralized so that it enters the political system only through the apex of the elite hierarchy. No longer do the Soviets or Americans or British work their ways with local officials or lesser notables of Tehran. With the centralization of political power, such influence now enters only at the top. The result, according to the more cynical observers of Iranian politics, is that corruption has been concentrated, moving Iran another step away from democracy.)

But the ab zire kah conception of politics has had several other untoward effects in Iran. One legacy is to contribute to that exaggerated quality of cynicism which has been so widely observed in Iran. Every one and every thing is assumed to be corrupt or, at least, corruptible. The more upstanding an individual appears, the more likely it is that he is at heart corrupt (again, ab zire kah). Not only were all political actors formerly viewed as corrupt, but members of the political elite were viewed as having more loyalty to foreign powers than to their own countrymen. This sentiment was certainly enhanced by the spectacle of members of the political elite striving to curry the favor of foreign nations and in the process creating internal political fragmentation on the basis of Anglophiles versus Russophiles, the pro-Germans versus the pro-French, etc. While the situation certainly differs today, a propensity to see Iranian politics in this way persists and individual members of the political elite are still branded *no kare Inglisi*—servants of the English—or the like.

Yet another effect of the indirect colonialism to which Iran was subject was the notion that events were essentially not controllable. That is, living in that system of indirect colonialism before Reza Shah came into power made it very difficult to know where responsibility for any act was to be found. "Bogeymen" were everywhere since no one was sure who was responsible for the perpetration of any given policy. Somehow, everything could all too easily be explained away by noting that "it's really the British (or the Americans or the Russians, etc.) who are in charge here anyway." Yet, since it was impossible to establish that with any sense of assurance, the Iranians were left with no clear sense of how their own lives were being affected or controlled. With no way to establish responsibility, villains were seen everywhere and a propensity for fatalism and an inclination to act in one's own self-interest irrespective of broader public concerns was reinforced. All these consequences of Iran's having successfully avoided the status of a direct colony can be found to operate in contemporary politics.

Interestingly, it is possible to analyze much of those politics in terms of the colonial analogy. That is, the present distribution of political forces in Iran and resultant policies can be fruitfully understood by retaining analogies derived from studies of colonial exploitation.

In its relations with the villages and cities of Iran, the central government in Tehran and its political and economic elites are in the role of colonizer to colonized. Simultaneously, in its relations with the populace as a whole, the regime and its political elites are also in a relationship of colonizer to colonized. The capital extracts resources, both human and economic—especially oil—from the provinces. It returns manufactured and processed goods for the raw materials it needs. Occasionally, it establishes its own administrative or economic outpost in the provinces for initial processing or a more efficient distribution of its output helping to create a labor force which will serve as the basis for an industrial proletariat.

Tehran's political control is constantly extended over the countryside, its administration strengthened, its gendarmerie expanded, its corpsmen dispatched. The government does provide services—the rebuilding of villages, the construction of streets. But villagers who benefit frequently have to tax themselves to build their schools and the government will never share its power to the extent of allowing the countryside to participate effectively in the making of political or economic decisions. Instead, the power, wealth, and comfort of the center grow at the expense of the periphery which becomes more integrated into the national system all the while losing its distinctiveness. Simultaneously, the periphery, the "colonized," becomes more dependent, more powerless, and more exploited.

The relationship of the political center to the political periphery is similar to the relationship between geographic center and periphery. A variety of examples might be spelled out. The political socialization of the youth of Iran is one. From a great variety of sources, both formal and informal, in both explicit and implicit ways, the youth of Iran are taught that the Shah always knows best and is possessed of superior wisdom. His rule is equated with tutelage and is viewed as beneficent for the people. The transcendent imperative of the society becomes law and order and a willing subjection to the beneficent tutelage of the ruler and his agents. Changes which do occur in the system occur because of the freely given gifts of His Imperial Majesty and not as the result of popular political forces which operate on the ruler—such popular political forces only serving to impede the operation of his beneficence. The principal factor which affects the rate and volume of the gifts which the ruler bestows on his wards, the Iranian people, are his perceptions of their ability to receive them and to utilize them effectively rather than their own opinions of these factors. Finally, democratic government, to be thought of as self-rule, will be granted when the ward is capable of exercising that right, a determination to be made, of course, by the regime.

In the course of the exercise of this tutelage several other factors must follow. For one, all organs of the mass media must be rigidly controlled to reflect the wishes of the ruler and the regime. "Subversive" thoughts are excluded from public dissemination because they may bend the people from their "true course" as determined by the regime. Similarly, independent political institutions are not allowed to exist for the same reasons. The regime sees their only purpose as questioning the basic tenets and doctrines which are used to maintain the distribution of power and to challenge the allocation of resources.

The consequences of politics in Iran, like the process, can also be analyzed in terms of the colonial analogy. Iran is a society characterized by the "trickle effect" whereby cultural innovations, consumption patterns, standards of proper behavior, political power, and economic wealth are located in or enter the society through an expanding but still very small political, economic, and social elite based in Tehran.[12] These phenomena trickle down the social ladder with most of the significant changes never reaching the large mass of the population. As a result, the gap between rich and poor continues to expand. Iran is a society characterized by far more growth than development.

One can visit the Hilton, La Residence, the Key Club, the Darband Boite, The Imperial Country Club or one of the staggeringly large number of boutiques in Tehran and not realize he is in one of the poorest nations in the world. Talk with a member of that upper social class and learn that "everyone" is going to Paris for holidays or "everyone is selling their Iranian made Peykans to buy a better car." Or read that the twin sister of the monarch, Princess Ashraf, boasts of her $10,000 lace dresses from Paris.[13]

The regime no longer denies that SAVAK permeates the society. It is a recognized instrument of rule. At a press conference in 1971 a SAVAK official boasted that his organization in addition to full time employees utilized ". . . individuals who cooperate with SAVAK, some of whom would even refuse to receive money and desire only to serve their country." After confirming that the number of the latter were far larger than the former he went on:

> Members of the second group work in various segments of the society—workers, farmers, students, professors, teachers, guild members, political parties, and other associations. They may also be civil servants receiving salaries from the government. The job of these individuals is to collect reports of grievances among various sections of the society and report them to SAVAK. SAVAK sifts through the material it receives and attempts to remove the factors responsible for dissatisfaction so as to remove any fertile ground which saboteurs might feed on.[14]

Despite this unusual view of its secret police, the government is in the midst of a major campaign against subversion in which the secret police plays a more conventional role. Since 1970, "urban guerillas" have committed many acts of terrorism—the shooting of policemen, numerous bank robberies, the assassination of two prominent military generals, the explosion of numerous bombs including one in the car of a U.S. Army General, the attempted but unsuccessful kidnappings of the U.S. Ambassador, the son of Princess Ashraf, and the Lebanese Ambassador, and the murder, in early 1973, of a U.S. Army Colonel being only the most publicized of their acts. The government has responded by the roundup and imprisonment of suspected subversives and the more general restriction of civil liberties.

Much like a challenged colonial regime the ardent devotees of the regime point to Iran's economic growth. The rise in Gross National Product is seen as justifying the existence of other less palatable facts of Iranian life or as necessitating them in the short run. The growth in Iran's GNP has, indeed, been one of the two or three fastest in the world, recently surpassing the rate of growth in Japan and Israel. From 1962 to 1967, the GNP of Iran grew at an average yearly rate of 8.5 percent (in constant prices). Since 1967, the GNP has been increasing at a rate above 10 percent.

Signs of economic growth are everywhere in Iran. The annual consumption of diesel oil, a fuel used only for industrial purposes, increased from 11,830,000 barrels in 1966 to 20,800,000 in 1971.[15] In the ten years from 1959 to 1969, the number of savings accounts in Iranian banks increased from 1,409,000 to 2,986,000 while the amount of deposits increased from 5,743 million rials to 19,446 million rials.[16] Or, again, from 1967 to 1970 the number of radios per 1,000 persons increased from 110 to 200, automobiles increased from 9 per 1,000 to 16 per 1,000, while telephones increased from 7 to 10 per 1,000 persons.[17] This economic growth is not slowing. In the first six months of 1972, the overall index of production in major industrial groups was up 17.1 percent, employment was up 3.8 percent and wages and salaries to all employees were up 13.5 percent.[18]

What accounts for this steady, impressive rate of growth? To restrict the answer to the one word "oil" would be a gross simplification. Certainly the relative domestic political stability and the intelligence of the Iranian people must be counted very highly. But oil revenues cannot be slighted as the major source of Iranian economic growth. In 1972, the Government of Iran earned over two billion dollars from oil—a 33 1/3 percent increase over the previous year alone.

These revenues promise to continue to grow rapidly. Thus, in 1965 Iran's oil production constituted 22.7 percent of all Middle East production. By 1969, the percentage had risen to 27.5, with the figure in 1971 over thirty percent. For the same period, Iran's share of world oil production went from 6.2 percent to 10 percent.[19] Moreover, Iran has such a large share of the world's proven petroleum reserves (some 11.7 percent in 1968) and offers such a sure source of supply that there is every expectation of Iran's revenues continuing to expand rapidly. In 1973, for instance, oil revenue amounted to more than four billion dollars. In 1974, Iran's oil income will total 20 billion dollars—a tenfold increase in three years![20]

Expanded oil revenues have had two immediate consequences—the share of GNP constituted by oil has increased from fifteen percent in 1960 to over twenty percent in 1970. In addition, the percentage of the Government budget provided by oil has increased to above 60 percent in the same period. In short, Iran's dependence on oil has increased.

Given her immense oil reserves, this is a dependency which can continue for the foreseeable future. There are certain steps which the Government of Iran has taken to build an infrastructure for future economic growth, particularly investment in roads, telephones, television, dams, and education. Education in particular has shown impressive results as the number of pupils in primary school has doubled, the number of secondary school students has quadrupled and the number of students at institutions of higher education has tripled in the past decade.[21]

But there is a pattern of expenditures which is more significant in that it represents a far greater share of Government revenues and yet does not justify the abuses of civil liberties and the untrammeled exercise of state power; that is, building the national strength of Iran. The Shah's vision entails, primarily, a major emphasis on the armed might of the Iranian state. Between 1967 and 1970, the budget of the Gendarmerie was increased by 33 1/3 percent. The budget of the National Police was raised by 50 percent, while the budget of the Imperial Armed Forces increased one hundred percent. In 1970-71, the defense allocation was budgeted at 781.3 million dollars.[22] In addition to the regular authorization, the Government makes special purchases of military equipment: more than $400 million from the U.K. and $110 million from the U.S.S.R. in 1968. More recently, Iran has negotiated for the purchase of over eight billion dollars of arms from the U.K. and primarily the U.S. These staggering expenditures are, or course, accompanied by huge additional outlays for personnel, the construction of bases, communications networks, and other facilities.

Another component of the kind of national strength which the Shah is intent on creating irrespective of economic merit is heavy industry. One of the Shah's favorite projects has been the "Aryamehr Steel Mill" as it was dubbed after a contract for its construction was signed with the U.S.S.R. in 1965. Initially built to produce 700,000 tons of steel annually, it may be expanded to a total production of 4,500,000 tons. Suffice it to note here that five years after the signing of a contract for its construction, the Government was still pouring money into it. In 1970, it cost Iran more than any of the Iranian Government Ministries save War, Education, and Roads. Some 64 percent of the allocation of the Plan Organization of Iran for industries and mines was allocated to the Steel Mill, some 11.8 billion rials.[23]

These extraordinary expenditures to build state power are one form of the frequently noted imbalances in Iran. For example, that Tehran "produces" the political elites has already been noted. But the city attracts resources as well. For example, the capital with one-tenth of the population boasted one-half of the new private construction in the entire country in 1971.[24]

Another example of the imbalance between the political center and periphery may be found in caloric intake. The Food and Agriculture Organization of the United Nations has estimated that the basic food requirement for the inhabitants of Iran is 2400 calories per day. In 1948-49, the average daily caloric consumption was estimated at 1600; in 1961-62 it had risen to 1800—a level still below that of Turkey, Egypt, Lebanon, Syria, and Iraq. In 1969, the daily average caloric intake was estimated, by the Government of Iran, to have risen to 2000.[25] Conditions below the median of 2000 can be judged by an article which appeared in the pages of the newspaper published by the ruling Iran Novin Party in 1969: "A survey conducted in some provinces in Iran has shown that about one-third of the child patients consists of those suffering from nothing more serious than malnutrition. Out of every two of such children, one died within fifteen days of hospitalization."[26]

The per capita average figure, then, tells us very little about the welfare of the vast majority of Iran's subjects—such information is, by definition, not part of a statistical average. How informative then is the average per capita national income of which the Government proudly boasts? The figure for 1960 was $179; for 1965, $263; and for 1970 it had leapt to $341.[27] This of course is not what the people of Iran individually receive but only the national income of Iran divided by the total population. The actual distribution of income in Iran is difficult to determine. One indication can be derived from a 1972 survey of Tehran residents which indicated that two-thirds of the families had incomes of less than $200 per person per year. The situation in rural areas is considerably more drastic. The Iranian Statistics Center has released figures which indicate that 35.3 percent of all rural families earn less than $400 per year, while another 41.3 percent of the families earn $400 or more but less than $800 per year. Thus, slightly over three quarters of Iran's rural families earn less than $66 per month.

Given that food prices in January of 1972 were 10.2 percent higher than in January of 1971 and given the abysmally low incomes of so much of the population, widespread malnutrition comes as no surprise. Neither do the near riots over prices which occurred in February of 1972 in Iran.

Many explanations can be advanced for these low family incomes in Iran and their concomitants—low wages. (In 1970 the Government estimated that the wages of an ordinary laborer averaged $1.25 per day; of industrial and commercial workers, $2.25 per day; of rural laborers, 70 cents to $1.00.) One key explanation can be located in the nature of Iran's economy and the political relations which determine the distribution of that economy's output. Put simply, while the Gross National Product doubled between 1962 and 1971, employment increased by only 23 percent. Thus, much of the new wealth with which Iran has been blessed—although some in Iran refer to it as the "black gold curse"—has not found its way to the hands of the population. This new wealth comes predominantly from oil and oil revenues and goes to the Government of Iran. The Shah and the Government of Iran are not primarily interested in a widespread dissemination of that wealth, but rather in augmenting the power of the state.

The political process in Iran, then, takes the form not of proposing new directions for political life or even a more proper or efficient allocation of resources within the existing codes, but, rather, an arduous and ardent pursuit of values on two levels. For the Shah, those prime values are an increase in the power of the state and of his ability to direct that power.[29] For his second stratum, the more conventionally defined political elite of Iran, the values of money and power are pursued.[30]

The astounding fact of contemporary Iran is that these values have been realized beyond the expectations of both the regime's supporters and detractors. In early 1971, the Shah claimed, "Already Iran's military power is being taken into account. By 1976, the Iranian armed forces will reach such a degree of qualitative progress that they will definitely be taken into account on an international scale."[31] From the parade of high level diplomats who come to court the favor of the Shah, it is evident that even the Shah was overly pessimistic in his prediction of Iran's arrival to international prominence and the monarch's control over the internal situation is at its zenith. It is undoubtedly true that no Iranian ruler has ever exercised as much power or commanded as responsive a political system as does Mohammad Reza Shah Pahlavi in 1974, "urban guerillas" and censorious foreign critics notwithstanding. Simultaneously, the political elite of Iran has never before enjoyed the material benefits or status which they currently command.

The genius of the Shah and his political elite plus oil revenues and good fortune are responsible for the enviable present situation of the regime. But there is at least one persistent possibility for the undoing of the system. In 1970, the then Managing Director of Iran's Plan Organization realized that ". . . economic abundance without regard for economic and social justice . . . is bound to cripple economic development, leading to mounting resentment and political and social unrest which could overnight spoil the fruits of the economic achievement of many years . . ."[32]

Insofar as such "justice" requires fundamental alterations in the distribution of power in Iran, the regime will be faced with hard choices which it has successfully avoided to this time. The Shah has been willing to countenance alterations in the forms of political relations as long as his own power remains unfettered. The social background of deputies to the Iranian parliament has changed, for example, from a rural, land-owning elite to that of technically educated urban dwellers, but this has brought no basic changes in the distribution of power. Similarly, the structure of the ministries, their responsibilities and representation in the cabinet have altered considerably over time without any fundamental alteration in the programs of the Government of Iran or internal power arrangements. But it is undoubtedly only a basic change in power relations which will result in that degree of "economic and social justice" necessary to preclude the dire possibilities to which the Director of the Plan Organization alluded. Yet the fundamental relations of the Shah and the political elite argue against such a change. The Shah seeks to preserve his ultimate control. He encourages the political elite to seek material rewards and that level and scope of power which he has relegated to them. Those members of the elite who refuse to accept the limits he has set are swiftly excluded from the elite. Thus, as long as the Shah preserves his power the political elite will be composed of those who shun any alteration in the fundamental distribution of values.

In short, at present, the political system of Iran is closed to basic realignments. As a colonial elite to its colony, the Shah and the political elite of Iran will continue to strengthen the center at the expense of the periphery.[33]

NOTES

1. James Bill conceptualizes the class structure in Iran in this fashion. See his *The Politics of Iran; Groups, Classes, and Modernization* (Columbus: Charles E. Merrill Publishing Co., 1972), esp. Figure 2, p. 17.

2. Mircea Eliade has noted that, "Where history is on the march, thanks to kings, heroes, or empires, the sun is supreme." For a provocative treatment of the relationship between astronomy and political absolutism, see Lewis Mumford, *The Myth of the Machine—The Pentagon of Power* (New York: Harcourt, Brace, Jovanovich, 1964), esp. pp. 28-39.

3. For the Shah's own view of this, see his *The White Revolution* (Tehran: Imperial Pahlavi Library, 1967).

4. For a more detailed analysis of royal decision-making in Iran see my *The Political Elite of Iran* (Princeton: Princeton University Press, 1971), esp. pp. 95-100.

5. For an initial presentation of the notion of a second stratum, see Gaetano Mosca, *The Ruling Class*, trans. by H. D. Kahn, (New York: McGraw-Hill Book Co., 1939), esp. pp. 329-337 and 430-433. The notion has been developed with greater detail in a forthcoming study of rural elites in Egypt by Leonard Binder.

6. For more information on the religious leadership and their relation to the regime see Hamid Algar, "The Oppositional Role of the Ulama in Twentieth Century Iran," in *Scholars, Saints and Sufis, Muslim Religious Institutions in the Middle East Since 1500*, ed. Nikki Keddie (Berkeley: University of California Press, 1972), pp. 231-255 and Zonis, *Political Elite of Iran*, pp. 44-47 and passim.

7. U.S. Army, *Area Handbook for Iran*, (Washington: Special Operations Research Office, The American University, 1963), pp. 85-95.

8. See, for example, the essay by Wenner in this volume.

9. See Harold D. Lasswell, "The World Revolution of Our Time: A Framework for Basic Policy Research" in *World Revolutionary Elites*, eds. H. D. Lasswell and D. Lerner (Cambridge, Mass.: The M.I.T. Press, pp. 29-96.

10. For more detailed information on the last two centuries of Iranian history, see Rouhollah K. Ramazani, *The Foreign Policy of Iran, 1500-1941, A Developing Nation in World Affairs* (Charlottesville, Virginia: University Press of Virginia, 1966); and Firuz Kazemzadeh, *Russia and Britain in Persia, 1864-1914, A Study in Imperialism* (New Haven, Conn.: Yale University Press, 1968).

11. For a perceptive study, see Howard J. Rotblat, "Stability and Change in an Iranian Provincial Bazaar" (Ph.D. dissertation submitted to the Department of Sociology, The University of Chicago, 1972).

12. Lloyd A. Fallers, "A Note on the Trickle Effect," *Public Opinion Quarterly* 18, (1954): 314-321.

13. Chicago Daily News, September 23-24, 1972, p. 13.

14. "Iran News and Documents," a publication of the Ministry of

Information, Vol. III, No. 8, April 12, 1971, p. 16.

15. Bank Markazi Iran, *Bulletin* 2, 61 (May-June 1972): 70-71.

16. Echo of Iran, *Almanac-1971*, (Tehran: Echo of Iran Publishing Co., 1972), p. 452.

17. Ibid., p. 256.

18. Bank Markazi Iran, *Bulletin*, p. 473.

19. Echo of Iran, *Almanac-1971*, p. 343.

20. Subcommittee on the Near East, Committee on Foreign Affairs, U.S. House of Representatives, 92nd Congress, 2nd Session, *The United States and the Persian Gulf*, 1972, p. 5. These projections take into account the oil crisis of 1973-74 and the new, sharply increased prices that resulted from it. See also *Middle East and African Economist* 28, 7 and 8 (July-August 1974): 91.

21. For a survey of the educational system of Iran, see this author's, "Higher Education and Social Change: Problems and Prospect," in *Iran Faces the Seventies*, ed. Ehsan Yar-Shater (New York: Prager Special Studies, 1971), pp. 217-259.

22. This figure represents approximately 30 percent of the total local, regional, and national governmental budget. The percentage understates Iran's true commitment to defense for a number of Ministries expend parts of their budgets on projects of direct benefit to the Armed Forces—sums which are not counted in the defense budget.

23. Bank Markazi Iran, *Bulletin* 10, 60 (March-April, 1972): 582.

24. Bank Markazi Iran, *Bulletin*, 2, 61 (May-June, 1972): 7-13.

25. *United Nations Statistical Yearbook, 1970*, Table 161, p. 520.

26. Echo of Iran, *Almanac*-1971, pp. 275-276.

27. *United Nations Statistical Yearbook, 1971*, Table 185, p. 595.

28. Echo of Iran, *Almanac*-1971, p. 269.

29. Note that there is no intention here of denying the ruler's interest in other values—those exemplified in the White Revolution, for example. Rather, the point is that such values are subsidiary interests for him.

30. Again, this is not to deny the presence of other values or of a different priority of values for any given member of the political elite or second stratum but, rather, to represent a generally valid set of priorities.

31. Echo of Iran, *Almanac*-1971, p. 144.

32. Mehdi Sami'i, "The Role of Foreign Private Investment in Iran's Economic Development," A Speech at the Iran Investment Conference, May 19, 1970, as reprinted in Bank Markazi Iran, *Bulletin* 9, 53 (January-February 1971): 530. Of course, Mr. Sami'i was not thinking of the staggering oil revenues which began to accrue to Iran after the Shah quadrupled oil prices on the heels of the Arab boycott. Money is to some extent, after all, a substitute for justice.

33. I am indebted to the seminal article by Edward Shils, "Centre and Periphery," in *The Logic of Personal Knowledge*, ed. Edward Shils (London: Routledge and Kegan Paul, 1961).

BIBLIOGRAPHY

Arasteh, Reza. *Education and Social Awakening in Iran.* Leiden: E. J. Brill, 1962.

Avery, Peter. *Modern Iran.* London: Ernest Benn, 1965.

Baldwin, George B. *Planning and Development in Iran.* Baltimore, Md.: The Johns Hopkins Press, 1967.

Banani, Amin. *The Modernization of Iran, 1921-1941.* Stanford, California: Stanford University Press, 1961.

Bill, James A. *The Politics of Iran—Groups, Classes and Modernization.* Columbus, Ohio: Charles E. Merrill Publishing Co., 1972.

Binder, Leonard. *Iran: Political Development in a Changing Society.* Berkeley, California: University of California Press, 1962.

Cottam, Richard W. *Nationalism in Iran.* Pittsburgh, Pa.: University of Pittsburgh Press, 1964.

Kazemzadeh, Firuz. *Russia and Britain in Persia, 1864-1914.* New Haven, Conn.: Yale University Press, 1968.

Keddie, Nikki R. *Religion and Rebellion in Iran: The Tobacco Protest of 1891-1892.* London: Frank Cass, 1966.

Lambton, A. K. S. *The Persian Land Reform, 1962-1966.* London: Clarendon Press, 1969.

Ramazani. R. K. *The Foreign Policy of Iran—1500-1941, A Developing Nation in World Affairs,* Charlottesville, Virginia: University Press of Virginia, 1966.

Rotblat, Howard J. *Stability and Change in a Provincial Bazaar.* Ph.D. Dissertation submitted to the Department of Sociology, The University of Chicago, 1972.

Upton, Joseph M. *The History of Modern Iran: An Interpretation.* Cambridge, Mass.: Harvard University Press, 1960.

Zabih, Sepehr, *The Communist Movement in Iran.* Berkeley, California: University of California Press, 1966.

Zonis, Marvin. *The Political Elite of Iran.* Princeton, N.J.: Princeton University Press, 1971.

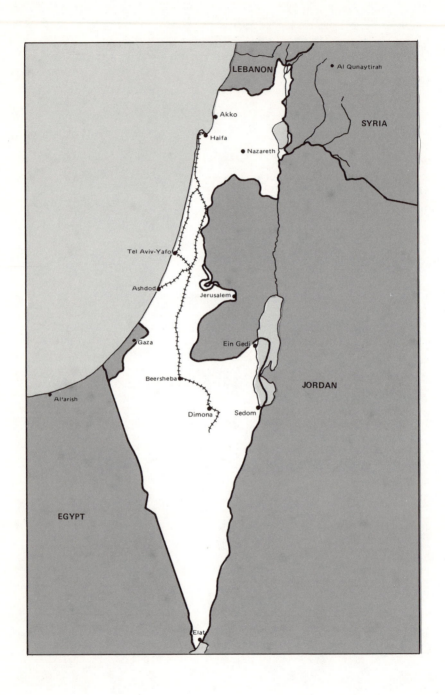

6

Israel:
The Persistent Elite

Efraim Torgovnik*

The establishment of the State of Israel in 1948 was a sublime moment for the Zionist Left which had secured the laobr leadership of the pre-State Jewish Settlement (Yishuv) in Palestine. Twenty-six years later, the labor leadership is still dominant in Israeli politics.

Several key factors explain the emergence and continuous domination of Israel's political elite. Foremost among them is the superior political organization established by the Zionist Left (specifically, the Mapai party) in the early 1930s. Understanding the capability of a party to mobilize and sustain the support of followers, the Zionist Left created political institutions before any other kind of institutions. This study deals with: (1) the origins of the political parties in the Yishuv (the pre-State Jewish community in Palestine); (2) the ideological base of the dominant elite; (3) the method by which the elite used various organizations to establish and maintain its dominance; and (4) the uninterrupted pre-eminence of the old guard of Eastern European origin.

Israel's political elite manifested great skill in political organization—including mobilization of the masses around popular ideologies, and control over the institutions which channeled economic resources from world Jewry to the Yishuv. Thus, throughout the years, an interactive process was apparent between political power and economic power.

*Special thanks are due to Dr. Avraham Brichta of Haifa University who provided updated data for the latter portions of this essay and the tables below. Some of the data have not been published previously.

Most members of the elite came to Palestine with the Second Aliya (wave of immigration) during the first decade of this century. The approximately 10,000 people of the Second Aliya established the effective political organization of the Yishuv in an inhospitable environment, under the rule of the British Mandate authorities. When they arrived in Palestine, the Yishuv was small and consisted of concentrations of religious communities (notably in Jerusalem) and agricultural communities, which had been established during the twenty years of the First Aliya. Major anti-Semitic outbursts in Russia had sent millions of Jews fleeing to the West from 1882 to the turn of the century; of these, 20,000 to 30,000 had come to Palestine. The best known group in the First Aliya was the *Biluim* (a Hebrew acronym for "House of Jacob, Let Us Go Forth"). The members of this first wave of immigration sought normal lives, secure from persecution. They showed little capacity for local organization and relied heavily on philanthropic help—notably from Edmund de Rothschild of France.

By contrast, members of the Second Aliya elite tended to be intellectual ideologues and agitators. They desired new forms of political and social organization, and set out to implement their ideas in Palestine. Unlike the members of the First Aliya, they did not seek mere normalization of a safe economic base as individuals. Instead, they had a futuristic outlook—and their efforts were geared to the national scene. They had been activists in Russia, where they had been involved in revolutionary movements. Having been disillusioned by the 1905 revolution in Russia, during which some of the most notorious anti-Jewish pogroms took place, the immigrants' outlook was for a new solution.

While world Zionist circles were debating Jewish integration in Europe, esoteric plans such as the settlement of Jews in Uganda, and whether the Zionist movement should support settlement in Palestine, the Second Aliya members were working hard at organizing their lives in Palestine. They gave special meaning to their act as the vanguard for others. They glorified hard work, especially toil on the land, as a means of purification; eventually this resulted in the establishment of unique communities such as the kibbutz (collective settlement) and the moshav (cooperative settlement). These agricultural settlements were also expressions of a collectivism of purpose which became the backbone of a strong national movement guided from a political center of power. These early settlers were not a homogenous group. There were political factions such as Hapoel Hatzair and Poale Zion, and numerous local worker organizations. There were programmatic groups—each believing in its capacity to offer the ultimate solution. Indeed, S. N. Eisenstadt labels their stands as extreme, a condition which could have prevented unified action.[1] This danger was averted, according to Eisenstadt, because: 1) they were compelled to act in some measure of unison within the world Zionist movement; 2) the dependence of the various groups on resources from the Zionist movement modified extreme positions—although separate allocations were made to each group; 3) they were constructive—channeling their energies into economic and social development as a substitute for revolutionary activity; and 4) city and agrarian worker groups chose to co-exist with other groups such as the middle-class urban settlers of Jaffa and Tel-Aviv (established in 1911) and professional groups.

The Yishuv was multi-centered during World War I. The various groups were supported by outside resources; the Palestine bureau of the World Zionist Movement channeled funds to the Yishuv. In such a setting, it would seem unlikely for one group to emerge as the dominant force—yet this did occur. Hapoel Hatzair and Achdut-Haavoda merged to become Mapai (1930), thus organizing a strong political party decades before statehood. Mapai became an important spokesman for the Yishuv, and fought for its way within the Zionist movement.

In 1918, more than a decade before the establishment of Mapai, the Achdut Ha'avoda party already controlled the major institutions of the Histadrut labor federation (the latter was formed by parties—contrary to the prevailing model where trade unions form parties). It gave the party much control over political spoils and appointments and the administration of many state-like activities such as employment, housing, workers' bank, industrial development and the sick fund. Thus, the Histadrut controlled the important Yishuv activities of absorbing newcomers and the allocation of Yishuv national resources.

The Zionist movement and its local representatives were fully committed to a wide-ranging program of settling Palestine with Jewish immigrants. This coincided with the normative orientation of the Mapai factions: hard work and reclamation of the land.

Hence, Mapai implemented the purposes of the Zionist movement while strengthening itself; it emphasized a socialist orientation, to which, interestingly, the Zionist movement was somewhat indifferent. The ultimate strength of this socialist group was in its organization into a political party able to mobilize people and to shape the development of the country. In cooperation with the Zionist movement, they helped achieve international recognition for Jewish national aspirations in Palestine. By dominating the Zionist movement's programs and institutions, they facilitated their role as the dominant socialist elite—the conveyer of change and inculcator of values, whose operational meaning was hard work directed toward the ultimate purpose of statehood.

The Yishuv's political organization was juxtaposed to the British Mandate authorities; it was a state within a state. Mapai, at the helm of national institutions such as the Histadrut, fulfilled many state-like functions. The authority it wielded was clearly like that of a legitimate ruling government.

In the 1920s, the concern of various labor factions with labor problems led to the establishment of the powerful Histadrut labor federation. First, they lobbied for economic aid from the Zionist movement to aid immigrant workers; second, they struggled to obtain employment for Jewish immigrants, who were easily replaceable by cheaper Arab labor. In the 1930s, the struggle shifted to the political scene; this change was epitomized by David Ben-Gurion's switch in 1932 from secretary-general of the Histadrut to chairman of the executive committee of the Zionist movement, a step which confirmed the recently established Mapai as the new center of power.

From its establishment, Mapai was the dominant political force; yet it always needed coalition partners in order to rule. Its traditional partners in the Zionist Executive Committee were the religious faction and the General Zionist faction, the political base of the middle-class center groups.

The political development of the Yishuv was thus marked by two major factors: (1) the emergence of the leftist Zionist labor movement as the dominant political element; and (2) the emergence of political structures and patterns which have survived to this day, inspired by the normative system of the Second Aliya: pioneering, dedication, voluntarism, hard work, and complete submergence of the individual to collective needs. These norms had their concomitant ultimate operational meanings: one was national consciousness, and the other was the return to the land.

The elite's constituency was both urban and rural. Socialism and collectivism were soon to be manifested in collective settlements (*kibbutzim*) and semi-collective settlements (*moshavim*) linked to Mapai. The link with the emerging rural sector was strengthened through intermediary institutions such as the moshavim movement and various kibbutz organizations which eventually came to comprise the major factions of the leftist Zionist movement. The link with the labor populations was, as mentioned earlier, through the labor federation—the Histadrut. As noted, it was established and controlled by the same factions which organized Mapai later in the decade. In fact, the Histadrut may be viewed as the first step in the political unification of labor factions. It not only organized the urban workers, but also served as a convenient bridge between the urban and the rural sectors. It was more than a trade union. From the outset, the Histadrut defined its role as overlapping with pioneering Zionism. While one definition of pioneering was return to the land, its conterpart was the utilization of collective efforts to develop industry, thereby utilizing the Yishuv's economic potential and assuring employment. The Histadrut's dominant role in Israel's economy today is traceable to this orientation.

The primary thrust of the Zionist Left and conceivably, the reason for its success, was the emphasis on a nationwide ideology and national organizations. With the establishment of the State, mass immigration flowed into Israel. (See Table I below). These waves of immigrants unlike those of the pre-State period were not all affiliated with political groups. They found a stable political system and a dominant ruling socialist party. They had the potential to change the political structure of Israel (see Table 1 below). To the dominant elite, mass immigration may have posed a threat—but this was easily averted.

TABLE I Population of Israel—1948-1970

1948	1951	1955	1965	1970
867,000	1,577,000	1,789,075	2,606,200	3,034,000

Leonard Fein has noted some reasons for the remarkable consistency in the political alignment in Israel.[2] It should be noted: (1) many immigrants, especially those of the five major immigration waves pre-1948 had belonged to movements abroad which were identical to those which operated in Israel; (2) in the post-statehood period immigrants were faced by the hardship of adjustment to a new life and new social values and they found it convenient to conform to the existing ideology, symbols, and leadership. This leadership was identified with the State of Israel, and consequently, the Mapai party, led by David Ben-Gurion, was identified with Israel. In the words of Duverger: "... a party is dominant when its ... doctrines ... and methods ... coincide with ... the epoch."[3] Not only was the ruling socialist Mapai identified with the epoch, but it also was indentified as the provider of basic sustenance.[4] (3) In absorbing the immigrants, a network of instructor-socializers was formed; their task was to help immigrants. Each of the established political groupings received a share in this network. These instructor-socializers lived with the immigrants, often in remote new settlements or abandoned Arab villages. They were the link to the outside world.[5] Unlike many other developing countries, the political elite of the Jewish community in Palestine emerged with little strife. True, there was much dissension within the Left, and between the Left and the Zionist Right—but the dominance of the Left was never seriously threatened. As noted, they organized on a national basis—providing a unifying ideology, and merging the rural and urban sectors into one movement. Mapai was not the only political group in the country, but it amassed great political and economic power—and the dogged devotion and persistence of these socialist Zionists resulted in their dominance. They facilitated this dominance by making accommodations with competing groups—while always assuring a key role for themselves.

Thus, Mapai achieved the key position in the Israeli Left, but we have yet to explain how its leaders became the dominant elite in the society as a whole. To begin with, Mapai and its predecessor factions consisted of people who were skilled in the art of organization of and for power. Their experience in the Russian revolutionary movement showed them the value of a system of total commitment. From the outset, they realized that what was essential for the preservation of power was a bureaucratic structure—not merely to mobilize masses around popular ideologies, but mainly to retain loyalty under changing conditions and to absorb new members, Hence, the very fact that a party emerged in Palestine prior to the existence of a state, a government or other institutions, illustrates Mapai's organizational skill. Before statehood, Mapai was already acting like a governing party, and sought to fulfill the functions of a state party. This program for the future blended well with the ideology of Zionism.

Defining its role in terms of a popular ideology—the dream of rebuilding a sovereign state for Jews—had many advantages. Mapai did not have to appeal to a diverse population for support and loyalty, as is the case in many newly developed countries; the Jewish population of Palestine was already united by a common cause. By articulating this popular goal, Mapai established itself as the major political force. It carried the banner of state-building, a function which Almond and Powell aptly describe as penetration—a process involving most segments of society through controls, regulations and manipulation of resources.[6] Although Mapai's origin was in the pre-State period, it was instrumental in the formation and domination of many state-like institutions such as labor exchanges, health funds and educational programs. It created positions of power around political, economic and social functions. It was part of the process of penetration. These roles helped to establish Mapai as the dominant force; not merely by offering rewards but mainly by setting itself up as a party responsive to the needs of the population.

Mapai appropriated domains and issues, so that other parties were Johnny-come-latelies at best, or poor imitators at worst. The control of service organizations was secondary, however, to the skill with which Mapai maintained its own system of support. At the same time that Mapai managed to become a political party in the commonly known sense of aggregating and articulating interests, it linked its membership through the service organizations. Such organizations earned tremendous loyalty among the members. Although the services were carried out indirectly—through the Histadrut, for example—the link to Mapai was not lost. Thus, Mapai, "by 1935 . . . led all the main bodies of Palestine Jewry. It welded the community together and brought about an important degree of coordination and unity."[7] From the outset Mapai controlled most of the national economic resources that were received through world Jewry.

The use of various intermediary organizations by Mapai for

the purpose of penetration was not limited to service organizations. Through a network of organizations, Mapai was able to link several segments of society to itself. It penetrated, for example, the kibbutzim, the moshavim, the labor force and other sectors of society.[8]

Mapai emerged as the dominant political force during the British Mandate in Palestine, under which the Yishuv enjoyed a measure of self-government. Mapai's leadership became synonymous with Yishuv leadership. The Mandatory government limited its activities to major functions such as security, taxation, transportation and postal services. The Jewish community was free to provide services such as education and religious services. But, more importantly, the Jewish community was free to organize—and it did. There was an elected assembly and a National Executive Committee (*Havad Haleumi*).[9] The latter was the representative body of the Yishuv, linking the Jewish community with the British authorities. The committee was responsible for numerous public services, notably education and development. The Jewish Agency (the Palestinian organ of the World Zionist Organization) financed new Jewish settlements. The important point here is the fact that by the early 1930s, Mapai had penetrated and gained control of all elective and executive organizations in the Jewish community, including the Histadrut labor federation. This situation naturally strengthened Mapai and brought it a great deal of support. Other blocs did emerge—in particular, the religious bloc and the center-right bloc—but they only gained minimal representation and few leadership posts in Yishuv institutions. The three blocs co-existed; each had its own settlements, health funds, youth movements, etc.

Any national challenge that emerged, either from the outside (such as Arab opposition to Jewish settlement and land reclamation) or from within, was taken up by Mapai-dominated organizations. Perhaps the strongest challenge came from the Arabs. The Palmach and the Hagana which were the Yishuv's military organs, were directly linked to labor organizations. The Palmach drew its ranks mainly from the kibbutzim; the Hagana, mainly from the urban sector. The Hagana was established by the Histadrut itself. New settlements were protected by Palmach and Hagana units. Day-to-day security in these settlements was openly undertaken by units of *Notrim* (guards) who were recognized by the Mandate authorities, but whose link to the clandestine Hagana was no secret. With the birth of the State of Israel in 1948, the Hagana became the foundation of *Zahal,* the Israeli Defense Forces. The Jewish Agency became the foundation of the provisional government—and later, of the elected government of Israel.

It is in this setting that nearly two million immigrants were absorbed into the State of Israel without significantly altering the dominance of the Left. Mapai had gained much experience in the use of power during the pre-State period. When the mass immigration began, Mapai presented itself as a flexible organization—ready, willing and able to absorb people of different backgrounds and ideologies. On this point, Lissak states: "The pluralistic characteristic of . . . Mapai is not accidental, but on the contrary, it is a direct function of . . . the absorption processes."[10] Indeed, the composition of Mapai's membership changed from predominantly rural kibbutz members in the early 1940s to predominantly city dwellers today.[11]

Mapai became the major faction in the Labor Party at its formation in 1969. Both before and after the formation of the Israeli Labor Party (I.L.P.), Mapai controlled the most important Cabinet portfolios—the Prime Ministership, Treasury, Foreign Ministry, and Defense. Table II indicates how election results have consistently assured a key role for Mapai, with 35-38 percent of the vote, far more than any other single party or faction.

Mapai's link with pressure groups and other organizations was not direct, that is, they were not part of Mapai's formal hierarchy. These organizations were separate, with their own governing bodies. But the governing bodies consisted of Mapai members, and their policies were linked to Mapai.

The link with Mapai has been established in a number of ways. Leaders of the various movements are employed in Mapai-affiliated organizations. Members of the movements are also members of Mapai. They view themselves as party missionaries (*Shaliach Hatnoah*). Candidates for offices within the organizations are backed by the party—and those elected become brokers on behalf of the members. It is clear to the members that Mapai-backed officers carry more weight and can secure more rewards for them. After the establishment of the State, this link became particularly important, because organizations competed for influence over government policy (mainly economic). To the agricultural kibbutzim and moshavim, policies on water, prices and subsidies are a matter of survival. It is no coincidence that the Minister of Agriculture has traditionally been a member of the kibbutz movement. The minister in 1973, Haim Gvati, was secretary of the movement. In the new government which came to power after the 1973 elections, the minister was a member of the moshav movement.

Kibbutzim and moshavim are able to secure favorable benefits or block policies repugnant to them. The interests of these two movements do not coincide; they compete for influence within the party and over government policy. Kibbutzim are collective farms, whereas moshavim are semi-private. Their differences manifest themselves in the movements' competition over the Ministry of Agriculture. The Ministry not only deals with production quotas, but also influences water quotas and policy. It was not until 1959, after heavy pressure on Prime Minister David Ben-Gurion that Moshe Dayan, identified with the moshavim, was appointed Minister of Agriculture. It was no accident that the kibbutz representatives were more successful than the moshavim. From the early 1930s the kibbutzim were a major, perhaps the major, organizational and ideological forces backing Mapai. The dominant values of pioneering, voluntarism, conquest of the land and reclamation were all put to practice by the kibbutz. Army units based on volunteers are still disproportionately manned by kibbutz members. Because its membership is more highly selected, the kibbutz movement has been more politically coherent. Moshavim are more open. This form of settlement was used in communities of new immigrants. Because they are less selective, moshavim have many unresolved conflicts between old-timers and new immigrants.

Both moshav and kibbutz movements serve important functions for their members. In the case of the moshav, the need is based on immediate economic factors: more land, more water, more credit at lower interest, and membership in moshav shopping organizations. The individual moshav member deals with many organizations; he has, therefore, learned to manipulate his environment and retains a measure of independent action.[12]

Another major link between Mapai and large segments of Israeli society is Histadrut, the Labor Federation. The Histadrut is different from the moshav and kibbutz movements in that Mapai faces competition from other political parties for domination of the labor federation's governing organizations. Membership in Mapai has few conditions attached and interestingly, these are not even ideological: members of the Histadrut are automatically eligible to join the party. Mapai and the Labor Party dominate not only the Histadrut—but, more importantly, many of its trade union groups such as metal workers, masons, etc. The Histadrut owns an important part of the country's industry, and has a giant construction company. The construction enterprises go back to the Yishuv period when the Histadrut attempted to create favorable conditions for the absorption of labor-class immigrants. Today, its housing is no longer selectively assigned to one class. In this regard, its policy blends well with the public sector. The Secretary-General of the Histadrut has usually been a member of the Knesset from Mapai; more recently, he has been from another Labor faction. There are many interlocking arrangements between the leadership positions of the party and the Histadrut. It is extremely important for the government to have these links: the implementation of economic and wage policies depends heavily on the Histadrut's agreement, because of its dominance of organized labor. An example is the "package deal" (an agreement on price and wage controls) signed by the government, the Histadrut and the association of manufacturers in 1970. The Histadrut is generally able to control its diverse membership and to assure consensus on government policy. When the Secretary-General attempted to project an image of separate Histadrut interest, party discipline tamed him—but not before he earned some impressive cost-of-living allowances for the major labor group. What appeared to be a split between the party and the Histadrut was probably no more than a temporary difficulty with an honest but temperamental Secretary-General, whose position at the helm is wholly dependent on his party's nomination. The political pay-off of Mapai's control over the Histadrut is highlighted by the fact that Histadrut members were the major element in the vote for the Labor party in the 1969 elections.[13]

Thus, the leading position of Mapai is due to a combination of factors: its identification with the state and with Israel's success; the interdependence of supporting organizations; the party's responsiveness to internal pressure groups; its identification as supplier of demands; and the loyalty of voters. This loyalty is reinforced in many ways, not the least of which is the service provided by many of the Mapai-affiliated organizations.

The support system consists of: 1) the governing organizations: the government, the Jewish Agency (which absorbs new immigrants), the Histadrut; and 2) the membership organizations: the kibbutz movements, the moshav movement, and the party itself. The army and police should be mentioned—not necessarily as support organizations, but rather as non-threatening organizations to the party regime. When the State was established, the army and police were depoliticized; the forces of the Palmach, Hagana and Irgun (a militant rightist group) were merged into a national army. Although the army commanders and police chiefs have been either members of Mapai or known supporters of the party, this description may not do justice to army-party relations. The great success of Ben-Gurion was not the removal of factional generals, but rather the creation of a culture of *mamlachtiut* (state service) in the security forces. The forces are clearly subordinated to civilian rule, which means, of course, the rule of Mapai. In this connection, Israel's experience should be compared with that of other countries which have had liberation armies, specifically Turkey and Algeria among those included in this volume.

Mapai, in achieving and maintaining its dominant position, rarely suppressed opposition; instead, it accommodated the opposition. The religious bloc was allotted a share in various institutions, notably education. The Zionist Right strengthened its local economic bases, inadvertently giving up its ability to organize nationally. Opposition groups, in a manner similar to the dominant Left, evolved service organizations such as health funds for their members. In the pre-State era and the early years of the State, parties had their own labor exchanges to secure jobs for their members. The various military groups were associated with different political blocs prior to the establishment of the State. Even the educational system was sectorially organized in a manner which reflected the major political groupings— notably the Left and religious blocs.

Mapai and other political parties are instruments for the realization of certain ideas; they try to implement their political ideologies in all spheres of life—social, cultural and economic. Since the ideologies are all-embracing, the activities of the political parties are manifold. Thus, the parties maintain (or exert great influence over) such institutions as theaters, sport clubs, youth movements, consumer and producer cooperatives, suburban developments, housing projects, health insurance programs, and convalescent homes. They publish their own newspapers, and organize various recreational and cultural activities. In short, not only is the Israeli political system party-dominated, but to a large extent, so is the entire society.

It appears that throughout the Yishuv period and since independence, a measure of pluralism has been retained, enabling the Labor Party to keep its position as a central source of authority (see Table II p. 237 and Table XII p. 248). Other groups appeared to accept Labor dominance, recognizing or adjusting to the exclusivity of its authority in domains involving statehood. Labor's success in this domain expressed to various degrees the wishes of the different groups. Yet the dominant factor which retained the distinction between Labor and others was Labor's willingness to allow others to dominate such areas as culture, education, and service activities. This approach lent much support to the national institutions led by Mapai. It ruled in the coalition with the religious and center blocs. The center bloc (the General Zionists), especially the faction headed by Chaim Weizmann, Israel's first president, was particularly bent on cooperation with Labor. Weizmann exerted his immense influence in the Zionist movement abroad in order to divert resources to the settlement and defense programs of Labor-dominated institutions. The Right bloc (notably the Revisionist group) was less cooperative with Labor. Its positions on the road to statehood were extreme, at times advocating a militant struggle as opposed to Labor's gradual building of the nation and institutions. The Revisionists seceded from the Zionist movement and attempted to establish an alternative, but were unsuccessful. Interestingly, however, even after their secession, which expressed disaffection with Labor-headed institutions, they were not able to take with them other rightist and center groups from what was called the organized Yishuv (*Hayeshuv Hameorgan*). This refers to the division between those who recognized the authority of national institutions and those who did not (like the Communists and Revisionists).

Up to World War II, the share of the Left in the private economic resources of the country (excluding agriculture) was rather small compared with their control of national development resources. Most investment was made by private capital. Even in agriculture, the share of privately owned farms was equal to that of the public sector. The private share appears more impressive when we consider that the emphasis on agriculture resulted from the ideological commitment of the Zionist Left and its success in mobilizing the support of the world Zionist movement, which placed much of its resources behind the endeavor.[14]

Why did the free-enterprise center and rightist groups fail to emerge as a cohesive opposition to the Left prior to Statehood? They were economically strong, by far stronger than the Left at least up to World War II. It was only then that American Jewry undertook heavy financial support of the World Zionist movement and consequently of the Zionist Left. The non-Left groups were many, and were organized in different forms and structures. D. Giladi lists at least seven organizational frameworks of the free-enterprise and rightist groups: (1) merchant organizations (mainly locally based); (2) *Benei-Binyamin,* sons of old, established farmers, who emphasized private farms and attempted to act as a political group against the Zionist leadership (which frowned on locally based efforts outside the collective national program); (3) local governments dominated by free-enterprise groups, whose share in the building of small and middle-size enterprises was impressive; (4) the Revisionist Party, the rightist militant group mentioned above; (5) the religious Mizrachi party; (6) intellectuals; and (7) economic entrepeneurs.[15] These groups had the potential to organize on a class basis as a countervailing force to the Zionist Left. But they did not, for many reasons. First, most of these groups were locally based. They never succeeded in organizing nationally. Dizengoff, the strong mayor of Tel-Aviv in the 1930s, attempted to form a national organization of middle-class commercial civic groups, but failed. Second, they did not provide a competing ideology to that of the Left. Third, the Revisionist Party, which could have been the nucleus of a national Zionist Center-Right front, failed because it was too extreme in its program and alienated many Europeans of the Liberal tradition. These groups and the Revisionist party were still debating the major purposes of Zionism and the ways to implement them at a time when Labor already enjoyed a measure of consensus on ends and means, and in a setting where economic conflicts among groups found their modus vivendi in mutual accommodation. Fourth, perhaps the most damaging element in weakening the Center-Right as an opposition was its lack of success in linking with the World Zionist Movement—thereby losing much economic and other support.

In the late twenties, the private farm communities isolated themselves from the Jewish community, and especially from people of similar views in the cities; they were also removed from the world Zionist organizations. It was noted above that the general economic ideology of the Left was alien to world Jewish leaders; nevertheless, it received economic support from them. The leftist Zionist group had clearly linked itself to the Zionist movement by serving as its vanguard in Palestine. The Left, in turn, became instrumental in defining the Zionist movement's purposes. Economically independent civic groups (consisting of merchants and small industrialists) did not need the world Zionist movement's immediate support but neither were they able to help define its purposes to their liking. Moreover, private farmers were verbally and physically attacked, mainly by Histadrut labor organizers. This was a period of unemployment, and the Left attempted to force itself on the farmers by waving the banner of building the country through Jewish labor. By contrast, the farmers were employing cheap Arab labor, an action which weakened their position vis-à-vis the Left.

By the early forties, the domination of the Left was a fait accompli. Economically, it had penetrated all sectors through the Histadrut's holding companies. Socially, it had translated the ideology of Zionism into operational terms and symbols. Politically, it became the bearer of the flag of independence. With the establishment of the State of Israel in 1948, the Zionist Left and notably Mapai, were in an undisputed position of leadership.

In his study of voting patterns in Israel, Arian notes that the dominance of the labor bloc is reflected not only in the popular vote. More importantly, it is widely *perceived* as being dominant.[16] One commonly hears in Israel: "Yes, I would like to change—but who can I vote for? There is no alternative." Even opposition parties do not view themselves as alternatives to the ruling labor bloc. In the 1969 election, the strategy of *Gahal* (the Zionist Center-Right bloc) did not aim at gaining a majority or plurality. It simply wanted to increase its share of seats counting on its militant stand on security to attract new young voters.[17] Even the labor bloc clearly views itself as the governing party. In the 1969 campaign, for example, Pinhas Sapir, the Minister of Finance and past secretary of the Labor Party, told an election meeting that the party's aim was not a plurality; this, he implied, was self-evident. The aim, he said, was a majority.[18]

The ruling labor bloc is identified with the epoch of independence, with Israeli successes. Mapai, as Etzioni has pointed out, is viewed not merely as a political party; it is identified with the State.[19] Indeed, Etzioni proceeds on the assumption that the party will continue to be dominant. Democracy, therefore, is to be sought not in a formal trimming of the system but in the accommodation of forces within the party. The dominance of the labor bloc is supported by many factors. The continuous strain of security is clearly not amenable to radical change. Furthermore, in the three major armed conflicts up to 1967 in which Israel was involved, it was always successful, and it was under the leadership of the labor bloc during these wars. Consensus in Israel is therefore very high, especially on the most important issues facing the State: security, economics and the policy of continuous immigration.[20] Finally, the labor bloc is sensitive to divisive issues such as the separation of religion and state; it has shown a capacity for avoiding head-on confrontations over these issues. This was illustrated in 1972 by labor's opposition to a test vote in the Knesset on the legalization of civil marriage.[21] This ability to avoid divisive issues enables the Labor Party to retain broad support. Even voters who are not ideologically attuned to its purposes may vote for it, recognizing the party's leadership role. It should be mentioned that politics is very much an issue for the average Israeli; he/she is interested in national politics, which would be most likely identified with the traditional labor leadership.

Perhaps the best indication of this ability of political groups in Israel to maintain their strength is their tight control over the recruitment and nomination of candidates. This was particularly true of Mapai, and is still true of the ruling labor alliance, which is dominated by the large Mapai faction. The other factions are *Achdut Ha'avoda* (moderate Left), *Mapam* (leftist) and *Rafi* (Center-Left).

Within Mapam, significant policies are outlined and decided upon by a secretariat. In Achdut Ha'avodah, the important policy decisions are made by the central committee. In Mapai, a small group of the top leaders, composed of the cabinet ministers, the secretary of the party, and the secretary-general of the Histadrut, decide upon the most important matters of general policy and party actions. Some decisions are forwarded to the central committee and, on rare occasions, to the party's conventions.[22] The selection of representatives to the Knesset and the Cabinet, as well as to other responsible bodies, is made by a very small group within the party leadership. "The usual course," writes Benjamin Akzin, "is for the group of leaders in the smaller body to initiate the decision and to have it prevail. Reversals, when they do occur, signify that opinion within the leadership groups is sharply divided."[23]

The process of candidate recruitment to the Knesset is carried out by small centralized nomination committees, which are the least representative bodies in the hierarchy of party institutions. A nomination committee is usually sovereign, that is, it rarely submits its decision for approval to a more representative body, such as the party central committee. There are some variations among the parties, however, in some cases where the list of nominees must be submitted to a more representative body such as the central committee. In some parties the approval of the central committee is a mere formality. In others, the members of the central committee have the right to add names to the proposed list of candidates and rank the candidates on the list. Where the party branches participate in the process, it gives the grass-roots membership a voice in the selection of candidates. This system has been adopted in a limited way by Mapai since the 1959 elections. The top party leadership's tight control of the nomination process plays the most significant role in the self-perpetuation of the political elite in Israel. Tight control, in turn, is due mainly to the institution of proportional representation and the multi-party system.

Israel has a proportional electoral list system, whereby the whole country is a single constituency. The system deprives the voter of any influence in determining the composition of the lists of candidates to the Knesset; he has no way of adding or eliminating candidates, or of changing their ranking on the ballot. Since the lists of candidates are drawn up by the political parties' central executive bodies, and the voters cannot change them, the parties are virtually omnipotent in determining the composition of the Knesset.[24]

An additional factor augmenting the dependence of the candidates on the party organs is the manner of financing election campaigns in Israel.[25] The main sources of income for the parties are various domestic and external funds which are allocated among the existing parties on the basis of a "party key." Government funds are also allocated to the parties, and not to individual candidates.[26] Thus, in addition to the power to nominate candidates, the existing parties have been given further power by the provision of significant funds to finance their election campaigns, so that candidates are, in effect, entirely dependent on the parties for coverage of their election expenses.

The far-reaching control of the parties over the recruitment of candidates may be ascribed partly to their history and development prior to the establishment of the State of Israel, and partly to their amazing capacity to adapt to the new conditions and challenges which faced Israeli society after 1948. Israeli parties were not created as a response to the exigencies and opportunities of statehood or to creeping political development. Instead, they evolved in the pre-State period as voluntary organizations with the ultimate aim of establishing an independent Jewish state. Members could view their parties instrumentally; the parties provided them with social, cultural, and economic institutions that helped them realize the good life. The fact that parties in Israel have such an important influence on the political and social life of the country grants the party leadership a decisive role in molding and controlling the party's affairs, including the selection of candidates. Here again, one may detect significant parallels with other societies which experienced comprehensive nationalist movements, such as Algeria, Egypt, and Turkey.

The power of the Israeli political elite in controlling the process of elite circulation is further enhanced by the unusual stability of voting patterns. The rather amazing stability of party strength, clearly demonstrated in Table II, is due to the fact that the parties not only offer their adherents programs covering a wide range of services, but also try to influence the lives of their followers in a great many respects. Formal membership is encouraged by giving members the advantages and conveniences of the above-mentioned party-controlled social, economic, and cultural institutions, which also explains the unusually high ratio of party members to voters. One-fourth to one-third of all Jewish voters in Knesset elections are estimated to hold membership in a political party.[27]

The stability of party strength affects the nomination process in two ways. First, confident of the continuous support to its members and followers, the party leadership has almost complete free-

TABLE II Knesset Elections: Distribution of Votes and Seats (1949-1969)*

	Knesset												
Parties	First 1949		Second 1951		Third 1955		Fourth 1959		Fifth 1961		Sixth 1965		Seventh 1969	
	%	Seats	%	Seats	%	Seats	%	Seats	%	Seats	%	Seats	%	Seats
Communists														
Maki	3.5	4	4.0	5	4.5	6	2.8	3	4.2	5	1.1	1	1.1	1
Rakah	-	-	-	-	-	-	-	-	-	-	2.3	3	2.8	3
Total	3.5	4	4.0	5	4.5	6	2.8	3	4.2	5	3.4	4	3.9	4
Workers														
State List	-	-	-	-	-	-	-	-	-	-	-	-	3.1	4
Mapam	14.7	19	12.5	15	7.3	9	7.2	9	7.5	9	6.6	8		
A.H.					8.2	10	6.0	7	6.6	8			46.2	56 (A)
Mapai	35.7	46	37.3	45	32.2	40	38.2	47	34.7	42	36.7	45		
Rafi	-	-	-	-	-	-	-	-	-	-	7.9	10		
Total	50.4	65	49.8	60	47.7	59	51.4	63	48.8	59	51.2	63	49.3	60
Religious														
Mafdal			8.3	10	9.1	11	9.9	12	9.8	12	8.9	11	9.7	12
AG	12.2	16	2.0	3					3.7	4	3.3	4	3.2	4
PAG			1.6	2	4.7	6	4.7	6	1.9	2	1.8	2	1.8	2
Others	1.7	-	0.6	-	0.3	-	-	-	-	-	-	-	-	-
Total	13.9	16	12.5	15	14.1	17	14.6	18	15.4	18	14.0	17	14.7	18
Centre, CR														
New Centre													1.2	2
PLA	4.1	5	3.2	4	4.4	5	4.6	6			3.8	5	3.2	4
L (GZ) G	5.2	7	16.2	20	10.2	13	6.2	8	13.6	17				
Herut	11.5	14	6.6	8	12.6	15	13.5	17	13.8	17	21.3	26	21.7	26
"New Force"	-	-	-	-	-	-	-	-	-	-	1.2	1	1.2	2
Others	8.4	7	3.0	3	1.6	-	2.2	-	0.3	-	1.2	-	1.1	-
Total	29.2	33	29.0	35	28.8	33	26.5	31	27.7	34	27.5	32	28.4	34
Arab Lists	3.0	2	4.7	5	4.9	5	4.7	5	3.9	4	3.9	4	3.5	4
Total	100.0	120	100.0	120	100.0	120	100.0	120	100.0	120	100.0	120	100.0	120

KEY: Maki = Israeli Communist Party; Rakah = New Communist List; Mapam = United Workers' Party; AH = Ahdut Haavoda (Labour Unity); Mapai = Israel Labour Party; Rafi = Israeli Workers' List; (A) = Labour Alignment; Mafdal = National Religious Party; AG = Agudat Israel; PAG = Poalei Agudat Israel; CF = Centre Right; PLA = Independent Liberals (Progressives); L (=GZ) = Liberals (General Zionists); G = Gahal.

*See Table XII for 1973 Knesset Elections.

dom in determining the composition of its list of candidates. In the framework of the parliamentary system prevailing in Israel, the Knesset is also the central body from which almost all cabinet members, including the Prime Minister, are selected. Second, the political parties are able to divide their lists of candidates quite accurately into three parts: safe positions, marginal positions, and unrealistic positions. The placement of a candidate in the first part of the list, containing the safe seats, is tantamount to election.

The electoral system, the rigid party structure, the stability of voting patterns, and the tight control of the nomination process result in a very select group of nominees. They are predominantly party functionaries. Thus, two-thirds to four-fifths of all Knesset members in the seven Knessets between 1949 and 1973 were party leaders or party functionaries.[28] Moreover, the negligible number of Knesset members elected as representatives of "special" interest associations (such as associations for industrialists, merchants or contractors) demonstrates the weakness of the right-wing bloc. The special interest groups have never attained more than 6 percent of the Jewish seats in the Knesset.[29]

The distinct overrepresentation (see Table III) of the kibbutz movements, which are affiliated with the Zionist Left elites, demonstrates the great influence of the Left leadership in the distribution of power in the Israeli political system. High kibbutz representation reflects the prevalence of the worker-kibbutz ideology.

People of Eastern European origin (*Ashkenazim*)[30] are clearly overrepresented, as shown in Table IV. However, the percentage of native-born Israelis has increased from 11 percent in the First Knesset to 18 percent in the Sixth Knesset, while the percentage of Afro-Asians has increased at an even higher rate from 3 percent in the First Knesset to 14 percent in the Sixth Knesset. The percentage of Europeans decreased from 86 percent in the First Knesset to 68 percent in the Sixth Knesset. The serious underrepresentation of Oriental groups and native-born Israelis has motivated continual demands on their part for a greater share of representation. It appears, however, that the underrepresentation is due to historical factors, and not to a deliberate policy of discrimination against ethnic or demographic groups. The founding fathers and leaders of the parties immigrated to Israel prior to its independence. Consequently, the Knesset is composed predominantly of politicians who came to

TABLE III

Members of Knesset Belonging to the Kibbutz and Moshav
Sectors; Comparison of Actual Seats in Relation to Electoral
Strengths of the Sectors in Israel.

Knesset	1		2		3		4		5		6	
	R*	D**	R	D**	R	D	R	D	R	D	R	D
Kibbutz	23	7.3	17	-	22	5.4	19	7	19	6	18	5
Moshav	4	3.5	5	-	7	6	6	5	5	5	5	4.4

*R = Seats Received

**D = Seats due = $\dfrac{\text{no. of votes}}{\text{no. of votes required for one Knesset seat}}$

NOTE: The calculation of the number of seats due each sector in proportion to its
share of the population is based on the following sources:
For the First Knesset:
Statistical Abstract of Israel No. 2 (Jerusalem, Central Bureau of Statistics
1950-51), pp.112-114.
For the Second Knesset we could not obtain a detailed distribution of votes
for the Kibbutz and Moshav sectors.
Since the Third Knesset, the Central Bureau of Statistics has published
special issues with complete elections results. *See Results of Elections to the
Third Knesset and Local Authorities* (Jerusalem, Central Bureau of Sta-
tistics, Special Series No. 51, 1956).
For the Fourth Knesset: Special No. 111, 1961.
For the Fifth Knesset: Special No. 116, 1964.
For the Sixth Knesset: Special No. 216, 1967.

Israel before its establishment in 1948, and this naturally works
against the native born and the Orientals (most of whom immigrated after independence).

The plurality of members of the First Knesset (49 percent)
immigrated during the Fourth and Fifth Aliyot (waves of immigration) between 1924 and 1947. Members of the Second and
Third Aliyot (1904-1923) comprised 39 percent of the Jewish
M.K.'s in the First Knesset. The number of new immigrants (i.e.,
those who immigrated after statehood in 1948) was negligible.
In the Sixth Knesset, the number of M.K.'s who immigrated
during the Fourth and Fifth Aliyot (1924-1947) increased to 58
percent. While the number of new immigrants increased significantly, they comprised only 11 percent of the total number of
Jewish members in the Sixth Knesset. However, most of the new
immigrants elected to the Sixth Knesset were of Afro-Asian
origin (8 out of 13).

The significantly larger number of native-born Israelis of

TABLE IV Knesset Elections: Members of Knesset by Period of Immigration and Country of Origin (Number and percentage) (1949-1969)*

Country of origin	Period of Immigration	First Knesset seats	%	Second Knesset seats	%	Third Knesset seats	%	Fourth Knesset seats	%	Fifth Knesset seats	%	Sixth Knesset seats	%
Total in Knesset		127**	100	124**	100	125**	100	120	100	124**	100	125**	100
Eastern Europe	Second Aliya 1904-14	20		20		13		8		8		5	
Asia, Africa		2		-		-		-		1		1	
Balkan		-		-		-		-		1		1	
Total		22	(17)	20	(16)	13	(10)	8	(7)	10	(8)	6	(5)
Eastern Europe	Third Aliya 1915-23	26		19		15		12		14		9	
Asia, Africa		1		2		1		1		1		1	
English speaking countries		1		1		1		-		-		-	
Total		28	(22)	22	(18)	17	(14)	13	(9)	15	(12)	10	(8)
Eastern Europe	Fourth Aliya 1924-31	23		20		29		26		25		25	
Central Europe		4		4		3		3		3		3	
Asia, Africa		1		2		2		1		1		2	
Total		28	(22)	26	(20)	34	(27)	30	(25)	29	(23)	30	(24)
Eastern Europe	Fifth Aliya 1932-47	23		32		34		35		36		30	
Central Europe		7		7		8		6		6		6	
Western Europe		2		-		-		-		-		-	
Asia, Africa		-		1		1		3		3		6	
Balkan		1		2		1		-		1		1	
English speaking countries		1		-		-		-		-		-	
Total		34	(27)	42	(34)	44	(35)	44	(38)	46	(47)	43	(34)
Eastern Europe	1948	1		2		1		1		1		3	
Central Europe		-		-		1		1		1		1	
Asia, Africa		-		-		2		4		4		8	
Balkan		-		-		1		1		1		-	
English speaking countries		1		-		-		1		1		1	
Total		1	(1)	2	(2)	5	(4)	8	(7)	8	(7)	13	(11)
Israel	East	7		5		2		4		3		7	
	West	7		7		10		13		13		16	
Total		14	(11)	12	(10)	12	(10)	17	(14)	16	(13)	23	(18)

*All data in this table pertain only to Jewish M.K.'s, at the end of every Knesset.

**The Knesset consists of 120 seats. Higher numbers represent the number of individuals who served during a four-year period. Upon death or resignation of members, parties appoint the person next on their list of candidates to fill the vacancy.

Ashkenazi (Western) than of Sephardic (Afro-Asian) origin stems mainly from the weakness of the ethnic elites. According to Lissak, "The organizational helplessness of the ethnic leadership which was mainly religious and rigid and did not grasp the social and political events which were taking place at the time, also contributed to their failure. Moreover, the potential followers of this elite were extremely passive in all the prevalent entrepreneurial activities and therefore, were very far from the creative centers. This combination of circumstances 'perpetuated' the backward political position of the Oriental communities at the time of the Yishuv. Their leaders, even those who attained important status, such as membership in the Knesset, did not attempt to go further and their membership did not usually serve as a springboard to higher office.[31]

We may assume that the gradual disappearance of the old guard will bring about greater representation for native-born Israelis and Afro-Asians. However, this process had been rather slow, as shown by Table V. While the average age of the Jewish M.K.'s in the First Knesset was 49.4 years, it increased to 54.3

TABLE V Composition of the Knesset by Age (1949-1965)*

	Total Jewish Members of the Knesset	Under 40	40-60	Over 60	Average age
First Knesset	117	22	76	19	49.4
Second Knesset	112	15	76	21	50.5
Third Knesset	113	9	82	22	51.8
Fourth Knesset	113	9	80	24	52.5
Fifth Knesset	114	6	76	32	54.0
Sixth Knesset	113	7	73	33	54.3

*All data pertain to Jewish M.K.s at the date of entering each Knesset. Thus, the discrepancy between this and Table III is expected.

in the Sixth Knesset. More significant, however, than the average age is the distribution of the M.K.s. While only 19 members of the First Knesset were over 60, their number rose by 60 percent to 33 in the Sixth Knesset. Similarly, while there were 22 members under the age of forty in the First Knesset, their number decreased to seven in the Sixth.

On the basis of our data on recruitment and domination, we may draw the following conclusion: the continuous increase in the average age of the M.K.s, evident to almost the same extent in all the larger parties, was due mainly to a low rate of turnover, a result of leaders' reluctance to give up their seats. Furthermore, able young men turned to technocratic and military careers. Thus, the aging of the Knesset is an indication of the process of oligarchization so clearly reflected in the nomination practices of the ruling Mapai. The process is similar in all the Jewish parties.

The political dominance of the Labor Party is most conspicuous in its overrepresentation in the Cabinet, which is the most important decision-making body in the Israeli political system (see Table VI). While Mapai polled 32-38 percent of the total votes in the first five elections, and was allocated approximately those percentages of Knesset seats, it always retained an absolute majority of ministers in the Cabinet. Furthermore, it should be

TABLE VI* Cabinet Members by Party Bloc (1948-1972)**

		No.	%
Labor Parties	(1)	39	60.9
Religious Parties	(2)	9	14.1
Right and Center Parties	(3)	12	18.7
Ethnic Parties	(4)	1	1.6
No Party	(5)	3	4.7
	Total:	64	100.0

NOTES: *All the data in this and the following tables pertain to 64 ministers serving in the cabinet from the establishment of the provisional government in 1948 until 1972. The bibliographical data on which the tables are based were taken from the following:

(Hebrew) A. Zidon, *The Knesset-Israel's Parliament* (Jerusalem, Achiasaf, 1960), p. 382-389.

Who's Who in Israel (annual), (Manut Ltd., Tel-Aviv), and periodic "Bibliographical Notes" on government ministers published by the Government Press of Israel.

**Based on the date of entrance.

1. Includes ministers from the following parties: Mapai, Mapam, Achdut HaAvoda, Rafi.

2. Hapoel-Hamizrahi; Misrahi; Agudat Yisrael; Polaei Agudat Yisrael.

3. General Zionists; Liberals; Independent Liberals; Herut.

4. Refers to B. Shitrit, Minister of Police, who joined the Cabinet during the First Knesset as the representative of the Sephardic List, and thereafter joined Mapai.

5. These were ministers who were recruited to the Cabinet as experts: J. Gerry, an industrialist, served as Minister of Commerce and Industry in the Second Cabinet; Haim Cohen, a member of the Supreme Court, who served as Minister of Justice in the Third Cabinet; and Rabb J. M. Toledano, Minister of Religious Affairs in the Eighth and Ninth Cabinets.

recalled that Mapai has always maintained control over the most important ministries, that is, the office of the Prime Minister, as well as posts in Foreign Affairs, Defense and Finance. Among the eighteen members of the inner circle, who Brecher says belong to the top decision-making elite, all but one belong to Mapai or its splinter factions.[32] The nature of the parliamentary system prevailing in Israel requires most members of the Cabinet to be members of the Knesset. Legally, ministers may be recruited from outside the Knesset, but this is an exception rather than the rule. It is therefore no wonder that the social profile of the top decision-making elite resembles that of the membership of the legislature. Thus, the overrepresentation of Eastern Europeans is even more pronounced in the Cabinet. Close to 80 percent of the ministers in the Cabinets between 1948 and 1972 came from Europe; more than two-thirds were from Eastern Europe. The underrepresentation of native-born Israelis and Afro-Asians is distinctly greater in the Cabinet than in the Knesset. Even the symbolic representation of Orientals is much smaller in the Cabinet than in the Knesset; in the last Cabinet included here, there is only one minister of Afro-Asian origin (see Table VII).

As in the case of the Knesset, the vast majority of Cabinet members immigrated to Israel prior to the establishment of the State in 1948. The striking difference between the composition of the Cabinet and the Knesset is the almost complete absence

TABLE VII Cabinet Members by Country of Origin (1948-1972)

	No.	%
East Europe	44	68.8
West Europe	6	9.4
Balkan	2	3.1
Anglo-Saxon	2	3.1
Asia-Africa	3	4.7
Israel	7	10.9
Total:	64	100.0

of new immigrants in the Cabinet (see Table VIII). The only "new immigrant" who was named to the Cabinet (Abba Eban) could hardly be regarded as a newcomer, since he had served for almost a decade as Israel's Ambassador to the United States and the United Nations *before* moving to Israel.

TABLE VIII Cabinet Members by Period of Immigration (1948-1972)

	No.	%
2nd Aliya 1904-1914	7	10.9
3rd Aliya 1919-1923	9	14.1
4th Aliya 1924-1931	19	29.7
5th Aliya 1932-1947	20	31.3
New Immigrants 1948-	1	1.6
Israeli born	7	10.9
Not known	1	1.6
Total:	64	100.0

The majority of the Cabinet members (67 percent) immigrated to Israel during the Fourth and Fifth Aliyot (1924-1947); however, the most important portfolios, prior to the formation of the Thirteenth Government in 1966, were in the hands of members of the Second and Third Aliyot. Thus, the Cabinet, even more than the Knesset, is an exclusive body composed of the pre-State Yishuv elite. But in the last Cabinet, it seems that the torch was being passed to a somewhat "younger" generation. The most important portfolios (except the Premiership) were now in the hands of a member of the Fourth Aliya (Finance); a native-born Israeli (Defense); and a new immigrant (Foreign Affairs).

The relatively large number of kibbutz members in the cabinets reflects the movement's focal position as the chief exponent of the pioneering ideology and a major reservoir of the Labor Party's political leadership. Almost 30 percent of the Cabinet members were or had been kibbutz members (see Table IX). The important political role played by the kibbutz movement has been described by Medding, as follows:

> Mapai was established as a pioneering Zionist-Socialist party, and in this sphere none excelled the highly prestigious kibbutzim. They reclaimed the land and settled it; used self-labour and exploited

TABLE IX Cabinet Members by Membership in an Agricultural Settlement Movement (1948-1972)

	No.	%
Kibbutz Member	12	18.7
Former Kibbutz Member	7	10.9
Former Moshav Member	2	3.1
Not Member	40	62.5
Not Known	3	4.7
Total:	64	100.0

none; made demands upon themselves in the service of collective
ideals; lived a life of strict economic equality; and carried a major
defense burden. They were highly politicised, strongly aware of
the political implications of their activities, and motivated by
political goals. It is little wonder then that the kibbutzim assumed
the leadership of Mapai, and the rest of the party seemed, at first,
hardly more than an appendage of its sector.[33]

Examining the occupations of ministers before they entered
the Cabinet, we again see a great preponderance of professional
politicians. More than two-thirds were recruited initially from a
prominent position in the party, or from a position which they
had held on behalf of their party in the Knesset, the Histadrut
or the Jewish Agency. Moreover, most of the ministers who had
served as diplomats before joining the Cabinet were assigned to
their posts by the party and, therefore, cannot be regarded as
career diplomats (see Table X).

TABLE X Cabinet Members by Occupation* (1948-1972)

	No.	%
Professional Politicians: Party	27	42.2
Professional Politicians: Jewish Agency	6	9.4
Professional Politicians: Histadrut	1	1.6
Professional Politicians: Knesset	9	14.1
Diplomatic Service	5	7.8
Military Service	5	7.8
Government Bureaucracy	7	10.9
Business	1	1.6
Religion	3	4.7
Total:	64	100.0

*Last occupation before entering Cabinet.

The close and durable ties between the ministers and the
party assures them of efficient control over party affairs,
including the process of elite circulation. The political elite has
had remarkable success in maintaining itself continuously in the
Cabinet. This is evident from the comparison of the age distribution of ministers at their entry into the Cabinet with the age
distribution of members when leaving the Cabinet (see Table XI).
Thus only 44 percent of Cabinet members were over 56 years old
when leaving the Cabinet. Such a sharp increase in age clearly reflects long tenure in Cabinet posts. It cannot be explained by the
simple process of natural aging (see Table XI).

TABLE XII Election Results 1973*

Party	Maarach	Likud**	Mafdal	Independent Liberals***	Moded***	Civil Rights List****	Others****
No. of seats	51	39	10	4	1	3	12

*Compare with Table II, p. 237.

**The Likud is a newly formed center right alignment consisting of the following parties; Herut, Liberals, Hamerchaz Hochofshi, State List.

***Moded, the Independent Liberals and the Civil Rights List are expected to support a government lead by the Maarach-labour alignment on matters of foreign policy.

****Parties and seats in Knesset of this group are Arab Lists (affiliated with the Maarach) (2); Rakach (4); Bedouin List (1) and the Religious Front (5).

was not fully prepared for it; Golda Meir, Israel's Prime Minister and leader of the Labor alignment, publicly admitted that a "fatal mistake" had been made by the government in wrongly assessing intelligence reports on Egyptian and Syrian preparations for war. General Arik Sharon, who headed the Israeli counter-offensive that carried Israeli troops across the Suez Canal to within sixty miles of Cairo, had been a key figure in the formation of the Likud—an alignment of center and rightist parties—prior to the war.

The war started just before the Israeli national elections were to have taken place; consequently, many people anticipated that judgment day had arrived for the long-ruling Labor coalition alignment, and that it might lose its dominant role in Israeli politics. However, this did not occur, at least not in terms of election results. The alignment lost only five seats in the Knesset (dropping from 56 seats to 51 out of 120). In spite of this erosion, it is still dominant in one important sense; no other party or combination of parties can form a government (see Table XII). It is interesting to note that two divergent aspects of Israeli politics such as split-ticket voting, and local political alignments outside the regular party structure have intensified.

Although it is beyond the scope of this chapter to discuss in detail how and why Labor maintained its dominance this time around, the reasons are basically the same as those stated above.

First, Labor's organizational skill and capacity were overwhelmingly superior. The party apparatus managed an election campaign against ominous odds. Factional division in the Labor alignment was very high. The popularity of many of the party's leaders was tarnished. The military situation was at a stalemate, and a large part of the Israeli public was mobilized. Consumer prices rose steeply. In spite of all this, the party conducted an effective campaign. It used scare tactics, pointing to the opposition's extremist positions. Interestingly, Likud asked the voters to give it the power to establish a national unity government perhaps because the opposition in Israel does not yet feel free to ask voters for a mandate.

Second, Labor openly admitted its responsibility for mistakes. It stressed its capacity to rule and its ability to seek the middle of the road in future negotiations with the Arab states.

Third, fearing a punitive shift in the vote to the Likud, it reminded the voters that the desire to punish Labor might bring into power the inexperienced extremists of Likud; a voter who tried to punish Labor would be voting against himself and his views, and against responsibility.

Fourth, the party apparatus had the organizational capacity to mobilize every possible segment of society for its support. It even succeeded in coopting a group which had been extremely critical of the party (consisting of university professors and intellectuals) under the cleverly conceived slogan of "Labor Alignment nevertheless"—implying that in spite of all inadequacies, mistakes and mismanagement, one should still vote for Labor. This group had started its public criticism of the party with small, self-financed newspaper ads which demanded, for example, the resignation of Defense Minister Moshe Dayan; it ended by publishing huge ads, paid for by the party, in support of Labor.

Such a campaign could be conducted only by an apparatus confident of the overt and tacit support of a public that still identified the party with the national goals.

After the war, many began to question Labor's ability to remain the dominant party in Israel. This, of course, is a matter for future research. The dominance of the Labor alignment in Israeli politics was perhaps best summarized in the following paraphrased newspaper comment: if this time, after the Judgment Day War, Labor had not been left in mourning, the country was bound to have the party around for some time to come.

The Zionist Left has overcome many challenges. During the Yishuv period, it organized in areas where the Old Yishuv had not. It accommodated itself to changing conditions (lessening its socialistic fervor), actively sought to integrate newcomers, organized and penetrated into many spheres of national life, and identified itself with the epoch. Despite splits and fragmentation, it survived well. Opponents were generally accommodated. Extremists were isolated. Its foundation was and still is a well organized party able to mobilize support. Already in power at independence, it became virtually invincible. It has a strong hold over centralized power through identification with the state, effective vote-getting machines, a monopoly over state spoils, continued support for its pragmatism and the failure of its opponents to make any institutional impact.

NOTES

1. S. N. Eisenstadt, *Israeli Society* (Jerusalem: Magnes Press, 1960).

2. L. Fein, *Politics in Israel* (Boston: Little Brown, 1967).

3. Duverger, *Political Parties: Their Organization and Activity in the Modern State* (New York: Wiley, 1963), p. 308.

Recent public opinion surveys show a drop in the support of Labor among the young; older generations are more strongly Labor oriented. Furthermore, support for Labor is weaker among the highly educated, so education may conceivably be a cue to future shifts; this has been shown in works of Arian cited below. The pattern has been confirmed in four surveys conducted by Arian and Torgovnik during August-December 1973, results of which have not yet been published.

4. See A. Etzioni, "Alternative Ways to Democracy: The Example of Israel," *Political Science Quarterly* 24, 2 (June 1959): 196-214.

5. See Eisenstadt, *Israeli Society*. A discussion of the role of the instructor socializer is given in E. Katz and S. N. Eisenstadt, "Response of Israeli Organizations to New Immigrants," *Administrative Science Quarterly* 5, 1 (June 1960). On the mode of living in a moshav in Israel and its response to the environment see: A. Weingrod, *Reluctant Pioneers: Village Development in Israel* (Ithaca, New York: Cornell University Press, 1966).

6. Gabriel A. Almond, and G. Bingham Powell, *Comparative Politics* (Boston: Little Brown, 1966).

7. P. Y. Medding, *Mapai in Israel* (Cambridge: Cambridge University Press, 1972), p. 10.

8. Medding, Ibid.

9. For an elaborate description of the Yishuv institutions see: S. Sager, "Pre-State Influences on Israeli Parliamentary System," *Parliamentary Affairs* 25, 10 (Winter 1971/2) and D. Horowitz and M. Lissak, *From Yishuv to State* (Papers in Sociology), (Jerusalem: The Elizer Kaplan School of Economics and Social Sciences, 1972).

10. M. Lissak, *Social Mobility in Israeli Society* (Jerusalem: Israel Universities Press, 1969), p. 72.

11. Medding, *Mapai in Israel*.

12. Weingrod, *Reluctant Pioneers*. The relationship of various labor

factions with kibbutz movements and the Histadrut is a highly complex matter deserving separate analysis. In the history of the labor movement in Israel, one may find cardinal importance attached to the exact definition of the role of the various factions, groups and movements. Among the most important issues was, for example, the conflict between kibbutz and early Histadrut leaders over the dominance of Labor.

13. A. Arian, *The Choosing People* (Cleveland, Ohio: Press of Case Western Reserve, 1973).

14. See R. Sharshevsky, *The Structure of Jewish Economy in Early Israel* (Hebrew), (Jerusalem: The Falk Institute for Economic Research, 1968).

15. D. Giladi, "Private Initiative National Capital and the Political Formation of the Right, in *The Social Structure of Israel (Hebrew)*, ed. S. N. Eisenstadt (Jerusalem: Akademon Press, 1965), pp. 85-97.

16. A. Arian, *The Choosing People*.

17. E. Torgovnik, "Election Issues and Interfactional Conflict Resolution in Israel," *Political Studies* 20, 1 (March 1972): 79-96.

18. Ibid.

19. Etzioni, "Alternative Ways to Democracy."

20. A. Arian, "Consensus and Community in Israel," *The Jewish Journal of Sociology* 12, 1 (June 1970): 39-53.

21. Marriage and divorce are based on Jewish law and are controlled by the Rabbinate, not by the State.

22. See Scott D. Johnston, "The Multi-Party System of Israel: Some Aspects of Party Policies in the Parliament (Knesset)," *Studies on Asia* (Lincoln, Nebraska: University of Nebraska Press, 1962), pp. 65-72.

23. A. Akzin, "The Knesset," *International Social Science Journal* 13, 4 (1961): 569.

24. The electoral system is set out in a series of electoral laws, the latest of which are: Knesset Election Law 5719, Laws of Israel (Jerusalem: Government Printer), p. 148; Basic Law: The Knesset, Sefer HaHukim No. 244, 1958; Knesset Elections Law 1969, Sefer HaHukim No. 550. For a discussion of the electoral system and its impact upon the social and political structure of Israel, see Emanuel E. Gutman, "Some Observations on Politics and Parties in Israel," *The Indian Journal of Public Administration* 17 (January-March 1961).

25. For an elaborate treatment of the intricate problems of politcal financing see Emanuel E. Gutman, "Israel" in the "Symposium on Comparative Political Finance," *Journal of Politics* 25 (1963): 703-717.

26. Law of Elections to the Knesset and Local Authorities in the Year 5730 (Finance, Restriction and Control of Expenditure)–1969. The Electoral Law regarding Finance, Restriction and Control of Expenditure and the electoral system in general have been discussed recently by the Chairman of Central Election Committee to the Seventh Knesset. See Chief Justice Alfred Witkon, "Elections in Israel," *Israel Law Review* 5 (January 1970). See also Boim, "Financing of the 1969 Elections" in *The Elections in Israel–1969*, ed. A. Arian (Jerusalem: Jerusalem Academic Press, 1972).

27. B. Akzin, "The Role of Parties in Israeli Democarcy," *Journal of*

Politics 17 (November 1955): 515-520, and Marver Bernstein, *The Politics of Israel* (Princeton: Princeton University Press, 1957), p. 56.

28. A. Brichta, *The Social, Political, and Cultural Background of Knesset Members of Israel* (Hebrew). Ph.D. Dissertation (Hebrew University of Jerusalem, 1972), p. 101.

29. Ibid. The data for the Seventh Knesset are based on A. Brichta, "The Social and Political Characteristics of Members of the Seventh Knesset" in A. Arian, *The Choosing People,* p. 119.

30. The discussion of the Ashkenazi-Sephardic split in Israel is beyond the scope of this paper. It is no doubt an important issue in Israeli politics. In this paper the issue is projected by the discussion of Knesset and Cabinet only. Generally speaking, differences between Ashkenazi and Sepharadi are related to country of origin. The former refers to Jews of European and American origin. Sepharadi origin is Asian and African. For an insightful discussion of the issue in Israel see S. Avineri, "Israel; Two Nations," *Midstream* (May, 1972).

31. M. Lissak, *Social Mobility,* pp. 69-70.

32. See M. Brecher, *The Foreign Policy System of Israel* (London: Oxford University Press, 1972), ch. 10.

33. Medding, *Mapai.*

34. A. Arian, and S. Weiss, "Split Ticket Voting in Israel," *Western Political Quarterly* 23, 2 (June 1969).

35. E. Torgovnik, S. Weiss, "Local Non-Party Political Organization in Israel," *The Western Political Quarterly* 25, 2 (June 1972).

BIBLIOGRAPHY

Arian, A. *The Election in Israel 1969.* Jerusalem: Jerusalem Academic Press, 1972.

Curtis, Michael, and Cheztoff, Mordechai S. eds. *Israel: Social Structure and Change.* New York: Dutton and Co., 1973.

Etzioni, A. "Alternative Ways to Democracy: The Example of Israel," *Political Science Quarterly* 74, 2 (June 1959): 196-214.

Halpern, B. *The Idea of the Jewish State.* Cambridge, Mass.: Harvard University Press, 1961.

Medding, P. Y. "Institutions of the Israeli Labor Party." In *Political Institutions and Processes in Israel,* edited by M. Lissak and E. Gutman. Jerusalem: Academon, Hebrew University, 1971.

Nachmias, D. "A Note on Coalition Payoffs in a Dominant-Party System: Israel," *Political Studies* 3 (September 1973): 301-305.

Nadav, Safran. *From War to War: The Arab-Israeli Confrontation.* New York: Pegasus Press, 1969.

—————. *The United States and Israel.* Cambridge, Mass.: Harvard University Press, 1963.

Perlmutter, Amos. "The Israeli Army in Politics: The Persistence of the Civilian over the Military," *World Politics* 20, 4 (July 1968): 606-643.

Seligman, L. *Leadership in a New Nation.* Chicago, Ill.: Aldine-Atherton, Inc., 1964.

Zweig, F. *Israel: The Sword and the Harp.* London: Heinemann, 1969.

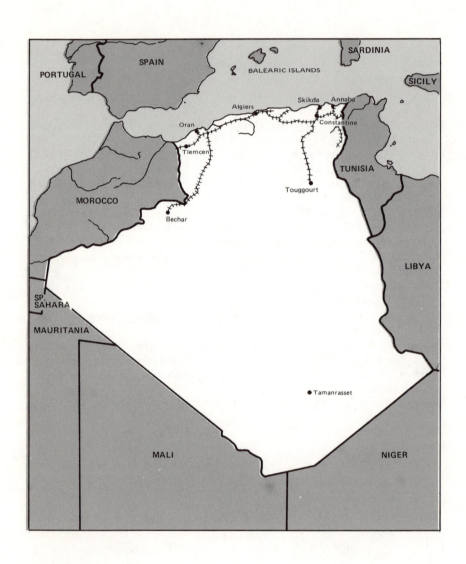

PORTUGAL
SPAIN
SARDINIA
BALEARIC ISLANDS
SICILY
Algiers
Skikda
Annaba
Oran
Constantine
Tlemcen
TUNISIA
MOROCCO
Touggourt
Bechar
LIBYA
SP. SAHARA
MAURITANIA
● Tamanrasset
MALI
NIGER

7

Algeria:
A Post-Revolutionary Elite

I. William Zartman

The following analysis seeks to explain the nature of Algerian policy and policy-makers in terms of elite circulation. Colonial elites followed by those of independent Algeria have instituted policies of development which gave rise to particular types of elite aspirants. Such aspirants and incumbents can be described in many ways and grouped along many dimensions—generational, regional, social, ideological—although many of the data for a full analysis are still elusive. This brief survey will be divided into three parts: Algerian elite circulation in the colonial period, particularly from 1920 to 1962; Algerian elite circulation in the first independent decade (1962-1972); and the production of elite aspirants for the future.

I

Independence in many African and Mideastern countries was won by a Great Coalition of political groups centered about new social forces which had arisen as a result of the modernizing impact of colonialism. Their demands initially grew out of frustrated attempts to overcome the disjuncture between their ascriptive inferiority (native status) and their achievemental equality or superiority (*evolué* status). Nationalist protest evolved through several political stages. When individual imitation of the colonial conquerors' Western ways proved insufficient to secure equal treatment for members of the small modernizing elite, they joined together in reform groups (the first stage). These interest-oriented elite associations militated for equal treatment on the basis of modern skills. In rare cases, independence was achieved at this stage, granted rather than being won. In most cases, the modernized elite saw that their efforts were not achieving equality but were separating them from their own national compatriots and national culture. They then turned back to the mass as a source of both power and identity and formed a nationalist movement (the second stage). The nationalist movement no longer recognized the legitimacy of the colonial system, which had proven incapable of accomplishing assimilation, but sought to set up its own system of national sovereignty. In the process of creating a mass-type movement, however, the modernized elites were obliged to dilute their modernism and to include traditional leaders whose shared characteristic was nationality, not modernity. Thus, a Great Coalition was formed. In most cases, independence was achieved at this point. In some cases, however, the nationalist movement was also unsuccessful and it was necessary to invoke the ultimate form of power, violence. The result was a revolutionary force (the third stage), in which the mass was no longer in an instrumental stage as before but provided its own leadership. To this group, independence was not enough; social change was also deemed necessary. Such has been the case in Algeria.

The winning form of the nationalist protest has had much to do with the form of political organization after independence.[1] When reform groups win independence, a competitive patron-party system has generally evolved. When nationalist movements win independence, a cooptive single-party system has tended to occur. When revolutionary forces win independence, a controlled technocratic no-party system has usually arisen. This essay will consider the three-stage evolution and its outcomes as a hypothetical model, and use it to give greater coherence to the explanation of events as well as to suggest the need for alternative explanations for those that do not "fit." In one of the original formulations of the model, emphasis was placed on the natural unfolding of the stages, which provided for the maturation of aspirant elites in each stage before going on to the next.[2] In another, each stage was considered as a socialization period, shaping the elites' attitudes and values.[3] Related to these notions is the idea that there are appropriate levels of power for the given goals of particular situations, and that frustration in achieving those goals leads to a new type of elite that either accepts reduced goals or seeks a power base necessary for the accomplishment of the original aims. These notions will be developed further in the discussion of each stage in Algerian nationalism. In the process, comparisons will be noted to bring out differences and similarities with Algeria's North African neighbors and with the other countries of the Middle East.[4]

Located on the northern coast of Africa, across the Mediterranean from France and Spain, Algeria is the second largest (after Sudan) but the sixth most populous country of the Middle East (after Turkey, Egypt, Iran, Sudan and Morocco). For the most part its 1970 population of 13 million was located along a 100-mile coastal strip, in cities and on plains and plateaus running parallel to the coast, with grazing highlands and vast desert reaches stretching southward to black Africa. The Muslim Algerian population increases at a rate of slightly over 3 percent and will thus double every quarter-century (as it did in the preceding quarter-century, despite wars); at that rate, half of the population is younger than 18. Despite an old tradition of urban life dating from Greek, Roman and Arab conquests and reinforced by the French colonization, less than a fifth of the Muslim population lived in towns over 10,000 at the end of World War II and only a tenth lived in cities over 100,000 (Algiers, Oran, Constantine and Bone [later renamed Annaba]); twenty years later, these proportions had risen to a third and an eighth.

This population distribution has left its imprint on social patterns. Unlike Tunisia and Egypt, Algeria's life has not been centered around one predominant urban center; it is only recently that some signs in this direction are appearing and they are not yet conclusive. The pattern of life around several provincial centers is still strong, but it has not taken on the political forms of inter-urban rivalry that would make apparent parallels with Syria appropriate. Nor has the division between Arabs and Berbers (about 18 percent of the population) reached the constant and characteristic position of political pluralism in Lebanon. Nevertheless, the historic tripartite provincial division (as among the eighteenth-century Turkish beylics of Mascara-Oran, Medea, and Constantine, plus *dar el-soltan* at Algiers), the ethnic differences between Arabs and Kabyles (the largest

TABLE I: Social & Economic Strata at the Outbreak of the Revolution

(Source: *Rapport du groupe d'étude des relations financières entre la Métropole et l'Algérie* [Maspetiol Report], [Algiers: Gouvernement général, 1955]. pp. 79-80, as calculated by Joan Gillespie, *Algeria* [London: Benn, 1960], p. 34).

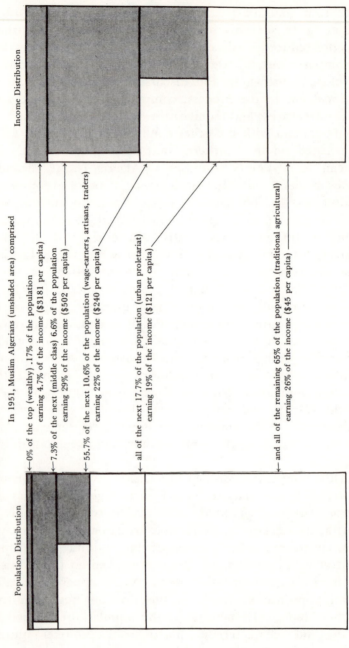

Population Distribution

Income Distribution

In 1951, Muslim Algerians (unshaded area) comprised

←0% of the top (wealthy) .17% of the population
earning 4.7% of the income ($3181 per capita) ——

←7.3% of the next (middle class) 6.6% of the population
earning 29% of the income ($502 per capita) ——

←55.7% of the next 10.6% of the population (wage-earners, artisans, traders)
earning 22% of the income ($240 per capita) ——

←all of the next 17.7% of the population (urban proletariat)
earning 19% of the income ($121 per capita) ——

←and all of the remaining 65% of the population (traditional agricultural)
earning 26% of the income ($45 per capita) ——

Berber group), the growing separation between traditional Islamic and Europeanized Algerians, and the personal and geographic bases of political divisions during the nationalist struggle has meant that national unity has been more of an item to be forged in Algeria than in Tunisia, Turkey, or Egypt, and probably even more than in Morocco.

The dynamics of modern nationalism began with the involvement of Algerians in the colonial society, economy and polity, their promotion and blockage, and the consequent production of leaders of demand-bearing groups in each area of activity. This involvement was accomplished through the entrance of Algerians into education, labor, and organized political activity, all during the interwar period. The first reaction of these inchoate groups was thus to imitate the conqueror and take on his ways. The dynamics of nationalization began when imitation provided individuals who qualified achievementally for equal status with the settlers but who found themselves blocked ascriptively by their native status (See Table I).

Figures drawn from an official French investigation just before the outbreak of the revolution can be presented to show very graphically how the ascriptive ethnic barrier—shown in the "population distribution" in the accompanying Table—combined with an unequal income distribution, created conditions ripe for a social protest movement couched in nationalist terms. Although the process which created a revolutionary force may be said to have begun with the arrival of the French in the nominally Turkish beylics of Algeria in 1830, the modern stages of nationalist protest began to evolve a century later, with the coming of the inter-war depression and the ripening of earlier, slower social changes.

By 1930, at the edge of the depression, about 70,000 Algerian children, or 7 percent of the school-age population, were in modern (French) elementary schools and a tenth of that figure were in Muslim "free" (semi-modern) schools. These children came primarily from two social groups, the traditional notables' families and the families of the petite bourgeoisie.[5] The economic power base of the first generally came from land, and of the second from commercial incomes, although there was a good deal of overlap between the two. Some of the primary graduates went on to secondary and higher education and entered the liberal professions, where they sought equal treatment with the settlers in the same situations.

The largest labor group—about 100,000 in 1930, falling to 30,000 in 1936, and rising again thereafter—was found among the Algerian immigrants to France, with a smaller number in Algeria where industry was less developed. The abnormally low social position of the first group, uprooted and transplanted into an alien society, led to early political action. Labor was not only urban, however; the settler acquisition of the best land pushed many families into villages and towns or directly into agricultural labor or tenant farming, where they often led a more dependent and precarious economic life than they had as smallholders or as *khammes* (traditional sharecroppers).[6] Finally, since the end of the nineteenth century, a small number of elected positions for Algerians were provided on municipal, regional, and territorial councils. For the most part, these members tended to come from the landed notables, with a lesser mixture of civil servants, liberal professionals, and merchants.[7]

If these individuals had been able to pursue their work on an equal basis while still retaining their Muslim status and not suffer any discrimination because of it, the evolution of Algerian political elites might have been quite different. The conditions to permit such a development did not exist; the very minority nature of the colonial overlay, which needed to rely on ascriptive criteria to maintain its advantage, forced the Algerians to take political action to seek equality. As a result, they banded together along socio-economic lines into reform groups, usually with limited, reformist, assimilationist goals.

The most moderate group, as might be expected, was already among the political elite working within the colonial political system. In 1927, a pharmacist and *qaid's* son named Ferhat 'Abbas and other Muslim representatives formed an association (the Federation of Elected Officials) to foster assimilation.[8] Its members came primarily from the liberal professions and thus, represented the social or educated elite as a demand-bearing group. The hopes of this group were dashed by the defeat of the Blum-Violette bill for limited assimilation just before World War II and their political activity was soon curtailed by the war itself. Two other groups created by the colonial impact were scarcely assimilationist. On one hand, teachers and students of the free schools and their religious mentors combined in 1931 to form an Association of the *'ulama* to proclaim a religious reformist nationalism that undercut the collaborationist folk religious sects and prepared the seedbed of future elite members. The fact that the 'ulama were clearly a demand-bearing group with their own interests does not diminish the widespread appeal they had among the general population. On the other hand, workers and other emigrants to France fell under the sway of the charismatic nationalist leader, Hajj Messali, and his successive organizations, the North African Star in 1927 and, when it was banned in 1937, the Algerian Peoples' Party (PPA). The Messalists' demand for independence was far ahead of the goals of the other organizations and groups and totally out of tune with any current possibilities. As a result, they were frustrated and grew increasingly desperate.

Within this early stage, some unusual characteristics of the Algerian nationalist protest become evident. The newly promoted (evolué) elite aspirants were working their way through the business of seeking reforms for their personal problems within the political system and learned gradually, through trial and error, of the inadequacy of their limited, political methods. Second, there were also other groups which were dislocated and had not profited by contact with the colonial economy and society, and which had already totally rejected the system and were even on the verge of adopting violence as their method. Furthermore, this latter segment of the protest movement did not suffer from separation from the masses and from their traditional culture as did the reform groups, and hence, were not to feel the need for a return to the people: they were the people.

As a result, smooth passage to the next stage—the nationalist movement—was replaced by a temporary stumbling move in that direction accompanied by some equally transient and inadequate stabs at revolution. Only when these various currents came together was it possible to overthrow the colonial system. While the war in North Africa was still going on in February 1943, 'Abbas in consultation with some of the Messalists issued a *Manifesto of the Algerian People,* calling for a sovereign, autonomous, but not specifically independent, Algeria and for a list of explicit social, economic, and political reforms, to which others were added in a *Supplement* in May. Initially, the move was effective: official negotiations between the French and the Algerian Muslims were begun toward the implementation of the *Manifesto* and the Friends of the Manifesto and of Liberty

(AML) were organized in March 1944. Middle-class followers of 'Abbas also joined lower-class followers of Messali and the 'ulama, over half a million in number, to form a nationalist movement much larger than the party-movements of Morocco and Tunisia at the same time.

In the same month, a new decree was issued, applying in expanded form the provisions of the Blum-Violette bill. It was nearly a decade—and, indeed, an entire War—too late. The "success" of the nationalist movement in accomplishing changes that were only meaningful for a modernized elite—changes that were the goals of the reform groups—quickly showed that political means and those who espoused them were inadequate to the situation; the current demands far outstripped the belated reforms. The Messalists took over the AML in March 1945 and two months later, on V-E Day, tensions between the Algerian Muslims and French escalated a popular, Messalist-led demonstration in Setif and elsewhere into a bloody encounter followed by a savage repression.[9] It was Algeria's "December Revolution." The repression cut short PPA plans for a general insurrection and the early institutional debates of the French Fourth Republic provided a political interlude during which the last hopes rose and were finally and completely destroyed. The organizations of this period were the Messalist Movement for the Triumph of Democratic Liberties (MTLD) and the 'Abbasist Democratic Union of the Algerian Manifesto (UDMA). At the same time, however, the interlude provided a chance for a new leadership to arise. Had the revolutionary war broken out in 1945, as a continuation of the Setif demonstration, hardly any of the eventual elite would have been old enough to take part. Not only were specific individuals not yet available, but an entirely new group with certain characteristics had not yet been propelled into political activity.

Who were these new leaders? Quandt's and Michel's detailed research shows them to be of a low social status with little education and of an average age of 20 at the end of the war, coming from rural towns and villages.[10] Unlike their predecessors, they had little to lose and could, therefore, engage in a total struggle with violence as a weapon and elimination a sure risk for one party or the other in every encounter. Yet, certainly, such people were not lacking in Algeria at any time. The newly educated or newly salaried needed time to appear in sufficient numbers, to be prepared for their aspirations to rise, and then to feel the frustration of ascriptive rejection. But why did "those who had nothing to lose" need to await their moment to appear? The most convincing argument, if somewhat circular, is probably that although people in their objective condition were never lacking, the realization that positive action against colonial subjection could be initiated had yet to come. Previously, people had not yet accepted the idea that violence could be used successfully against those who until then had monopolized violence. The realization that the mass was both available and a useful tool had also been missing. In other words, subjective awareness had yet to be added to an objective condition for both the leaders and an inchoate group of followers. Once the revolutionary forces stage was begun, it was a slow but cumulative process to use violence to develop support among those masses that the 'ulama and the Messalists had prepared but also among those traditional and modernized elites that had been deceived by the colonization. Thus, it took a revolutionary force to create a nationalist movement acting in the name of the overriding goal of independence, but as a result, some sharp divisions over social policy were both exacerbated and plastered over.

The process began in 1948, when rigged elections and the arrest of Algerian Muslim candidates showed with finality the futility of attempts at assimilation and of the old political methods. A few Messalist leaders set up a Special Organization (OS) dedicated to total independence through violence. This organization grew into the Revolutionary Unity and Action Committee (CRUA) that began the revolution in 1954, into the successful National Liberation Front (FLN) with its National Liberation Army (ALN) that fought the revolutionary war after 1956, and into the Provisional Government of the Algerian Republic (GPRA) that negotiated independence after 1958.

Although the revolutionary war period covers less than a decade, it is possible to discern quite distinct phases within it, each with its own particular incumbent and rising elites. The first phase covers the initial two years of the war, in its pre-institutionalized stage, when leadership was composed of those young radicals left over from the previous period and their small guerrilla bands. Revolutionary violence was seen by this group as a doubled-edged sword, designed to accomplish two goals that previous political action had failed to achieve: mobilization of the Algerian Muslim mass and destruction of French military control over the country. Their efforts were significantly more successful in achieving the first goal than the second one but the very process of mobilization brought on a new stage of evolution and eventually won by political means the ends that could not be attained militarily.

By the end of 1956, most of the former nationalist leaders (with the notable exception of Messali) had joined the FLN, the interior guerrillas had been organized into regional forces or *wilayas*, but the young "historic chiefs" of the revolution were almost entirely eliminated. An important new collection of guerrilla forces had grown up within the country, more representive of a mass organization than were the leaders who manned the external office in Cairo. Although these guerrillas shared the title of FLN, they organized themselves into a National Liberation Army (ALN) when 50 of their leaders met clandestinely in the Soummam river valley in August 1956. In addition to the ALN, they also established a 17-man proto-parliament, the National Council of the Algerian Revolution (CNRA), and a five-man Coordination and Execution Committee (CCE) as an executive. The Congress affirmed the primacy of the interior over the exterior, of the political over the military (two contradictory assertions that were to trouble Algerian politics for the next decade), and of collegial decision-making over *zu'ama* (charismatic leadership).

Yet, it was a new leadership that inherited the fruits of this situation. By the beginning of 1956, all but two of the nine "historic chiefs" had been killed, jailed, or exiled. By the end of the year, out of this group only Krim Belqasim was alive and out of jail. Nine of the CNRA were dead or jailed, and the leadership was forced to flee to Cairo and Tunis. At the beginning of 1957, the Battle of Algiers was lost and the guerrillas withdrew back to the maquis in the countryside; by the end of the year, they were cut off from sources of arms and messages by the fortified barrier along the Tunisian frontier, soon to be complemented by a similar seal on the Moroccan side. Nevertheless, recruitment continued. In the interior, peasants and townsmen, farmers and workers, joined the guerrilla bands. In both Algeria and France, a students' strike called by the CCE in 1956 started an important influx toward the FLN. In France, a bloody battle went on between the FLN and the Messalist organization, the Algerian National Movement (MNA), until the latter was destroyed. The CNRA meeting in August 1957 reacted to all these developments by cancelling the contradictory affirmations of Soummam (thus reversing the contradiction) and electing a new, larger CCE representing many views and backgrounds.

The Algerian nationalist movement was decisively influenced by changes in the French political scene in 1958 when the French army began to undermine the civil government. Spurred on by its success against the nationalists, the French army pursued the ALN into its Tunisian bases in February. The increased military activity in Algeria was met by political indecision in Paris and international political intervention in the war in March. In May 1958 the army overthrew the French government. The Algerian nationalists were uncertain about the best policy to adopt toward these events, since their direction was unclear. The FLN made a major shift, however, at a meeting of North African parties in April in Tangier. It abandoned its insistence on unconditional recognition of independence (leaving only the conditions of the transfer of sovereignty open to negotiation) in favor of a limited demand of the right to independence as a precondition to negotiations. In September, before de Gaulle was elected President, the FLN strengthened its international position by forming a Provisional Government (GPRA) which declared its readiness to negotiate. It was a comprehensive group of 14 men (with the addition of five "historic chiefs" still in prison in France) most of them had been active in pre-1948 politics; however, three individuals had risen from the *wilayas* and one had joined after the student strike. Ten days later, Muslim and French Algerians voted massively in favor of the new constitution of the French Fifth Republic, in reality a plebiscite of confidence in de Gaulle's ability to find a solution.

Yet neither side was strong enough to come to terms, although the French needed more time than did the Algerians. De Gaulle, trying to unite his country and disarm his opposition at first made an unenticing offer of amnesty and then, more than a year after taking office, announced the possibility of a solution by referendum and a choice of independence. The following January, 1960, in Algeria, the CNRA reorganized the Provisional

Government into a smaller group with increased representation from the wilayas and an Interministerial War Council of three wilaya leaders, Krim, Boussouf and Ben Tobbal who were charged with carrying out negotiations. The first round began in June 1960 at Melun and rapidly broke down; the second took place at Evian and Lugrin a year later and made some progress; and the third at Evian ended with a ceasefire on 19 March 1962.

The formation of the GPRA in Tunis and the shift in emphasis from guerrilla to diplomatic efforts created an opportunity for better trained individuals with political, administrative, and technical skills. A proto-administration began to grow, probably more active in training than in actual management. Following the Evian Accords, a Franco-Algerian caretaker administration, the Provisional Executive, was created until an Algerian government could be established. The Provisional Executive incorporated the services of Algerian civil servants in the colonial administration who wanted to stay, but it also brought in many of the young technicians and services of the GPRA.[11] Thus, by the time the independent government of "historic chief" Ahmed Ben Bella was installed, an administrative service of young technicians trained by the French educational system and liberated from the blockage of the colonial society by a change in the political system had come into existence.

The nationalist armed effort was not abandoned, but it underwent an important change. At the same time as the second GPRA was formed, the CNRA set up Military Operations Committees in Tunisia and Morocco, as the effective French grid tactics and frontier barriers had forced many of the ALN guerillas to take refuge in these countries. A few months later, in March 1960, a General Staff was established under the command of Col. Houari Boumedienne, a former Qoranic teacher and commander of the Oran wilaya. The forces that gathered on the borders were drilled into a modern conventional army.

The origins of the ALN officers were diverse, but they included students, workers, and farmers, technically and politically formed into a tight organization. Since they were in little physical danger but were trained for war, they developed a hard-line policy on the conditions of independence and possible future relations with France but also on social change and the eventual nature of the Algerian elite. Activist military rebellions such as the Colonel's revolt of 1959 and the Moroccan border mutiny of January 1962, in addition to the sharp debates in the CNRA in August 1961 and early 1962, were clashes caused by the hard-line military stand as well as personal rivalries.

In the maquis, a dwindling number (10,000-15,000) of guerrillas had become increasingly isolated from each other and the outside, in an endangered and expendable position which created considerable resentment. Once the French decision to discuss independence had been made, their role was to maintain enough pressure to keep the French settlers from changing de Gaulle's policy, but they were neither needed nor able to win the war militarily. As in the case of the French army, these strains produced fissures in the nationalist Front and added to the bitter debates in the CNRA.

It is not surprising, therefore, that at independence just as during the nationalist struggle, Algeria was to be led by a coalition of nationalists from diverse backgrounds and with conflicting views on social, economic, and political issues, until the regime could establish its legitimacy and its institutions.

II

At the end of the revolutionary war in 1962, Algeria appeared to be on the brink of a co-optive single party system, an outcome that seemed to diverge from the trends of the final revolutionary stage. The discrepancy was illusory, however: within a short period the State had slipped into a controlled technocratic system (judged by its attitudes toward elite circulation and nature of dominant elites). To understand this evolution and the first decade of independent Algerian politics, one must look more closely at the various elite groups inherited from the revolution and the sources of their power, and their demands within the context of development and its impact on elite circulation. Again, there are rather distinct phases, with differing elites, policies, and aspirants. After the 1962 struggle for power, Algerian politics could be divided into the Ben Bella (1963-65) and Boumedienne (1965-   ) periods, on the basis of the top leadership. A more useful division, based on a larger political group, would be to designate the first half of the independent decade (1962-1967) as the period of the *mujahidin* (warriors) and the second half and beyond (1968-) as the period of the technicians.[12] The following discussion will define the periods and focus on the groups active in them.

As in other states established after a revolution, Algeria at independence had a truncated economic and social pyramid; those who had enjoyed the greatest wealth and status under the colonial system had either left the country or were leaving. Certain wealthy Muslims remained but their power was weakened by the current ideology which associated wealth with collaboration. Even toward the end of the decade, a proclamation announcing the creation of a Revolutionary Court indicated that "History of the peoples of the world proves ... that no Revolution, because of its dynamism and its specificity, can please everyone. Those who are opposed often come from the former privileged classes, large landowners or industrialists, and those thirsty for power."[13] Many of these people were able to keep their wealth at the cost of lying low and using their economic power base politically for defensive purposes only. In mid-1963, when under attack in a wave of confiscations by Ben Bella's entourage, they were able to amass enough indirect pressure to have some of the seizures stopped, but there were others which were not annulled until two years later when Boumedienne seized power. Since then, they have shown that discretion is the better part of power; even the slowness in the promulgation of an agrarian reform has been due more to their allies within the governing elite than to their own efforts. Indeed, the wealthier Algerians, landowners and merchants rather than industrialists for the most part, have been joined by the governing elite rather than joining them. The sons of the landowners or merchants are not often found among the political elite; yet members of the political elite have bought up land and bought into commerce, developing common interests with the older wealthy families. The clash between the value of possession and the value of management, between consumer and producer ethics, has not yet developed beyond passing ideological references but its existence and implications will be important subjects for further inquiry as the current generation continues to hold power.[14]

The normal criteria for status were also disrupted by the war, and a new elusive basis was introduced—participation in the revolution.[15] "Those who struggled," the mujahidin, were accorded special deference, regardless of their actual role; they had made the revolution and were considered to be the most deserving of the Algerian people, and hence, should benefit from the revolution they had made. It soon became evident, however, that the skills which made them good fighters were not necessarily those required in the period of reconstruction. Neither the source of the mujahidin's power, the means of violence, nor the uncompromising, non-negotiable, action-oriented attitudes which it engendered, were suitable for government. The result was the creation of the politics of tension, since the qualities which made the new elite deserving also made them useless and even disruptive.

It took exactly half a decade to depoliticise the mujahidin leaders, either reintegrating them into civilian life or by encouraging them to join the army as professional soldiers. Curiously, the mujahidin were not the original governing force; in the struggle for power of late 1962, they lost out to a coalition of radical politicians and external army leaders (on the latter, see below). They were unable to overcome their own wartime heritage of clandestine activity and factional politics and come to an agreement on a governing coalition of their own in the wilaya conference of July 1962 in Tlemcen and al-Asnam. Thus, divided they fell before the persuasion of Ben Bella and the coercion of Boumedienne's forces. With the help of some allies among the wilayas, the Ben Bella-Boumedienne group was then able to overcome the others; in the process, from August to September 1962, the wilayas lost to the army most of their seats among the National Assembly nominees. The issues which separated them from the winners concerned the future organization of state and society and the distribution of the spoils of victory, but above all the question of who should rule.

But the men who fought in the tough guerrilla war could not be easily sent back to the farm. Neglected by the government, deprived of the spoils of war, they fell back on the only means they knew of calling attention to themselves—violence.[16] Either as individuals, or as groups based on the old wilayas, or even as parties (the Socialist Revolution Party—PRS—of Mohammed Boudiaf and then the Socialist Forces' Front—FFS—of Hocine Ait Ahmed and Mohand oul-Hajj), they took up arms again during the first year of independence until the Morocco-Algerian border war provided a rallying cause of patriotism and a diversion in the use of violence. In exchange for support, however, the respected mujahidin leader, Col. oul-Hajj of wilaya 3 (Kabylia), negotiated an agreement in November 1963, which provided for a full-scale congress of the FLN (whose membership was limited to those with a record of participation in the revolutionary war). In the Political Bureau that emerged from the Congress of April 1964, the mujahidin finally achieved some small representation on a major political body (4 of the 17 members of the Political Bureau were wilaya leaders and another 2 can be counted as mujahidin). During the year that followed, Ben Bella gradually shifted his alliances away from the army and toward the rebellious wilaya groups which the army had slowly been defeating. The president and the army had already had a major confrontation before the Congress, and before a major reversal in the alliances could take place, the army overthrew the regime on 19 June 1965.

Boumedienne's new coalition included, perhaps surprisingly, both mujahidin and technicians. The party's Executive Secretariat, successor to the party functions of the Political Bureau, had wilaya leaders as 4 of its 5 members, and the five wilaya commanders were members of the Council of the Revolution, which took over the Political Bureau's policy functions. Neither body worked well. The party Executive floundered in inactivity, and the Council split in two as the military technicians behind Boumedienne were challenged by the mujahidin, once again revealing a conflict between producer and consumer ethics. By letting the bitterness of personal and group rivalry run its course and envenom each substantive issue that came up in the Council, Boumedienne finally brought the mujahidin leader, Col. Tahar Zbiri, to a half-hearted and ill-planned coup against the regime and easily defeated him. With the coup manqué of December 1967, the power of the mujahidin was broken, and their major leaders blended back into civilian life.

One other group was inherited from the previous history of the nationalist movement and had to be worked out of the political system, if it could not be integrated into it. Like the mujahidin, the politicians, the pre-war reformist nationalists, were victims of their sources of and attitudes toward power, although these differed considerably in the two cases.[17] Politicians had a place in the nationalist struggle through the Provisional Government, where their belief and skill in the political exercise of power were useful in the diplomacy that finally won independence. Applying the doctrine of "my neighbor is my enemy" to ideological position, they supported Ben Bella in reaction to the second GPRA, of Benkhedda, and were rewarded with five seats in the National Assembly, over which 'Abbas presided, and two seats in the Council of Ministers. After the first year of independence, however, they became increasingly useless and obstreperous. As politicians in a revolution, they were ineffective against the rising military importance and they were unappealing to potential audiences. As liberals and democrats, trained in a bygone era, they felt that the elected Assembly was the seat of sovereignty and the voice of the people, and thus, conflicted with Ben Bella who had his own ideology.[18] They criticized his laws, wanted to write his constitution, and competed with his legitimacy. By the second year of independence, none of these members remained in the Council of Ministers or the Political Bureau, and only one remained in the Assembly. From the point of view of needed skills, it is not surprising that although some of the politicians were released from prison during Ben Bella's alliance shifts in the third year of independence, none reappeared in the Boumedienne coalition. Their skills were obsolete.

In addition to the old colonial elite and the new revolutionary elite, there were other groups, both inside and outside the broad mujahidin category who were products of the political, economic, and social changes of the previous decades. Although the term "mujahidin" has been used to describe a general category, it is best hereafter to assign it to a more restricted usage, referring only to the wilayists who fought in the interior of the country. The troops tended to be local peasants and townsmen whose major aim was to free themselves of the disruptive foreign presence and return to their work, and the officers tended to resemble their troops. Since the military fortunes of the wilayas during the war were not impressive, the best of the former wilaya (and smaller unit) leaders had made their way to the military camps in neighboring Morocco and Tunisia. In Morocco and Tunisia, however, the external National Liberation Army (ALN) was a different type of armed force. Many of their officers were either former officers from the French army (a major group joined the FLN in 1958) or former students from France or Algiers (many of whom joined in

1956). They had served their apprenticeship in the guerrilla interior but by 1960 were part of the new conventional army being set up on the borders. With the Evian cease-fire, the ALN began to move into the country, relieving the French army and displacing rival groups of wilayists, to take over local political control. This action was crucial to the struggle for power in the latter half of 1962 and the installation of Ben Bella with Boumedienne behind him.

Once its immediate occupation task was accomplished, the ALN began dividing in three directions. The best-trained and most ambitious of its young officers went on to Algiers, where 8 immediately became ministers and many more took over top positions of state management. The group below them remained in uniform in the new Algerian People's Army (ANP), perhaps 100-150 as majors and colonels but several thousands as captains and lieutenants, politically alert and technically well-trained. The least well-trained and capable (but perhaps equally ambitious) stayed on the spot and became local party officials. These three groups were to be the central elements of Algerian politics for the coming decade and more.

When people work together under conditions of solidarity, they are socialized into a cohesiveness that makes them a group. When the group dissolves and its members enter other working conditions and form other groups, their cohesiveness stays with them as a past experience but their new group exerts its own socializing influence. If the current group is demanding, organized, and rewarding, it will override past allegiances and identifications; if not, it will merely be a subordinate or an extension of the past experience. Although the three major units of Algerian politics—administration, army, party—have each had very different internal characteristics, they all fall in the first category of an overriding new allegiance to a greater or lesser degree. Since the generation in question was born during the thirties, with older members who were born during the latter part of the twenties, the socializing experiences of their youth were drawn from the war and the postwar context of nationalism as their families and schools were operating in that context. The wartime ALN experience has remained an important heritage for those who shared it, but it has become subordinate to their membership in one of the new groups, with its own natures and demands. Furthermore, the vast majority of the elite population under consideration was rapidly promoted to the three new groups of leaders in government, the army and local politics, without strong antecedent ties and obligations, and was therefore, ready to identify strongly with its particular new group.

These characteristics enabled the new managerial, military, and party elites to identify strongly with the new organizations. Unlike scions of old families who take their place in institutions (whether established or, a fortiori, new) as "delegates" from their social groups, the new elites of Algeria became organization men with the particular imprint of their organization.[19] Because both were new, the elites and the organizations grew together, the elites using the organizational power to defend and promote the organization's interests. What is particularly impressive is the stability of each group, despite the varying fortunes of their three organizations.

These three groups in government, army, and local politics which grew out of the ALN can also be analyzed as technicians since their roles and the particular type of skills demanded are specifically modern ones, related to inanimate sources of power and the use of tools. It is the predominance of people who possess this skill and fill this role among the Algerian elite which qualify it as a technocratic system (the second characteristic mentioned above, control, will be developed below). Whether the technicians deal in military, managerial, or mobilization matters (that is, whether they were army, administrative, or party technocrats), they were still part of the broad category and it was the technocratic aspect that was dominant.[20]

The young cadres of the ALN were not the only ones to fill the three variants on the technicians' role, however, although they were the predominant source. The regime's administrators have also continued to be recruited from elsewhere. The military, too, has also been recruited from other sources. The party, however, has had little personnel turnover since its establishment. These facts will be developed further, as they have important bearings on the nature of each group.

To form the administrators, the ALN cadres were joined by the young employees in the administrative services of the Algerian Provisional Government (GPRA), the Provisional Executive, and the colonial civil service. Although it was not until 1966 that GPRA technicians were named ministers, the group dominated the ministries holding most offices from that of the secretary-general to many junior ones following independence. Since independence, the civil service continues to expand and recruits are drawn from the secondary school and university graduates.

One of the major political disputes during the first year or more of the Algerian regime was the conflict over the proper size of the army. There was, in any case, an over-abundance of ALN cadres who could serve as new recruits. Once the conflict was resolved in 1963 with the expulsion of Mohammed Khider (one of the 3 "historic chiefs" left in the government) and the military reorganization subsequent to the Moroccan border war and Kabyle (PRS and FFS) rebellion, volunteers were admitted to the army. Two years after the June 1967 war, a two-year conscription was also put into effect to train reservists.

After the ALN officers had been incorporated as party cadres, there were few places for new recruits. An important means for recruiting new members, however, was the series of elections for the hierarchy of positions in the party structure. These elections were to be held to choose delegations to the Party Congress of 1964 and were part of the organizational plans of the Executive Secretariat and then the Leader (Ahmed Qaid) was to be installed under Boumedienne. Unfortunately, none of these recruitment devices has ever come to full fruition, and the only elections ever held were at the local level in 1969 and 1970.

We can now proceed to an analysis of the power sources and the demands made by the three technicians' groups in order to explain some of the above characteristics. We have already noted the characteristics of the National Liberation Front, Algeria's single party, as a less qualified elite with little turnover or activity. These attributes are all reinforced by its power and interests.[21] The FLN has had strikingly little power in Algeria, both before and after independence. In order to understand this situation we will need both a clearer idea of what "FLN" means and an evaluation of its available sources of power. If FLN is taken to mean something specific and organized (as opposed to general sympathizers), it must be separated from the ALN and the GPRA during the revolutionary war. Defined in these terms, the organization is reduced to the Federation of France, the FLN branch in the metropole. Similarly, during the Ben Bella period after the war, it is again necessary to separate the party from the Council of Ministers, Political Bureau (a sort of presidential council), and National Assembly, as it must also be distinguished from the Council of Ministers and Council of the Revolution under Boumedienne. Even the 1964 Central Committee of the FLN was composed of prominent political leaders (and allies of Ben Bella) who were set on top of the party structure and had not been drawn from or associated with the party's operations.

As a result, the party was either an uncoordinated series of local fiefs, a confederation of peacetime *wilayas,* as under Ben Bella, or a ministry of information and organization, a network of clubhouses and publicity offices, as under Boumedienne. Party offices were used neither for the formulation and execution of policy nor for influencing those who were policymakers, nor did party leaders develop or articulate a guiding ideology. Even minor favors that are indispensable to the operation of parties were not dispensed by the FLN; if an Algerian needed aid on matters of food, job, salary, education, health, security, or mistreatment by bureaucracy, he would find no help from the party, with some few local exceptions. Party elites simply had no power, and, paradoxically, powerlessness was the best way for them to defend their minor interests, since their jobs were not worth taking away from them. By the same token, the party elite's role was anything but a vanguard; its task was to propagate others' policy, defend others' candidates, and make sure it knew which leader to follow in a coup (as in 1965, when most local party leaders deserted Ben Bella).

The power and interests of the military elite in the ANP were more highly developed. Their origins provided them with the notion that they were the quintessence of the Revolution and the microcosm of the mujahidin, since they were the ones who had fought and were also trained and organized well enough to have had some ideological notion of the values of the revolution. As a result, they did not want any politicians or people with a less clear idea of their mission to govern their affairs, and the ANP officers, therefore, firmly held the notion of the army as the guardian of the Revolution. The military elite, however, have never been interested in governing directly but believe in intervention to correct the situation when necessary, followed by a return to the barracks to observe the political process with a keen eye and a discrete hand.

The two interventions were turning points in Algerian politics.

In the 1962 struggle for power, the external ALN was the major force behind Ben Bella, thrown into his arms by the attempt of the GPRA (Benkhedda) to fire the ALN general staff preparatory to a full "reconversion." When enough wilayas were defeated, undermined, or converted by the ALN to swing the balance behind Ben Bella, the military elite could return to the job of building a conventional army. During the next three years, however, Ben Bella gradually moved away from his military allies, using them more and more for internal policing while negotiating with the dissident elements that they defeated. An effort to clear the air before the 1964 Party Congress proved to be a failure and instead, Ben Bella began to remove the military representatives from the Council of Ministers. In response, the army removed him. Its representatives now firmly ensconced in the Presidency, the Council of Ministers and the Council of the Revolution, the army returned again to the barracks.

It is not merely the threat of intervention that gives the military elite its power, however. In addition to its role on national bodies, the ANP is an active participant in the other two levels of government, albeit within defined limits. On the local level, its members work closely with the local administration and the favors that the party is not able to distribute are often obtainable from military influence. On the intermediate level, the commanders of the six military regions function as surrogates for regional governors.

If the party elite has limited power and the military elite has limited interests, it is the administrative elite that has the most important political role. Its activities extend beyond the actual administration of the country (a function that occupies the Interior Ministry's segment of this group) into the substantive functions of various other ministries and their local networks (such as Education, Public Works, and Agriculture) and also of additional agencies that do not parallel the administrative structure, such as SONATRACH, the oil empire. As the administrative group grows and predominates, it tends to break down into component groups along these lines just as the ALN group broke down into three groups of technicians. Ever since the Boumedienne takeover, when the technocratic predominance began, bureaucratic politics within the ministerial and presidential councils have been largely conducted among the leaders of technician sub-groups. It is among this multiplistic administrative group, too, that the rewards have been the greatest and and the sense of a New Class most evident. Villas, cars, expense accounts and other tangible ways of getting around the civil service salary limitations are present if hard to prove.

However, the Algerian administration has not been so busy with internal maneuvers that it has neglected to contain its rivals from within the technocratic elite. The military elites have been kept in their important but restricted place—an intervening but not a ruling force, as in Syria, for instance, and the party elites have generally lost the battle for the newly created prize, the People's Assemblies elected on the local and provincial levels. Obviously, at this point it is difficult to ascertain with precision the comparative strengths of group identification and cohesion (although survey measures could be devised, if the data were obtainable). But the presence of "external" (administration versus party and army) and "internal" (inter-ministerial) rivalries provides enough sense of cohesion and competition to keep the bureaucratic elites both alert and under control.

Finally, unlike the other two technocratic elite groups, the bureaucrats are a highly productive elite with a real impact on the country's development and hence, on the production of new elites. Whether it is the school, the factory, or the local assembly, the policy output of the administration creates new skills, new opportunities, new demands, and new sources of power, that are the parameters of continuing elite circulation.

III

Elites in power defend their own positions, prepare new elite aspirants, and create a socio-economic context.[22] They may do this consciously or unconsciously, at varying speeds, and not necessarily with any compatibility among the three policy areas. Since, for many reasons, development proceeds unevenly from sector to sector, there is competition, friction and blockage among elite aspirants. It is the degree of concordance or disjuncture among these three activities that creates the political dynamics of elite circulation. The first has already been discussed in the previous description of elite groups. The other two activities need attention in order for us to understand the coming needs for Algerian elites and changes in Algerian society. The two will be treated together since they concern the supply and demand for elite members, qualitatively as well as quantitatively. The process of generating new elite aspirants and the context in which they function is a part of the modernization and development policies of the elite in power. Modernization, the process of industrialization and its concomitants, may be taken to refer to increasing reliance on inanimate sources of energy, complex tools, and specialized scientific know-how, creating in turn a new value system, a differentiated and complex society, and a centralized political system with increased power.[23] These elements find some correspondence in a notion of development that refers to increased growth and distribution in the economy, increased mobility and role expansion in society and increased participation and institutionalization in the polity. Although one may draw out parallel elements in all three areas of human activity, the political stands somewhat aside, since it is the polity that is concerned with the authoritative integration and allocation of goods, services and values that make up social and economic change.

Table II presents a summary of socio-economic changes over a 12-year period of important political change in Algeria. The first striking fact is nationalization, the reduction—although not removal—of the European sector. The proportions of Europeans and Algerians were reversed in the high socio-economic levels, and control and decision-making passed into Algerian hands. Second, the urbanization of the labor force increased, as did the two component characteristics within that trend—proletarianization and the rise of the middle class. The proportion of technical and liberal professions doubled and that of office employees and urban labor increased by half. It may be harder to draw as sharp conclusions on the remaining two characteristics: the drop in components of farm labor and the rise in general unemployment. The data indicate that both permanent and temporary salaried farm labor rose significantly while landownership and family agricultural labor fell, although the decrease in the last figure may be only definitional. The employment figures seem more accurate for the 1960s than for the previous decade, making it difficult to judge the rate of the rise in unemployment. The total labor force (not visible on the chart), however, fell about 5 percent from 2.534 million (2.180 million Muslims plus .354 million Frenchmen) to 2.400 million (2.335 million Muslims plus .065 million Europeans), despite a general population increase from 9.47 million to 12.093 million.

Aspirant elites can be created in two ways: by deliberate training (lifting them up) or by creating new social demand-bearing groups that require a spokesman (pushing them up), although sometimes it is hard to separate the two effects in a particular case. Through varying mixtures of the two methods, the incumbent elite in Algeria has slowly been producing a variety of new aspirant groups. At the same time, the incumbents have also been creating a socio-economic context by pursuing development policies which require certain skills, create specific employment opportunities, favor particular interests and conforming with particular values and attitudes. They, therefore, allow some kinds of elite aspirants to be absorbed, as opposed to others. These generating and absorbing processes correspond roughly to supply and demand functions for elites. The functions are performed in various ways, according to a country's development options.

One of the means of creating aspirants is through education. Algerian primary enrollment doubled in the first half-decade of independence and tripled by the end of the decade, until the primary-age education rate attained about 70 percent.[24] However, the biggest increase was in the first year of independence, when the places vacated by the French were filled by Algerians; thereafter, despite all efforts the population growth rate has outrun the education growth rate. Secondary and higher education both tripled in the half-decade and quintupled in the decade. Out of 1,000 primary school pupils per 1430 school-age children, 100 went to secondary school and ten to higher education, but only one graduated with a degree. At this rate of graduation, newly educated elite aspirants have every chance of being absorbed by the economy throughout the second decade. Indeed, their small numbers mean that they accede to a very favored status. In terms of this parameter, it is only when the supply of educated aspirants exceeds the demand, or they are otherwise blocked in their regular promotions, that challenges to the incumbents' control system may occur.

But who gets educated? Like other developing countries, Algeria shows an understandable imbalance of educational opportunity in favor of its urban areas.[25] Like most countries, it also shows an imbalance in favor of those whose families already hold wealth, status, or power. The extent of this imbalance is hard to document, however, although it has been suggested that

TABLE II: Socio-Economic Strata before and after Independence

(Sources: 1954 figures from Government General, *Tableaux de l'économie algérienne* [Algiers: Baconnier, 1960]; 1966 figures from Algerian Government, *Recensement général de la population et de l'habitat* [Algiers: Ministère des Finances, 1966]. There has been some slight telescoping of 1954 subcategories to fit 1966 categories, but the fit seems close. Unemployment figures appear to be neither exact nor comparable. Area between the solid lines and the center edge of each figure indicates Muslim Algerian unemployment; the 1954 area is undifferentiated by profession whereas the 1966 area is differentiated. Unlike Table 1, figures refer to laborforce, not total population, although the two are roughly the same. LF, below, means laborforce.

In 1954 & in 1966, respectively, Algerian Muslims (unshaded area) comprised

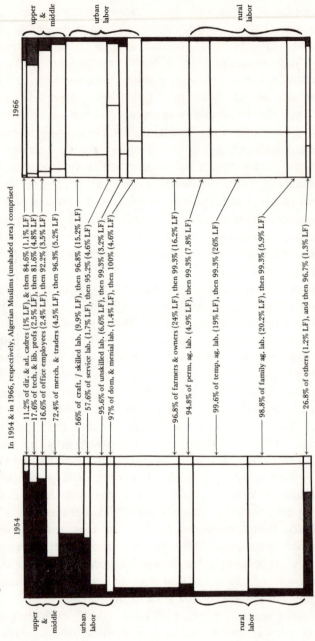

11.2% of dir. & ad. cadres (1% LF), & then 84.6% (1.1% LF)
17.6% of tech. & lib. profs (2.5% LF), then 81.6% (4.8% LF)
16.6% of office employees (2.4% LF), then 92.2% (3.5% LF)
72.4% of merch. & traders (4.5% LF), then 96.3% (5.2% LF)

56% of craft. / skilled lab. (9.9% LF), then 96.8% (15.2% LF)
57.6% of service lab. (1.7% LF), then 95.2% (4.6% LF)
95.6% of unskilled lab. (6.6% LF), then 99.3% (3.2% LF)
97% of dom. & menial lab. (1.4% LF), then 100% (4.6% LF)

96.8% of farmers & owners (24% LF), then 99.3% (16.2% LF)
94.8% of perm. ag. lab. (4.9% LF), then 99.3% (7.8% LF)
99.6% of temp. ag. lab. (19% LF), then 99.3% (26% LF)
98.8% of family ag. lab. (20.2% LF), then 99.3% (5.9% LF)
26.8% of others (1.2% LF), and then 96.7% (1.3% LF)

a New Class is in formation since "the children of liberal professionals, proprietors, merchants, and civil servants are proportionally more numerous in the university than are students from disfavored social levels."[26] Education is still conceived (by the incumbent decision-makers) as a means of preparing people for public service, but, as in most developing countries and notably in Iran and Egypt, that very doctrine plants the converse corollary, that government positions are the rightful reward for education.[27] Thus, typical expectations are forming which, if fulfilled, carry with them a certain birthright notion, and which, if unfulfilled in the future, will change current social and perhaps political structures.

It is more difficult to figure out the supplies and demands of elites arising from industrial or agricultural growth in the Algerian economy, although a non-quantitative appreciation can be obtained. Much of Algeria's economic leadership and training comes from the technocratic sector, since the petroleum, export, and other industries are under the management of national offices and companies. This sector of the elite has been briefly discussed. Corresponding to it, however, is a large labor sector, which, while not generally thought of in elite terms, does promote its members to positions of labor leadership and political activity.

Despite the size of the General Union of Algerian Workers, (UGTA), with a membership estimated between 350,000 and 200,000 at independence, dropping by half in 1965, and rising back to the original figures at the end of the first decade of independence, labor leadership has never been a vehicle to top political elite status in Algeria. The reason may be that salaried labor is extremely vulnerable in a society where non-agricultural unemployment was 44 percent of the labor force in 1970 and agricultural underemployment 69 percent.[28] When Ahmed Mahsas was Agriculture Minister, under Ben Bella, he created an agricultural labor union as his client group, but only a few labor leaders ever entered the Council of Ministers (Batel and Boudissa did, both under Ben Bella) and those who did were picked as individuals, not as labor representatives. Workers and union leaders fared particularly badly in the elections of 1967, 1969, 1971, and 1974. Similarly, labor was never strong (or ambitious) enough to take over the party apparatus, but was instead continually under fire from the party leadership which was trying to subdue the labor union. Twice in the process the labor leadership was evicted, making the top labor positions as precarious politically as the rank and file positions were economically. Yet, Algeria's major economic thrust is towards industrial growth and as industry grows so does labor and its importance.

Still, the supply of labor is so great that the characteristics of precariousness and vulnerability are likely to continue through the second decade, even if the planned growth goals are attained. Indeed, the potential for leadership among Algerian labor comes from the unemployed. The present political system gives no outlet for such activity and could doubtless control it if it arose, as it has, with the help of the army in the past under Ben Bella. A different situation would occur, however, if the labor outlet in Europe were suddenly closed. This is admittedly improbable in view of European solicitude for Algeria but not entirely impossible if one of the series of Franco-Algerian diplomatic tiffs should get out of hand. There were about half again as many Algerian workers in non-agricultural employment in Europe in 1974 as in Algeria (roughly 600,000 to 400,000), a safety valve of tremendous proportions for a segment of the population that the domestic economy will not be able to absorb for a long time. It is politically as well as economically important to maintain the expatriate employment opportunity.

The private sector of the economy is still important in socialist Algeria, and the liberal professions (doctors, lawyers and engineers, in addition to the teachers already mentioned) as well as businessmen are growing in numbers. In the long run, when the state technocratic sector becomes satiated, this private sector will have an important political role, as the Turkish example has shown.[29] In the meantime, the interests of these groups are clear and their small numbers make them important to the economy, since—unlike employed labor—they are not easily replaceable. They are, however, not organized and neither the Bar Association nor the Chambers of Commerce serve as spokesmen for their interest groups as yet.

The other side of the economy, the self-management sector, is less promising as a seedbed for new elite aspirants, despite the hopes and promises of the experiment in its early years.[30] When the French fled, and were expelled from their farms and factories, in 1962 and 1963, they were replaced as managers by committees of workers, while actual ownership gradually passed to the State. Although they controlled the best lands and industries and had a strong ideology and idealism behind them, the committees have not been a dramatic success. The industrial self-management sector has dropped from 450 industries at the beginning of the independent decade to half that number at the end; at the end of the decade there were also 1948 self-managed farms (including 300 Veteran's Cooperatives). Each unit had a self-management organization composed of an elected president, a management committee of 6-12 members, and a workers' council of 18-45 members, and a technical director or chargé. The original anticipation, valid and innovative in its conception, was that the new experiment in participatory economic democracy would bring to the surface new elite members hitherto hidden under the colonial overlay. Quite unfortunately, things worked out otherwise. The change was too sudden and the old habits too well ingrained; it was generally impossible to promote producer values when consumer values had not yet even been inculcated. There are some exceptions where self-management performed its economic duties and met or surpassed the colonial production norms; there are also some exceptions where social promotion and re-education in new values occurred as a result. But there are no cases where the self-management sector brought new individuals into the political elite. A few self-management presidents were nominated for local assemblies and some of these were elected, but none went on to hold the office of the assembly presidency. Of the 18 self-management presidents nominated to the wilayal assemblies, only a third were elected.[31] The ideological spark has gone out of the experiment and it is unlikely that the self-management sector will provide new elite aspirants in the future.

A decade after independence, the Boumedienne government tried to revive the spark by restoring a modified self-management idea to state and private industry. The measure was studied by the UGTA and the government in 1969-70, passed in 1971, and applied to a pilot industry (SNMetal) the following year. Revised through experience, it has thereafter been applied gradually to the state sector, and in a slightly different form, to the private sector, bringing workers into management councils and functions. Along with the Agrarian Revolution, the Socialist Management of Industry represents one of the two major prongs of structural reform under the Boumedienne government, full of promise and uncertainty.

If predictable consequences (even if not at a predictable date) can be discerned in Algerian policies and development concerning education, private professions, and bureaucrats, the implications of Algerian agricultural policy for elite circulation are far less clear, even though the policy decisions have been far more courageous and probably even significant. The pronouncements of the Algerian revolution have been rather vague from the start on agrarian reform. There are probably two reasons for this, both related to the colonization: on one hand, Muslim landownership was not highly concentrated in large estates, and on the other, the immediate brunt of any urge toward land reform fell on the European landholdings, which were largely concentrated.[32] Thus, the summary seizures and self-management developments took much of the edge off pressures toward agrarian reform during the first independent decade, and any pressure that was left was effectively stifled by the incumbent elite, many of whose members had taken advantage of the uncertainties of the early sixties to gather in a few acres for themselves. It was therefore against nearly unanimous opposition in the Council of Ministers that Boumedienne decreed a wide-sweeping agrarian reform in November 1971 and began its application in June of the following year, on the seventh anniversary of his take-over.

The core of the reform consists in the limitation of ownership to 125 acres and the distribution of public and recovered private lands to landless farmers, grouped into cooperatives, as their private freeholding.[33] Surveyors, agricultural agents and other types of technicians have had to be trained in both crash and long-range programs; physical and ownership surveys have had to be undertaken for the entire country (cutting through some of the remarkably complex ownership provisions of Muslim law); the efforts of the state machinery during 1972 and 1973 were dominated by the concerns of the reform. Politically, however, the policy represents an important option. Segments of the political elite who were also landowners have been seriously affected economically and perhaps socially, if not politically. On the other hand, it will be some time before the new smallholders constitute a group that is organized and politically active enough to be a viable counter-ally for the president against any disgruntled former owners. The chance that they develop rapidly into a demand-bearing group for their own interests is diminished by the rather complex administrative organization reaching down from the provincial governor (*wali*) to the cooperatives. However, it was just such a rapid agrarian reform and administrative structure that produced the Tunisian farmers' revolt and policy reversal of 1969.

The most direct device for elite recruitment, the election, has been used regularly under the Boumedienne regime, the future implications of which are still not entirely clear. Some 20,000 candidates were nominated in 1967 and a like number in 1971 for the 10,000 seats in the People's Communal Assemblies (APCs) and 1,300 were nominated for the 660 seats in the People's Wilayal Assemblies (APWs) in 1969 and 1974.[34] Nominations were controlled by the party but the army and administration were involved, and not all candidates (or successful ones) were strict party men. Yet, the element of continuity from one election to another has been slim. Less than a fifth of the APC candidates in 1971 were incumbents and only half of them were reelected. More than two-thirds of the incumbent council presidents ran again in 1971, however, and four-fifths of them were reelected. It is not known how many of the APW candidates in 1969 were APC members but a sixth of the winners came from the APC's. One-twentieth of the APW candidates were APC presidents and over two-thirds of these were elected to the APWs. Besides APC members, two or three other groups of candidates were favored by the voters in the three popular assembly elections: upper bureaucrats, liberal professions and to some extent (in 1971 only) party officials. However, none of these groups accounted for a tenth of the nominees. The largest groups of nominees for the APCs (15-25 percent) were lower bureaucrats, workers and farmers, and the largest groups for the APWs were lower bureaucrats and teachers; none of these were especially favored by the voters.

Since the most significant result of the elections (which were accomplished without individual candidate campaigns) was the randomness of the outcomes, it is difficult to draw sharp conclusions about their role in elite recruitment. To the extent that the voters favor one category over another, their choice does not bear on the same types as the nominating authorities. In the APW elections, where promotion was involved, the nominators appeared to want to promote ordinary citizens to higher political levels; the voters appeared to want to confer political power on people who had already occupied a comparable socioeconomic level. The people's assemblies have been a better school than the self-management committees for learning management responsibilities and both levels of assemblies have been serious administrative organs. In the process, they also provide an excellent outlet for those members of other groups—particularly liberal professions, labor, and bureaucrats—with political ambitions, who are now given a chance to work off their energies apolitically.

The next step is a potentially different matter. Elections for a People's National Assembly have been promised for a while, using the same electoral system with twice as many candidates as seats, but their occurrence raises problems. While its membership is likely to be as faceless and technocratic as the members of the lower assemblies (some of whom are likely to be promoted), it is more difficult to keep politics out of such a body and difficult to keep it, in the long run, from developing into an institution to which government is held responsible. Proto-parties may form as legislative coalitions and then as client groups of competing ministers, without changing the technocratic nature of the regime (which is by no means apolitical or even nonfactional, but simply nonpartisan). All these are steps toward the basic alteration of Algerian politics but they are distant indeed. Algeria's cooptive technocratic system is as far from a competitive multi-party system as it is from a mobilizing single-party system and is likely to remain so for a while.

Faced with such a situation, general studies on the evolution of developing countries at their best pose the question of the long-range impact of development on the society and hence on the polity. In its general terms, the model states that increased modernization, industrialization and development provide greater pluralism (role expansion) and mobility in society, providing differentiation of interests along with pressures for increased participation in the polity. A competitive system ensues and has a good chance of life if resources and perceptions are positive-sum. In addition to fixed-sum resources and perceptions, a number of other conditions may disrupt this rosy picture, however; a traditionalist backlash, distribution inequalities and promotion blockages among many others, may create enough dissension for the incumbent elite to try to "freeze" the system and institute control, constriction, centralization. In an even shorter run, the phenomenon of elite "bunching" in newly independent countries has been noted, resulting from a massive influx of new young nationalists into formerly colonial positions and ending in a pile-up of aspirants before a saturated system, eventually leading to political conflict.[35] These developments are likely to occur in Algeria too. But it does appear that a period of stability has been brought in since 1968 and is likely to last for a while, perhaps another decade or more. There are no groups that seek power *qua* groups in Algeria as a result of development, only (at most) isolated individuals. Until these individuals come together and control demand-bearing groups to challenge the incumbents, who will still be in power, ten to fifteen years on, there will be little chance of political upheavals.

There is much promise in such a situation, for it provides a stable base from which to exercise policy with continuity. It also contains theoretical confirmation, for it reflects the "bunching" model discussed earlier, in which development policy provides for the generation of new elite aspirants and new issue alignments after a period of stable incumbency. But it also contains a challenge to the elite and raises an important question about the nature of revolutions and elite circulation. A revolution is a phenomenon of rapid and sudden elite circulation, when blockages are wiped away and a waiting group streams into new opportunities and positions. In the process, creative energy is released, often to be harnessed to new constructs and products although sometimes to be wasted away in merely defending new *situations acquises*. But what happens once the initial circulation has taken place? Does it open the way for increased mobility and the expansion of roles? If so, social development can be said to be taking place, often with important spill-over effects into political development, aspects of participation and problem-solving. Or, does the newly promoted elite merely take root and set up its own form of blockage, so that a continual cycle of revolutions—each less and less substantive and simply increasingly procedural—becomes the mode of politics for a frustrated nation? In other words, is there something in the way elites circulate at one time that has determinant or predominant consequences for the future modes of elite circulation? Some studies have shown that rapidly promoted members of society tend to conservatism and defensive class awareness, since they tend to assure for their children advances that they do not believe will be freely available to them, or that they do not want them to have to struggle for in the same way as the parents did.[36] Observers of post revolutionary societies have noted the practical application of this phenomenon in the formation of a New Class.[37] Other chapters in this volume have shown the phenomenon at work in various forms in such Middle Eastern countries as different from each other as Israel, Iran, Saudi Arabia, Syria, and Egypt. Yet, the evidence is not conclusive, and even if a social trend were shown to exist, human beings still have enough free will to create exceptions. The Algerian elites are faced with this challenge.

NOTES

1. For a similar typology, see Raymond Hopkins, *Political Roles in a New State* (New Haven, Connecticut: Yale University Press, 1971), 242f. On the first alternative, see Thomas Hodgkin, *African Political Parties* (Baltimore, Md.: Penguin, 1961); Ruth Schachter Morgenthau, *Political Parties in French-Speaking West Africa* (New York: Oxford University Press, 1964). On the second, in addition to the above, see also Clement Henry Moore, *Tunisia Since Independence* (Berkeley, California: University of California Press, 1965) and "Mass Party Regimes in Africa," in Herbert Spiro, ed., *The Primacy of Politics* (Englewood Cliffs, N.J.: Prentice-Hall, 1967); Charles Micaud, L. Carl Brown and C. H. Moore, *Tunisia: The Politics of Modernization* (New York: Praeger, 1964). On the third, see John Kautsky, *Political Change in Underdeveloped Countries* (New York: Wiley, 1962) and *The Political Consequences of Modernization* (New York: Wiley, 1972). I am grateful to Ailon Shiloh, John Badeau and J. C. Hurewitz for occasions to discuss earlier drafts of this chapter, and to Charles Issawi, Janet and Donald Zagoria, Waldo Mazelis, Louis Cantori and, above all, Douglas Muzzio, for their comments.

2. By L. Carl Brown in Micaud, Brown and Moore, *Tunisia*.

3. William Quandt, *Revolution and Political Leadership: Algeria 1954-1968* (Cambridge, Mass.: MIT, 1969).

4. On Tunisian and Moroccan development analysed through the study of elites, see Henry de Montety, "Old Families and New Elites" and Octave Marais, "The Ruling Class in Morocco," in I. William Zartman, ed., *Man, State and Society in the Contemporary Maghrib* (New York: Praeger, 1973), 171-201, and John Waterbury, *The Commander of the Faithful: The Moroccan Political Elite* (New York: Columbia, 1970), as well as Micaud, Brown and Moore, *Tunisia*.

5. See John Damis, "The Free Schools in Tunisia and Algeria," *International Journal of Middle East Studies* (forthcoming); Roger LeTourneau,

"L'Afrique du Nord," in *Développement d'une classe moyenne dans les pays tropicaux et subtropicaux* (Brussels: International Institute of Different Civilizations, 1957); G-H Bousquet, "Les élites gouvernantes en Afrique du Nord," *Welt des Islams* 3, 1 (1953): 15-33; Augustin Berque, "La bourgeoisie algérienne ou à la recherche de César birotteau," *Hesperis* 35, 1 & 2, (1948): 1-29; anonymous, "Chefs indigènes du Département d'Alger," CHEAM (November 1951); M-G Berge, "Caids et Elus en Algérie," CHEAM (October 1953).

6. M de Peyerimhoff, *Enquêt sur les Résultats de la Colonisation Officielle de 1871 à 1895* (Algiers: Gouvernement général de l'Algérie, 1906); André Nouschi, *Enquête sur le niveau de vie de la population rurale constantinoise* (Paris: Presses Universitaires de France, 1961); John Ruedy, *Land Policy in Colonial Algeria* (Berkeley, California: University of California Press, 1967); André Nouschi, *La naissance du nationalisme algérien* (Paris: Minuit, 1962).

7. Robert Aron et. al., *Les origines de la guerre d'Algérie* (Paris: Fayard, 1962), esp. 52-54; Quandt, *Revolution*, 35.

8. See Jean Lacouture, *Cinq Hommes et la France* (Paris: Seuil, 1961) for a good biography of 'Abbas; see also Ferhat 'Abbas, *La nuit coloniale* (Paris: Juillard, 1962) and Amar Naroun, *Ferhat 'Abbas: les chemins de la sourveraineté* (Paris: Denoel, 1961). On the following events, in addition to Nouschi, *Naissance*, and Aron, *Origines*, see Roger Le Tourneau, *L'évolution politique de l'Afrique du Nord musulmane 1920-1961* (Paris: Colin, 1962).

9. See, in addition to Aron, *Origines*, and Quandt, *Revolution*, Manfred Halpern, "The Algerian Uprising of 1945," *Middle East Journal* 2, 2, (April, 1948): 191-202.

10. Quandt, *Revolution*, Chapter 5; Hubert Michel, "Algérie," in Réné Duchac et. al., *La formation des élites politiques maghrébines* (Paris: Librairie Générale de Droit et de Jurisprudence, 1973).

11. Gerard Chaliand, *L'Algérie est-elle socialiste?* (Paris: Maspero, 1964), 89. For other good works on Algerian politics, see David Gordon, *The Passing of French Algeria* (New York: Oxford University Press, 1966) and David Ottoway and Marina Ottoway, *Algeria: The Politics of a Socialist Revolution* (Berkeley, California: University of California Press, 1970).

12. For the themes underlying this classification, see I. William Zartman, "The Army in Algerian Politics," in Zartman, ed., *Man, State and Society*.

13. *El-Djeich* 72:7 (May, 1969).

14. For a development of these concepts, see I. William Zartman, "Revolution and Development," *Civilisations* 20, 2, (1970): 181-198.

15. For more on this theme, see Zartman, "The Army in Algerian Politics."

16. In 1963, at the time of the revolts, the enterprising *Algér-Republicain* (the Communist newspaper) interviewed a number of rebels who expressed this theme.

17. For more on this theme, see I. William Zartman, "Who's on First and What's He Doing There," *Comparative Politics* 6, 3 (April 1974).

18. See Mohammed Harbi, "The Party and the State," in Zartman, ed., *Man, State and Society*.

19. Cf Marvin Zonis' discussion of Iran, in this volume.

20. Note that the same institutional jobs could be performed very differently, in roles that might be called warrior, bureaucrat, and politician, respectively. The politician has already been mentioned.

21. There is no good full-length study of the FLN. For shorter studies, see William H. Lewis, "The Decline of Algeria's FLN," in Zartman, ed., *Man, State and Society*; Jean Leca, "Parti et état en Algérie" and Abderrahmane Remili, "Parti et administration en Algérie," in *Annuaire de l'Afrique du Nord 1968* 7 (Paris: Centre National de Recherche Scientifique, 1939), 13-56; and Mustapha Sehimi, "Le Parti et l'Etat," *Révolution Africaine* (7 November 1964) and "Le Parti et l'Etat," *Algérie Actualité* (28 December 1968).

22. Elites do not do these things alone, of course. Chance and other forces have their role to play.

23. Kautsky's variation on Levy's definition; see Frank Tachau's introductory essay in this volume.

24. See Gérard Viratelle, *L'Algérie algérienne* (Paris: Editions ouvrières, 1970), 228.

25. See André Tiano, *Le Maghreb entre les mythes* (Paris: Presses Universitaires de France, 1967), 47, 121; and also the reports, *Informations et Statistiques*, issued periodically by the Ministry of Education.

26. *Révolution Africaine* cited in Viratelle, *L'Algérie*, 230.

27. Cf Marvin Zonis, *The Political Elite of Iran* (Princeton: Princeton University Press, 1971), 173f; Malcolm Kerr, "Egypt," in James Coleman, ed., *Education and Political Development* (Princeton: Princeton University Press, 1965), p. 184.

28. Andre Tiano, "Human Resource Investment and Employment Policy in the Maghreb," *International Labor Review* 105, 2 (February 1972): 109-133. On the UGTA and structural reforms, see three articles by Nicole Grimaud, "Reformes de structure en Algérie," *Maghreb-Machreq* 49, (January 1972): 36-39; "Approfindissement de la 'Revolution socialiste' en Algérie," *Maghreb-Machreq* 56, (March 1973): 12-17; "Evolution du syndicalisme en Algérie," *Maghreb-Machreq* 57, (May 1973): 26-30.

29. Cf Leslie and Noralou Roos, *Managers of Modernization* (Cambridge, Mass.: Harvard, 1971) and Frederick Harbison and Charles Myers, *Education, Manpower and Economic Growth* (New York: McGraw-Hill, 1964), p. 76.

30. Some recent evaluations of self-management are Ian Clegg, *Workers' Self-Management in Algeria* (New York: Monthly Review, 1971); Thomas Blair, *The Land to Those Who Work It* (New York: Doubleday, 1970); Monique Laks, *Autogestion et pouvoir politique en Algérie (1962-1965)* (Paris: Editions et Documentation Internationales, 1970). The following figures and details come from Viratelle, *L'Algerie*, p. 259; Blair, *Land to Those Who Work It*, p. 75; and *Annales Algériennes de Géorgraphie* 4, pp. 206, 226, 217f (special issue on self-management). See also Damien Helie, "Industria! Self-Management in Algeria," in Zartman, ed., *Man, State and Society*.

31. On the other hand, half of the bureaucratic leaders (self-management directors and chargés) nominated were elected.

32. As of 1951, Algeria had a Gini index of inequality in Muslim land distribution of 67, a relatively moderate figure which was the same as

Morocco, Tunisia, Norway, South Vietnam and West Germany. Half the land was owned by 90 percent of the owners, another measure of distribution. See Zartman, ed., *Man, State and Society*, p. 494. At about the same time, Egypt had a Gini index of 74, with half the land in 98 percent of the farms; figures for Iraq were 88 and 99 percent; from Bruce Russett, "Relation of Land Tenure to Politics," *World Politics* 16, 3, (April, 1964): 442-454.

33. As of 1951, Muslim-owned land in plots over 125 acres comprised 38 percent of the Muslim-owned land and 4 percent of the Muslim owners.

34. See I. William Zartman, "Les élections départementales," in *Annuaire de l'Afrique du Nord 1969* 8 (Paris: Centre National de Recherche Scientifique, 1970), pp. 311-327, and I. William Zartman and Ahmed Rhazaoui, "Winning Chances in Algerian Single-Party Elections," (forthcoming).

35. See I. William Zartman, "Elite Circulation in the Middle East," in Zartman and Zonis, ed., *The Study of Elites and the Middle East* (Princeton, N. J.: Princeton University Press, forthcoming).

36. S. M. Lipset and Hans Zetterberg, "A Theory of Social Mobility," in Reinhard Bendix and Lipset, eds., *Class, Status and Power* (New York: Free Press, 1966, 2nd ed.), pp. 563, 569f.

37. Milovan Djilas, *The New Class* (1957).

BIBLIOGRAPHY

Amin, Samir. *Le Maghreb Moderne.* Paris: Minuit, 1970.

Blair, Thomas. *The Land to Those Who Work It.* New York: Doubleday, 1970.

Bourdieu, Pierre. *The Algerians.* Boston: Beacon, 1962.

Chaliand, Gerard and Minces, Juliette. *L'Algerie independante.* Paris: Maspero, 1972.

Clegg, Ian. *Workers' Self-Management in Algeria.* New York: Monthly Review Press, 1971.

Gordon, David. *The Passing of French Algeria.* New York: Oxford University Press, 1966.

Halpern, Manfred. *The Politics of Social Change in the Middle East and North Africa.* Princeton, N. J.: Princeton University Press, 1965.

Leca, Jean and Vatin, Jean-Claude. *L'Algerie politique.* Paris: Colin, 1974. 2 vols.

LeTourneau, Roger. *L'evolution politique de l'Afrique du Nord musulmane 1920-1961.* Paris: Colin, 1962.

Moore, Clement Henry. *Politics in North Africa.* Boston: Little Brown, 1970.

Ottoway, David and Ottoway, Marina. *Algeria: The Making of a Socialist Revolution.* Berkeley, California: University of California Press, 1969.

Quandt, William B. *Revolution and Political Leadership: Algeria 1954-1968.* Cambridge, Mass.: MIT Press, 1969.

Viratelle, Gerard. *L'Algerie algerienne.* Paris: Editions ouvrieres, 1970.

Zartman, I. William, ed. *Man, State and Society in the Contemporary Maghrib.* New York: Praeger, 1973.

periodicals

Annuaire de l'Afrique du Nord Paris: Centre National de Recherche Scientifique, annual.

Maghreb Paris: Documentation Française, bimonthly.

8

Conclusion

Frank Tachau

It is now appropriate to summarize the insights to be gained from the foregoing analyses. If we conceive of the process of modernization as moving along a continuum, some of the societies which have been the object of our scrutiny have remained closer to the traditional pole than others. Significantly, one of these societies, Saudi Arabia, is blessed with economic resources (in the form of oil) which provides a source of income and potential wealth equaled in few societies elsewhere in the world, particularly among developing nations. Apparently, this extraordinary wealth has given the traditional political elite the wherewithal to help maintain its political dominance and to keep some semblance of control over the process of modernizing change. Of the remaining societies within our purview four have undergone varying degrees of modernization, while one, Israel, was largely modernized to begin with. All of these societies have experienced some measure of economic growth, have wrestled (with varying degrees of success) with problems of political identity and authority, and have confronted (again with varying degrees of success) questions of governmental penetration and capacity.

SEGMENTATION VERSUS STRATIFICATION:

We have largely avoided explicit concern with theoretical questions of the nature of social stratification and its relation to social change and political conflict. Instead, we have focused on the empirical realities of the groups and societies under scrutiny.

Nevertheless, it is useful at this point to make some general observations.

It has been noted that some societies, particularly certain types of traditional societies, manifest cleavages along vertical axes rather than along horizontal planes. In other words, basic social and political divisions do not separate strata at various levels from higher to lower. Rather, the fundamental divisions separate groups which share in the exercise of power and include within their own ranks both higher and lower socio-economic strata (if, indeed, such strata are discernible at all). Fortes and Evans-Pritchard, for example, argued that societies based on lineage or patrilineal descent exhibit this type of segmentation. They distinguished segmented societies of this type from those based on bilateral kinship on the one hand (limited to relatively small-scale societies) and what they called administrative societies on the other (permitting larger-scale political organization).[1]

Vertical cleavage or segmentation is not, however, limited to tribal societies. In fact, all societies exhibit a certain degree of segmentation, especially in their political systems. It may be discerned even in the most complex industrial societies, particularly in pluralistic social settings in which a variety of economic, social, and other groups compete for a share of political power.[2] Thus, it may be said that most societies combine elements of vertical and horizontal differentiation, much as they combine elements of traditionalism and modernity (though we must take care not to link segmentation too closely to traditionalism, and vice versa).

To what extent do the societies we have analyzed manifest vertical and/or horizontal lines of division?

The traditional social structure of the Ottoman Empire clearly exhibited the principle of vertical segmentation. The *millet* system, under which the population of the Empire was divided into semi-autonomous groupings based primarily on ethnic and/or religious identity, manifested this type of division most clearly. Each community was left to its own devices so long as it did not challenge the legitimacy of the Ottoman system. To some extent, these cleavages also assumed functional significance; for example, commercial activities were largely in the hands of non-Muslim *millets*. Thus, groups were identifiable in terms of multiple and mutually reinforcing criteria, including ethnicism, language, religion, economic function or activity, and even mode of dress and place of residence. The resultant social pattern has been aptly called "a mosaic of peoples."[3] Superimposed on this segmented social system was the sharp distinction between governing elites on the one side and subject masses on the other.

With the Young Turk revolution of 1908, as Szyliowicz argues in Chapter I, this traditional Ottoman system was transformed. The process of national integration begun by the Young Turks was carried to completion by the Republican regime of Kemal Atatürk. When the legal basis of the *millet* system was dismantled, the vertical cleavages of the traditional system were undermined, although some of the attitudinal concomitants remained. Horizontal lines of stratification gradually appeared, especially after 1950, with the development of greater pluralism and the closer integration of national center and regional peripheries. The contemporary political system in Turkey is characterized by a relatively high degree of interest articulation and, at the same time, greater ideological polarization and dissensus than ever before. Segmental loyalties and lines of division remain primarily in the least developed and most remote regional centers.

The Saudi Arabian political system, by contrast, is still largely characterized by traditional style tribal segmentation. Wenner aptly reminds us that Western concepts of the territorial state seem somewhat incongruous in this milieu. Significantly, it is the territorial state which has been historically associated with the development of the archetypal class structure of modern Europe. Yet, with the phenomenal development of the petroleum industry, the Saudi regime has increasingly found it necessary to recruit and train cadres of modern-style technocrats, managers and functionaries. The coexistence of this essentially modern sector with the still highly traditional tribal structure (which would grant the modern technicians no clear status apart from traditional criteria of descent and religious orthodoxy) suggests the simile of a social structure which has been tilted somewhat from its vertical axis, but has not rotated a full 90 degrees to a horizontal base. The vast wealth produced by the petroleum industry and the responsiveness and political dexterity of the governing elite, to carry on the metaphor, have kept the system in balance so that it does not tilt too far too quickly.

Syria manifests a different combination of segmental and

horizontal lines of division. Regional and provincial centers of attraction have dominated Syrian politics, as Van Dusen shows, and this suggests a vertical type of segmentation. At the same time, horizontal divisions have also been apparent, especially between the traditional political elite, the quasi-middle class counter-elite, and what Van Dusen calls the "new" elite moving up from the ranks of lower socio-economic echelons. Significantly, as the latter group achieved political power in the 1960s, regional politics began to fade in importance, perhaps for the first time.

Israel presents another variation on this theme. The pervasive dominance of what Torgovnik calls the Zionist Left, particularly the Mapai faction of the ruling Labor Party, again suggests a vertically segmented system (but in this case not based on traditional criteria) in which lines of political power reach down into rural communes, labor organizations, social service facilities, professional associations, etc. Yet here, too, lines of horizontal stratification have been evident, especially those based on ethnic differentiation between the Ashkenazi and the Sephardic communities. In a sense, to stretch our Saudi Arabian metaphor a bit further, we may have here a system which is tilting in the opposite direction (from segmentation based on functional differentiation to stratification based on ethnic criteria). In this case, the system is kept in balance by a combination of high consensus on issues of national survival and immigrant absorption, an adaptive and essentially responsive political elite, and more mundane interest in political survival on the part of the various parties and factions.

The remaining cases, Algeria, Egypt, and Iran do not present such clear-cut pictures, although again one may find evidence of both vertical segmentation and horizontal stratification in each case. In the Algerian case, in particular, the alternative of what Zartman calls a single party cooptive system, which could easily have assumed segmental form, failed to develop. In Egypt, aspects which Akhavi has labeled neo-patrimonial also suggest a segmented pattern, but there are in addition, evidences of stratification in both urban and rural sectors. Finally, the Iranian case resembles the Saudi picture in terms of efforts by the political elite to coopt the burgeoning cadre of modern functionaries, technicians, and professionals, and in terms of the favorable economic base provided by the petroleum industry. In these

PATTERNS OF ELITE INTERACTION AND CHANGE:

Almost all of the societies within our purview have experienced changes in elite composition. Significantly, they exhibit common tendencies in the shifting social bases of elite recruitment. In particular, in five of our seven cases, either whole new elites or significant new elite segments have emerged from lower socio-economic levels. Let us briefly review these cases.

In Saudi Arabia, Wenner highlights the rather rapid infiltration of elite ranks by "commoners" (that is, persons not part of the Saudi kinship structure), especially those with modern skills. In Iran, the incumbent elite has itself tended to monopolize access to elite status as a means of maintaining its power. While, as Zonis notes, there has been some selective cooptation, there has been no widespread recruitment of new social groups into the elite. In Syria, by contrast, the traditional elite has been undermined and largely replaced by a wholly new elite. Significantly, this new elite is derived from lower socio-economic strata, and is less wedded to regional power centers and parochial concerns. Likewise, in Turkey, especially since 1960, individual aspirants to elite status as well as aspiring elite groups have increasingly emerged from lower socio-economic levels and from the provincial hinterland rather than the national urban centers. In Egypt, the new elite which swept into power in 1952 was largely of humble origins and used its power to undermine the traditional elite. Finally, in Algeria, the nationalist uprising has dominated the political and social arena. The replacement of the colonial French elite by indigenous leadership also represents, albeit in a special sense, the rise of individuals from low status both vis à vis the French and within the Algerian social structure. Only in Israel is this trend not clearly evident; and even here, the evidence shows some percolation of individuals of low status upwards through the system. It is, in any event, notable that in every case where there has been clear change in the composition or identity of political elites, the change has been in the direction of replacement of individuals of high socio-economic status with those of lower status.

In terms of elite training or education, the Saudi and Iranian cases are again characterized by the increasing relevance of modern secular education, paralleling the infiltration of individuals from lower status levels in at least the former case. There, too, completion of a course of study in a secular institution of secondary education or higher has become the only criterion for elite status other than kinship or membership in the Saudi family. The latter criterion remains critical for control of the most important positions in the political system, while the former increasingly characterizes second echelon members of the elite. In Iran, as Zonis points out, the incumbent elite has, by virtue of its advantageous economic and social position, tended to monopolize access to the relevant secular educational institutions and the consequent modern skills.

In Syria and Turkey, by contrast, expansion of the educational system has been one of the prime causes of change in elite composition. In Syria, the new elite is identified by Van Dusen largely in terms of the lowest socio-economic sectors with access to the secondary school system, which in turn was greatly expanded to accommodate them. In Turkey, new elite elements emerged in the late nineteenth century largely by way of new secular educational institutions. Such institutions were reorganized and expanded under the Republic, and the trickle of these new elite elements became a virtual flood during the last three decades or so.

In our remaining three cases, educational development has had less obvious effects on elite composition. In Algeria, indigenous control of the system is too recent for its effects to have become as visible as elsewhere, although here, too, technicians show the important effects of education. In Egypt, the members of the elite are less distinguished from their predecessors by education than by social background. In Israel, the educational system has been planned as a homogenizer and equalizer, and has to a large extent served that function.

Patterns of elite circulation are somewhat easier to discern. We noted in our introduction that elite circulation may take two forms: slow, evolutionary change of individual members of the elite, and sudden replacement of one elite by another. Of the societies under review here, four (Turkey in 1908 and after 1950, Egypt in 1952, Syria in the 1950s and 1960s, and Algeria in 1962) experienced the latter type of rapid elite circulation. This is, of course, an oversimplification. The two types of circulation, as noted earlier, are not dichotomously opposed to one another nor are they mutually exclusive. Thus, in Turkey both before and after 1950, elite circulation occurred in a more evolutionary manner than is indicated above; the election of 1950 serves only as a convenient historical marker to date the basic shift which was taking place, just as the 1960 military seizure of power represents an attempt by the older elite to reassert its former dominance. Similarly, in Syria, the shift was no less basic, in spite of the fact that it did not take the form of a single act of political transformation (that is, a single act of revolution or revolutionary coup d'état). In Egypt, there has also been remarkable stability since the upheaval of 1952, while the Algerian system has barely had time to work out the overwhelming tensions of the struggle against French colonialism.

Our remaining three cases are no less interesting. Saudi Arabia and Iran, as noted earlier, continue to be dominated by incumbent political elites. In both instances, the elites have been fully conscious of the pressure for modernizing change, and have sought to respond to that pressure while maintaining their dominance of society and politics. Their relative success to date may be attributed in no small measure to the material largesse which their vast oil resources provide. In essence, especially in Iran, pressure for change has been largely siphoned off by the offer of material rewards for acquiescence in the status quo.

In this regard, Israel is unique in the Middle East. Its persistent elite is hardly traditional in any sense of that term. Nor can it be said that Israeli society has been static or unchanging; if it were true, this alone might explain the unusual persistence of this small and highly cohesive political elite. The uniqueness of Israel lies precisely in the fact that the elite has survived unchallenged in an environment of great social flux. The explanation would seem to be that the overriding issues of national survival and the absorption of immigrants have simply postponed or overshadowed all other potential sources of conflict and thus muted any possible challenge to the ruling elite. The implication, of course, is that if these issues begin to fade, the remarkable consensus which has characterized Israel during its first quarter-century of statehood may well begin to erode. Subsequent challenges to, and changes in, the dominant elite may then begin to appear.

Closely related to the process of elite circulation is the phenomenon of impeded access to elite status. Whether there is or has been rapid circulation or replacement of elites or not, the question is to what extent aspirants to elite status, or aspiring counter-elites, are accommodated or satisfied by the existing system. In other words, unless there is a certain amount of "capillary action," social and political pressures from below are likely to develop. This would seem to be true regardless of the origins of the incumbent political elite or the manner in which it came to power.

Saudi Arabia and Iran, as has been noted, have had the benefit of oil wealth as a device to siphon off the resultant pressures. In the case of Iran, a pervasive system of political repression has also contributed to this outcome. In Egypt, the charisma of Nasser probably helped to maintain a stable political base; this is implicitly reflected in the partial liberalization of the political system in the early stages of the successor regime. Political stability has subsequently been maintained by a delicate balancing process among various elite segments, with the Israeli military presence east of Suez playing a definite role—exaggerated though this has been for rhetorical purposes. The Israeli case is once again to be explained in part by the overriding issues of survival and absorption of immigrants. So long as these issues dominate the political scene, it will be extremely difficult for a counter-elite to challenge the status quo. This is not, of course, the whole explanation; it is perfectly conceivable for counter-elites to challenge the political status quo precisely on the grounds that the incumbent elite is not dealing with these dominant issues in a competent manner; indeed, precisely such a challenge was raised in the aftermath of the war of October 1973. The Israeli elite has not only demonstrated competence, but, as Torgovnik argues, has also manifested a remarkable degree of adaptiveness and pragmatism, at least in domestic affairs. It has thus managed to keep most of the levers of power and channels of access under its control.

The Algerian regime has not yet been tested sufficiently by the passage of time to permit well founded conclusions. As Zartman implies, however, this may turn out to be an example of a revolutionary regime bringing a new elite to power and then blocking access for other groups pressing upward from below.

Syria and Turkey manifest the least impeded access to elite status. Significantly, of the seven regimes under review, these two have experienced relatively greater instability than the others, especially in recent years. This instability may be directly traced to competition among contending elites and factions. It is not true, of course, that there has been no impeded access in these two countries. The traditional Syrian elite in fact tried unsuccessfully to block access to counter-elites, leading to considerable strife and contention. In the end, it was unsuccessful. On the other hand, none of the counter-elites was strong enough to establish undisputed control in their own right. In Turkey, the rules of the game of competition among elites have been somewhat more clearly delineated. Moreover, the stakes of conflict have not yet reached the point at which the momentarily dominant elite refuses to countenance the continued survival of its rivals.

GENERAL OBSERVATIONS:

The analyses of political elites in the context of socio-economic change presented in this volume may finally be summarized by noting the general patterns that appear to emerge in terms of three interacting factors: the relative stability or instability of the elite, both in terms of composition and control; the level of institutionalization characteristic of the political system; and the rate of socio-economic change which appears to prevail. The accompanying table shows how each society stands in terms of these variables.

Political Elites, Political Institutionalization, and Socio-Economic Change

Country	Stability of Elite	Level of Political Institutionalization	Rate of Socio-Economic Change
Saudi Arabia	High	Low	High
Iran	High	Low	High
Israel	High	High	High
Egypt	High (since 1952)	Low	Low
Turkey	Moderate	High	Moderate
Syria	Low	Low	Moderate
Algeria	Low	Low	Moderate

Taking elite stability as our basic factor (though emphatically not in a causal sense), we find four societies with highly or relatively highly stable political elites, that is, Saudi Arabia, Iran, Israel, and Egypt. Not only have the political elites in these cases remained stable in composition, but they have apparently retained a remarkable degree of control over their respective political systems as well. Yet in terms of the other two variables, these societies are markedly different from one another. Neither Saudi Arabia nor Iran manifest a high degree of institutionalization in their political systems. Processes of institutionalization seem to have begun in Saudi Arabia as commoners have started to infiltrate upwards through the system, and as modern skills and training have assumed increasing importance. In Iran, on the other hand, the stability of the system is based precisely on the absence or lack of institutionalization in the political system, as Zonis has argued here and elsewhere. Both systems, further, are characterized by rapid development, particularly in the economic sector, based in both cases on oil wealth. As we have noted above, the very availability of oil wealth has, in fact, provided the wherewithal for the elite to maintain its control by increasing its ability to allocate material rewards to aspiring elites. On the other hand, as Zonis argues, oil wealth in Iran has not generally been translated into welfare for the masses; in fact the society is characterized by a widening gap between rich and poor. Thus, material wealth has not been accompanied by social development. A similar situation may be developing in Saudi Arabia.

Israel, of course, is a markedly different case; this is perhaps most evident in the very high degree of institutionalization characteristic of both its political and social systems. Economically, however, it, too, has benefitted from a high rate of development.

The only other country which has had a highly stable political elite is Egypt, and then only since 1952. Egypt differs from the other three societies with stable elites in that each of them is characterized by a high rate of economic development (and in the case of Israel, also a high level of political institutionalization). In the case of Egypt, however, the level of both political institutionalization and socio-economic development has been low.

The table shows Turkey to have a moderately stable elite, a high level of political institutionalization and a moderate rate of socio-economic change. The relation of these variables to one another is quite clear in this case. Political institutionalization has been quite high for a number of years, while economic development rates have fluctuated somewhat, with the overall rate lower than that of the oil-bearing countries and Israel, yet higher than most developing nations. Significantly, it was the relative success of socio-economic development which produced the conditions undermining the high level of political stability which prevailed in Turkey during the Atatürk years (roughly 1925-1950). The creation of new elites and elite aspirants produced a challenge to the dominant bureaucratic and military elite, with the result that this elite lost its dominance and became one among a number of contenders. Consequently, the Turkish system has been less stable in recent years than was the case earlier. In particular, as Szyliowicz has noted, a marked degree of ideological polarization has come to characterize Turkish politics. On the other hand, the system remains far more stable than many others in the Middle East or elsewhere in the Third World. It is especially notable that political conflict in Turkey has been largely carried on within existing institutional and procedural channels.

Syria, by contrast, has often stood out as an exceptionally unstable political system. Van Dusen's chapter outlines the nature of elite change which has taken place amidst this general instability. At the same time, there has been at least a modicum of socio-economic development—indeed, as Van Dusen notes, there might have been more had there been greater political stability. Unlike Turkey, the Syrian system has not yet developed generally acceptable institutional structures or procedures to govern political conflict.

Algeria, as has been said repeatedly in this conclusion, remains an unknown quantity, largely because of the relatively short time since the achievement of independence. The failure of the FLN to develop a single party regime, marked by the overthrow of its leader, Ben Bella, in 1965, prompts us to characterize both the stability of its political elite and the level of political institutionalization as "low."

The evidence is not conclusive; nevertheless, we have here at least a suggestion of the conclusion that political stability tends to be greatest at the extremes of the spectrum of modernization; i.e., the most stable societies tend to be those not yet subject to the stresses of modernizing change, or those which have undergone a good deal of modernization with relative success.[4] The greatest stress—hence the greatest instability—seems to occur in the intermediate phases where the modernization process has gone far enough to disrupt traditional patterns and institutions but not yet far enough to establish new ones in their place. It should be noted further that it is impossible to fix exact points or thresholds at which the stability of the traditional system or elite tends to break down, or at which stable new elites and systems tend to appear. As the case studies in this volume indicate, special factors operate in each case; for example, the incumbent elites in Saudi Arabia and Iran have undoubtedly been greatly assisted in their efforts to maintain their dominance and the stability of the systems over which they preside by the availability of a vast storehouse of material wealth.[5]

One such special factor may well be the character of the political elite itself. The tendency to view political elites as dependent variables—to explain their composition, value commitments and behavior patterns as the outcome of other factors— should not blind us to the fact that these elites are *acting* as well as *re*acting. To a large extent, the outcome of processes of social change depends on the ability and sagacity of members of salient political elites. The social, economic, and physical environment in this sense provides opportunities and possibilities to be exploited by the elite. Although it would be difficult to measure in absolute terms, it seems clear that at least some of the differences we have noted among the societies analyzed here are due to differential talents among their political elites.

Finally, we should note once again that analysis of political elites provides many insights into the character and developmental trends of political systems. We have attempted to provide such insights here. If our relatively brief reviews have provided some clues to the understanding of the dynamics of political, social, and economic change in these Middle Eastern societies, we can consider our endeavor successful. If we have raised questions and pointed the way towards more intensive study of these and similar societies, we will have had a greater impact than perhaps we had a right to expect.

NOTES

1. M. Fortes and E. E. Evans-Pritchard, *African Political Systems* (London: Oxford University Press, 1940), pp. 6-7.

2. John Waterbury uses the concept of vertical segmentation as a basis for analyzing the Moroccan political system in *The Commander of the Faithful: The Moroccan Political Elite—A Study in Segmented Politics*

(New York: Columbia University Press, 1970), chapter 3.

3. See Carlton S. Coon, *Caravan,* rev. ed. (New York: Holt, Rinehart, 1966), chapter 10.

4. Graphically, the phenomenon discussed here is described by a U-shaped curve. For a discussion of a similar relationship between incidence of violence and modernization, see S. P. Huntington, *Political Order in Changing Societies* (New Haven, Connecticut: Yale University Press, 1968), pp. 39-59.

5. The point has become redundant because of our frequent reference to it, particularly in this concluding chapter. We should add the qualification underlined by both Wenner and Zonis that oil wealth is by no means the sole explanation of the remarkable perseverence of these two political elites.